What People are Sa[ying] About *The Mezonic* [Agenda]

"Hackers and spies, what an a[...] for the sequel!"

—*Sarah Gordon, Security Researcher*

"Cyber threat hits home in a very realistic manner. This really could happen"

—*Greg Miles,Ph.D., CISSP, President Security Horizon, Inc.*

"This novel is scarily realistic and I know Herbert Thompson well enough that I am sure whoever he is voting for will win the next election!"

—*James A. Whittaker, Ph.D., Chief Scientist and Founder of Security Innovation*

"Entertainment is the best way to communicate complex ideas. *The Mezonic Agenda: Hacking the Presidency* is an enjoyable electronic crime novel that simplifies complex technologies and reveals the dangers of electronic voting, a page-turner that shows how people in power might manipulate electronic voting and undermine democracy - and how they might be stopped."

—*Richard Thieme, Author of "Islands in the Clickstream"*

Imagine a scenario whereby the U.S. presidential election could be manipulated through ingenuity, stealth, and the exploitation of flaws inherent in the technology used to tabulate the vote. Now imagine that the flawed technology isn't cardboard chads, rather, it's the allegedly hack-proof software used by the Federal Elections Committee to gather and calculate the popular vote. What's more, the culprits aren't overworked precinct monitors; instead they're brilliant programmers working for a foreign corporation committed to a favorable election outcome at any cost. You now have the essence *The Mezonic Agenda.*

Register for Free Membership to

solutions@syngress.com

Over the last few years, Syngress has published many best-selling and critically acclaimed books, including Tom Shinder's *Configuring ISA Server 2000*, Brian Caswell and Jay Beale's *Snort 2.0 Intrusion Detection*, and Angela Orebaugh and Gilbert Ramirez's *Ethereal Packet Sniffing*. One of the reasons for the success of these books has been our unique **solutions@syngress.com** program. Through this site, we've been able to provide readers a real time extension to the printed book.

As a registered owner of this book, you will qualify for free access to our members-only solutions@syngress.com program. Once you have registered, you will enjoy several benefits, including:

- Four downloadable e-booklets on topics related to the book. Each booklet is approximately 20-30 pages in Adobe PDF format. They have been selected by our editors from other best-selling Syngress books as providing topic coverage that is directly related to the coverage in this book.

- A comprehensive FAQ page that consolidates all of the key points of this book into an easy to search web page, providing you with the concise, easy to access data you need to perform your job.

- A "From the Author" Forum that allows the authors of this book to post timely updates links to related sites, or additional topic coverage that may have been requested by readers.

Just visit us at **www.syngress.com/solutions** and follow the simple registration process. You will need to have this book with you when you register.

Thank you for giving us the opportunity to serve your needs. And be sure to let us know if there is anything else we can do to make your job easier.

SYNGRESS®

THE Mezonic

HACKING THE PRESIDENCY

Agenda

HACK ALONG WITH THE HEROES
AND VILLAINS AS THE AMERICAN
PRESIDENCY HANGS IN THE
BALANCE OF CYBER-SPACE

Dr. Herbert H. Thompson
Spyros Nomikos

KEY	SERIAL NUMBER
001	HJIRTCV764
002	PO9873D5FG
003	829KM8NJH2
004	67GAW5PLDR
005	CVPLQ6WQ23
006	VBP965T5T5
007	HJJJ863WD3E
008	2987GVTWMK
009	629MP5SDJT
010	IMWQ295T6T

PUBLISHED BY
Syngress Publishing, Inc.
800 Hingham Street
Rockland, MA 02370

The Mezonic Agenda: Hacking the Presidency

Printed in the United States of America
1 2 3 4 5 6 7 8 9 0
ISBN: 1-931836-83-3

Publisher: Andrew Williams   Cover Designer: Michael Kavish
Acquisitions Editor: Christine Kloiber   Copy Editor: Adrienne Rebello
Technical Reviewer: Russ Rogers   Page Layout and Art: Patricia Lupien

Distributed by O'Reilly & Associates in the United States and Canada.
For information on rights and translations, contact Matt Pedersen, Director of Sales and Rights, at Syngress Publishing; email matt@syngress.com or fax to 781-681-3585.

Acknowledgments

We would like to acknowledge the following people for their kindness and support in making this book possible.

Jeff Moss and Ping Look from Black Hat, Inc. You have been good friends to Syngress and great colleagues to work with. Thank you!

Syngress books are now distributed in the United States and Canada by O'Reilly Media, Inc. The enthusiasm and work ethic at O'Reilly is incredible and we would like to thank everyone there for their time and efforts to bring Syngress books to market: Tim O'Reilly, Laura Baldwin, Mark Brokering, Mike Leonard, Donna Selenko, Bonnie Sheehan, Cindy Davis, Grant Kikkert, Opol Matsutaro, Lynn Schwartz, Steve Hazelwood, Mark Wilson, Rick Brown, Leslie Becker, Jill Lothrop, Tim Hinton, Kyle Hart, Sara Winge, C. J. Rayhill, Peter Pardo, Leslie Crandell, Valerie Dow, Regina Aggio, Pascal Honscher, Preston Paull, Susan Thompson, Bruce Stewart, Laura Schmier, Sue Willing, Mark Jacobsen, Betsy Waliszewski, Dawn Mann, Kathryn Barrett, John Chodacki, and Rob Bullington.

The incredibly hard working team at Elsevier Science, including Jonathan Bunkell, Ian Seager, Duncan Enright, David Burton, Rosanna Ramacciotti, Robert Fairbrother, Miguel Sanchez, Klaus Beran, Emma Wyatt, Rosie Moss, Chris Hossack, and Krista Leppiko, for making certain that our vision remains worldwide in scope.

David Buckland, Daniel Loh, Marie Chieng, Lucy Chong, Leslie Lim, Audrey Gan, Pang Ai Hua, and Joseph Chan of STP Distributors for the enthusiasm with which they receive our books.

Kwon Sung June at Acorn Publishing for his support.

David Scott, Tricia Wilden, Marilla Burgess, Annette Scott, Geoff Ebbs, Hedley Partis, Bec Lowe, and Mark Langley of Woodslane for distributing our books throughout Australia, New Zealand, Papua New Guinea, Fiji Tonga, Solomon Islands, and the Cook Islands.

Winston Lim of Global Publishing for his help and support with distribution of Syngress books in the Philippines.

Authors

Herbert H. Thompson, Ph.D., is Director of Security Technology at Security Innovation Inc. (www.securityinnovation.com). He earned his Ph.D. in Applied Mathematics from the Florida Institute of Technology and is co-author of *How to Break Software Security: Effective Techniques for Security Testing* (Addison-Wesley, 2003). Herbert has over 50 academic and industrial publications on software security, and frequently writes for industrial magazines including: *Dr. Dobbs Journal, IEEE Security and Privacy, Journal of Information and Software Technology, ACM Queue* and *Better Software Magazine*. He has spoken on software security throughout the United States, Europe, and Asia at conferences such as STAR, Quality Week, SD Expo, RSA, Gartner, RUC, ACM SAC and COMPSEC to name a few. He has won numerous best presentation awards for his lectures and is often asked to give conference keynotes. At Security Innovation, he leads research efforts on software security and trains security testers at some of the world's largest software companies. Herbert is also the principal investigator on several grants from the U.S. Department of Defense.

Spyros Nomikos holds a BS and MS in Chemical Engineering from the Florida Institute of Technology. He has worked for numerous fuel cell companies developing future hydrogen systems. His expertise is in systems design, safety analysis, and new product development. He is published and presented in various conferences on subjects such as hyperthermophillic bacteria, fuel cells and hydrogen.

Technical Reviewer

Russ Rogers (CISSP, CISM, IAM) is a Co-Founder, Chief Executive Officer, and Principle Security Consultant for Security Horizon, Inc; a Colorado-based professional security services and training provider and veteran owned small business. Russ is a key contributor to Security Horizon's technology efforts and leads the technical security practice and the services business development efforts. Russ is a United States Air Force Veteran and has served in military and contract support for the National Security Agency and the Defense Information Systems Agency. Russ is also the editor-in-chief of 'The Security Journal' and occasional staff member for the Black Hat Briefings. Russ holds an associate's degree in Applied Communications Technology from the Community College of the Air Force, a bachelor's degree from the University of Maryland in computer information systems, and a master's degree from the University of Maryland in computer systems management. Russ is a member of the Information System Security Association (ISSA) and the Information System Audit and Control Association (ISACA). He is also an Associate Professor at the University of Advancing Technology (uat.edu), just outside of Phoenix, Arizona. Russ is the author of *Hacking a Terror Network: The Silent Threat of Covert Channels* (Syngress, ISBN 1-928994-98-9). He has contributed to many books including: *Stealing the Network: How to Own a Continent* (Syngress, ISBN: 1-931836-05-1), *Security Assessment: Case Studies for Implementing the NSA IAM* (Syngress, ISBN 1-932266-96-8), *WarDriving, Drive, Detect, Defend: A Guide to Wireless Security* (Syngress, ISBN: 1-931836-03-5) and *SSCP Study Guide and DVD Training System* (Syngress, ISBN: 1-931846-80-9).

Contents

Part I

The Mezonic Agenda: Hacking the Presidency   1

In six days Chad Davis will testify before Congress on the security, stability, and safety of Advice Software Inc.'s e-vote software. He is a world-renowned expert on software security, and his testimony will determine if the software will be implemented for use during the 2004 U.S. Presidential Elections. All is well until he receives a cryptic CD on the software from a notorious hacker, which ignites a string of murders and uncovers a dangerous conspiracy. A race against the clock, Davis must use his knowledge of buffer overflows, format string vulnerabilities and zero-day exploits to penetrate physical and cyber defenses, ultimately uncovering Advice's plot to fix the US presidential elections. What's the software's secret? Will Davis find out before his testimony? What is *The Mezonic Agenda*?

Part II 243

The Technology behind *The Mezonic Agenda*

In *The Mezonic Agenda*, Chad Davis is a computer expert who must use all of his skills and knowledge to unlock the CD and solve the secret of Advice's software. The story may be fiction, but the science is all too real. Every day, real-life security experts use the methodology and tactics implemented by Davis in the story. The following appendices touch upon these technologies, their history, and their role in the present-day. From the origins of voting to the modern-era realm of buffer overflows, you'll be given a tour of the technology behind *The Mezonic Agenda*.

Preface

In six days Chad Davis will testify before Congress on the security, stability, and safety of Advice Software Inc.'s e-vote software. After his speech at a security conference in Amsterdam, notorious hacker Baff Lexicon hands Davis a cryptic CD with information about the software. Soon after, Baff is killed and Davis must unravel a plot to manipulate the U.S. presidential elections.

Welcome to the world of *The Mezonic Agenda*!

Our goal in writing this book was to create an engaging and most unique entertainment experience. In this first of its kind mix of techno-thriller and interactive hacking adventure, you, the reader, can face the same challenges as the novel's characters through the software on the included CD. With that in mind, there are several ways to read this book. You can choose to never open the CD and simply read what we think is a great novel. For the more curious reader, however, we invite you to "hack along" with the novel's characters and experience the adventure first hand.

In addition to entertainment, one of this book's aims is to educate, and empower the reader with information about software security and the challenges of implementing modern voting systems. We encourage you to also read Part II: *The Technology Behind The Mezonic Agenda* which is a collection of nonfiction appendices intended to enrich your knowledge of electronic voting and software security in general. One of the appendices focuses on voting history and its evolution from stone balls being cast into vases to today's optical scan and electronic systems. The other appendices take a piercing look at software security, cryptography, steganography, reverse engineering and software exploits.

We hope you enjoy reading this book as much as we've enjoyed researching and creating it. Please visit the books companion website at www.mezonicagenda.com for new challenges and more information on all of the topics discussed in the novel. Thanks and enjoy!

Herbert H. Thompson
Spyros Nomikos
August 2004

About the CD

Now you can hack along with the heroes and villains of *The Mezonic Agenda*! Don't just read it, experience it!

Notorious hacker Baff Lexicon has just handed internationally renowned software security expert Dr. Chad Davis a cryptic CD. Davis must decrypt this CD's contents to reveal the secrets behind Advice Software's e-voting system, a secret that has cost the lives of several people and holds the American Presidency in the balance.

Hack along with Davis as he tries to unlock the CD's mysteries. Unzip the contents to access the data on the CD. You will then have three files, and your first challenge is to decrypt one of them: encrypted.dat, where you will receive several more challenges. The CD's mysteries will be revealed in the story and you can either: read the novel and ignore the CD, perform the hacks as they appear in the novel, or the more aspiring techie can try and decrypt the CD contents without reading too far into *The Mezonic Agenda*. Do you have what it takes to expose Advice Software Inc. and ultimately save the Nation's general election from disaster? There's only one way to find out…

Visit www.mezonicagenda.com for more information and new challenges!

About the Contest

The Mezonic Agenda: Hacking the Presidency Contest challenges you, the reader, to interact with the book and CD, decrypt its contents, and ultimately control the fate of a mock U.S. Presidential Election. Contestants will attempt to vote for themselves as the winning candidate during our "simulated" election to be held in early 2005. Contestants must use their hacking skills, along with strategy, to manipulate the results of the Mezonic "mock" election. Visit www.mezonicagenda.com to enter.

Any eligible contestant can download the software from the Mezonic Agenda: Hacking a Presidency website (www.mezonicagenda.com) without having to purchase the book. The book, though, will help the reader better understand how the software works, teach them software hacking skills and ultimately aid in its exploitation.

Prizes include a free pass to the 2005 Black Hat Briefings in Las Vegas and a suite of security books from Syngress Publishing.

Syngress may require any participant receiving any prize to provide Syngress with proof that he or she is eligible to participate according to the eligibility requirements hereunder. See "The Mezonic Agenda Hack Contest Rules" in the back of the book or visit www.mezonicagenda.com for complete contest rules.

Author Acknowledgements

Herbert H. Thompson Acknowledgements

This book has been a huge effort and wouldn't have been possible without the support of many people. The staff at Syngress has been great and I'd like to especially single out Andrew Williams, Christine Kloiber and Amy Pedersen for their fantastic and sustained efforts and contributions. I'd like to thank my co-author (and more importantly great friend) Spyros. Because of him this book was possible, and working with him made it a pleasure, never a chore. My fiancé, Sasha, has been so understanding and encouraging during the time-intensive process of writing this book that a mere "thank you" doesn't even begin to express my gratitude and love. And finally, thanks to the greatest family one could ever hope for. I dedicate this book to them. To my mother, the strongest and most incredibly loving person I have ever met. To my father, my idol, a man who has the respect and admiration of everyone he knows, especially his son. And finally to my brilliant sister Maria, who is my constant teacher, friend, and one of my favorite people to spend time with.

Spyros Nomikos Acknowledgements

Having known Hugh for almost ten years now, I am honored that we have worked together on this book and he is without a doubt the first person I owe an immense *Thank You* to for choosing to work with me. I have spent countless nights on the road traveling from my home to his fiancé's place where Hugh and I would burn the midnight oil, chugging away at the chapters. It's been lots of laughs, stressful deadlines, lots of reading, and an exercise in humility. Hugh's expertise transcends computer and software security. I have grown to respect him even more not because of what he knows but because of how he's taught me! *Thank you Hugh*.

Additionally this book would not be possible without the support of my family. They have allowed me the freedom and time to dedicate nights and weekends to for almost a year. I think I can get some sleep now.

Finally a great thank you to Syngress for signing us and moving along on such a tight deadline. Thanks Andrew, Amy, Christine, Russ, and all!

Part One,
The Mezonic Agenda: Hacking the Presidency

Prologue: Seattle, WA

October 2, 2003

"Our country will never be the same, gentlemen. It is time for us to take matters into our own hands." The host spoke with authority, commanding the attention of the other two.

"The people will be behind us," the second man said, taking a deep and sustained drag from his cigar.

"We are taking a risk. What if the method is revealed?" The third man asked.

"The pilot project is underway in Washington. All we need is for Congress to ratify its implementation," said the host. He sat comfortably, yet still wielded control of their meeting within his mansion in Seattle, Washington.

"I am willing to fight for this campaign and win it for the people," the third man said, speaking with less confidence than the other two.

"With all due respect Senator, you have powerful forces pushing your campaign forward," the smoking man replied.

"Gentlemen," the host interrupted, "We did not meet here tonight to discuss specifics. We are here because a growing number of Americans feel the way we do. We are here because our leader has failed us. We are here because our country needs us."

"How big is our following?" asked the Senator.

"It grows daily. There is pain shared by many that cannot be soothed, an anger that cannot be suppressed. The *society* is strong."

Both men listened silently. They knew the host had suffered a great loss. They knew how passionate he was, and how deeply he felt for his brethren. The society sympathized. Hard-working Americans, once satisfied with a job and a roof over their heads, now wanted justice.

The host continued, "Tonight our campaign is working for us, Senator. It will not be won on the road; rather it will be decided on the Net."

Chapter 1: Seattle, WA

University of Washington, Six Months Later

Dr. Chad Davis's desk was overrun with research journals, notes, and month-old student papers waiting to be graded. Though his office was small, it had enough room for a desk, a large filing cabinet, two book shelves, and a couple of chairs for guests, both of which now held two tall and relatively unstable stacks of reference papers.

Davis had been at the University of Washington's Computer Science Department since 1990 where he had just been tenured the previous year. Right now, though, he was frantically stuffing his laptop case with papers and demonstration hardware.

"Relax Dr. Davis, you'll make your flight," his secretary, Anne, reassured him, as she helped him make his final preparations.

Davis was scheduled to be a keynote speaker at the RSA Conference in Amsterdam, where his topic would be reverse engineering. Pausing to reflect, he made sure he had stocked his carry-on with enough reading material on his most recent priority, analysis of Advice Software's e-voting initiative for the 2004 U.S. Presidential Election.

"That's what I thought last time, Anne," replied Davis, referring to the last planned flight to Washington D.C., which he missed. After spending most of the early morning at the airport, he arrived the next day, one hour late for his meeting with members of the Federal Election Commission and a number of electronic voting software and hardware vendors.

"This flight is a bit longer. I don't think there are many flights to Amsterdam that I can catch if I miss this one." She smiled and handed him a small stack of papers for him to cram into his briefcas, before returning to her desk in the next room. Anne was the glue that held Davis's life together. She would often joke that his mind was so preoccupied by his work that there was no room to maintain basic organizational skills. He knew she was right.

Before packing his laptop he checked his e-mail one last time. Only one of the 12 new messages required immediate attention:

```
Mr. Davis,


We have received your unofficial analysis of the Advice Software e-vote
system. I'm glad to see that it's held up to your testing so far so that
we can move to the next step. We look forward to your testimony a week
from Monday. As you can understand, this system will be of extreme
importance to us and, of course, to the voters of our country. We have
confirmed your hotel and travel accommodations in the attached file. Have a
safe trip and we look forward to seeing you.


Regards,


Grace Wilkinson
Voting Systems Director
Federal Election Commission
```

He quickly sent off a reply:

```
Ms. Wilkinson,


Thank you for the travel info. I look forward to seeing you a week from
Monday. As you may already know, I will be in Amsterdam for the RSA
conference this coming week. If you need to reach me please do so via e-
mail.


Chad
```

He quickly stuffed his laptop in his carry-on, and grabbed his now full briefcase.

"Thanks Anne, I'm sure that Delta will wait for me," he said wryly as he hurriedly walked past her desk.

"But, you're on KLM!"

Davis paused as he stood in the doorway, but only for a moment, "Right. I knew that! Thanks!"

"Have fun." She called after him, but the only answer was his quick footsteps echoing down the hall.

Hopping into his car, he double-checked that his suitcase was with him, before glancing at his watch. *Only 40 minutes behind this time!*

Traffic was surprisingly light for a mid-Wednesday trek to the airport. He had an eventless check-in and security pass followed by an hour-long wait at the gate before boarding. More often than not, Chad had enough on his mind to keep him occupied during a lengthy wait at an airport. This was no exception. While taking his seat on the plane, he reassured himself that his analysis of the Advice e-vote software had gone well. He had found no serious flaws in the system aside from a few of the typical functional bugs, but nothing that couldn't be fixed and certified in time.

"Sir, please buckle up, we're taxiing for take-off."

Davis was startled but quickly came to, realizing he had drifted for a few minutes. He buckled up and turned his attention to the window. *Maybe I should get some sleep.* There was plenty of time for sleep, reading, and the airline's finest meals during this flight. Somehow Davis knew his mind wouldn't let him sleep for long.

Chapter 2:   Macau, China

Mezonic Corporation: Corporate Headquarters

Sitting at his desk, Eric Tang's hands held his head in despair. *I can't do this anymore.* Between a gap in his fingers Eric spotted one of his business cards stapled to a fax,

Eric Tang, Chief Financial Officer

Mezonic Corporation

Macau, China

The word "Officer" amused him in an unsettling way. It wasn't too long ago that executive "officers" from Enron, Tyco, Adelphia, and the ever-popular Martha Stewart were publicly crucified for actions that seemed harmless compared to his own.

Eric's morality had been tested with his every business move over the course of his career; over time he had become a master of the "little white lie" justification. Early in his career, Eric had worked for a small start-up tech firm that relied heavily on venture capital and government money. He helped write many of the grant proposals that weathered the company through their pre-IPO years. He remembered paying company-wide administrative expenses by invoicing the government for the time of employees who didn't even exist.

"The government expects us to do this," his boss reassured him daily.

Although Mezonic had not yet sunk to defrauding its customers, he knew the time was near.

Eric was a remarkably tall Chinese man whose thinning hair, bad posture, and slight belly made him look much older than his 43 years. He had grown up in Macau and spoke fluent English, Cantonese, and Portuguese with little detectable accent. Other than his height and way with languages, Eric was unremarkable in every sense of the word. He'd never been particularly successful in his career as an accountant. He was one of those people who could slip in and out of a room, completely unnoticed. He wasn't assertive and caved to the will of his superiors as a matter of practice. Professionally, Eric's submissiveness had hurt him, but a stagnant career had never inspired him to change.

Two years ago, Eric heard about an opening in the newly formed Mezonic Corporation, a specialty video chip manufacturer, from Steve Watts, his former college roommate. They had both attended UCLA and graduated with MBAs, one year apart. Eric had always been quiet and passive whereas Steve took charge, volunteering their room for parties, securing drinks and kegs even when they were underage. After Steve graduated, Eric dreaded the thought of another roommate and decided to take up miscellaneous part-time jobs to pay the extra rent. Steve's departure was both a curse and a blessing for Eric. He became a complete social recluse but his grades improved, allowing him to graduate fifth in his class. Eric and Steve kept in close touch even after they both left UCLA, and it was Steve who Eric walked down the parchment floor of Mezonic's executive suite to confront.

He slowly opened the large oak door to Steve's office with an almost inaudible knock. As usual, Steve greeted him heartily like an old friend who had been absent for a while even though they saw each other every day in the company halls.

"Steve we need to talk," Eric said in a concerned voice.

"Sit down, Eric; sit down," Steve said. "You know my door is always open to you."

Like a familiar but dissonant tune, Eric began to go over the company finances. "Steve, these problems don't just fix themselves. We have to raise prices! If we don't do something now we'll all be out of a job in three months."

Steve was Mezonic's President, and in its short life of two years, he had led Mezonic to be a resounding success in the marketplace. Mezonic had seen exponential growth in its microchip sales, and both Eric and Steve had been there since the beginning. By most measures of success, Mezonic was a wunderkind, but Eric knew differently. He knew that the company was hemorrhaging money. Microchips had become a commodity business, and by undercutting the prices of their competitors, Mezonic took a loss on every chip that went out the door. As CFO, this had been frustrating for Eric, but time and time again, Steve chimed in with reassurance, "This is part of our grand vision," he'd say, "we need market share, and then we worry about profit."

In the latest quarter's figures, though, Eric could see that the company was spiraling toward bankruptcy. This was the all-too-routine subject of today's talk with Steve, but this time Eric's patience had finally run out.

"Eric…" Steve began to speak with a familiar air of condescension.

"No, NO!" Eric interrupted, suddenly smacking his hands onto the desktop, leaning towards Steve, "*You* may not care about getting a job when this company is through but I do! You know who the board, the stockholders, the press are going to blame if we go under? They're going to blame us, because only a fool wouldn't have been able to see this coming!"

This outburst was very uncharacteristic of Eric. He usually would acquiesce at the slightest hint of Steve's disapproval. Steve's mood immediately sobered at this display and his voice lowered.

"Eric, you're right…something has to be done. Something *will* be done."

"That's all I ask," Eric said more calmly, before nodding and leaving the office. A thrill of adrenaline rushed down his spine as he walked back down the hall. *Finally! Finally things are going to change.*

As soon as the large oak door closed, Steve picked up a cell phone from his locked drawer, punched in a few numbers, and was greeted by an accented voice on the other end.

"The problem isn't going away."

"I can solve your problem," replied the voice.

"But I think we can still trust him."

"Trust is a luxury we can no longer afford. Consider the problem solved."

It was almost 8 P.M. that evening when Eric took his nightly reprieve from balance sheets, transaction records, and the ever-growing mound of sales slips. The parking lot was nearly deserted, but this was how he usually met it. Eric's characteristic malaise was lifted tonight, though; he walked confidently and was oblivious to the security lights, which no longer hung above the executive parking area, and to the large Yugoslavian man hiding in the resulting shadows nearby.

Eric reflected on his time at the Mezonic Corporation, including the creative accounting he had done to satisfy the new reporting requirements beginning to take effect in Macau. *It was no accident that Mezonic ended up here,* he thought. Macau was an anomaly in China. Until 1999, the island had been a Portuguese territory. This made for an interesting landscape of ornate churches adjacent to Buddhist temples. It was Macau's reputation for liberal laws and cheap labor that led Steve Watts and Mezonic to its shores. Despite the handover to China, the island still prospered from casinos and prostitution. More than 20,000 people per day made their way from mainland China to Macau to indulge in pleasures that were illegal only a few kilometers away in the Chinese province of Guangdong. So strong were the ties with its neighbors that Hong Kong dollars, Macau pataca, and Chinese yuan renminbi all flowed freely in stores and on blackjack tables. However, Steve's and Eric's major interest was in their accounting practices: no intrusive audits, little mandatory reporting requirements, just the way that Steve and the major shareholder liked it.

As Eric approached his car, the streetlights faded, before finally extinguishing completely. Eric turned his head just in time to see the dim outline of his executioner. With a veteran move, the assailant covered Eric's mouth and plunged a large blade through his rib cage. Eric struggled only briefly, and when it was done, the man worked quickly and without emotion to load the body into the trunk of his car.

He had to hurry; a plane awaited him to Amsterdam. One more life needed to be taken.

Chapter 3:
Amsterdam, the Netherlands

RSA Conference: RAI Convention Center

"Thank you. I'd be happy to answer any questions you may have."

The room erupted with applause. At heart, Chad Davis was a showman. The applause of a crowd, no matter how perfunctory, always gave him a charge. This was the second year that he had spoken at the RSA European Security Conference. The number of attendees had grown substantially from the previous year. He overlooked the crowd of about 700 and glimpsed a few familiar faces in the audience from the year before: a software developer from an Israeli pharmaceutical company, a system administrator from Poland, and a small American man whose insightful questions last year lead Davis to believe that "State Department" on his name tag belied his true employer, the National Security Agency.

By the now-steady din of the crowd and some occasional camera flashes, Davis could sense his lecture had gone well. He had stood in front of a crowded room many times over the past three years and had grown accustomed to—almost dependent on—the enthusiasm of the audience. Today's topic, *Reverse Engineering*, was one of the most controversial Davis had broached.

"Dr. Davis," a faint voice said as an usher fumbled to switch on the cordless microphone in the hands of a small blond woman.

"Dr. Davis. Ah that's better. Dr. Davis, aren't you concerned that teaching people how to bypass security and essentially steal software, data, and much worse will increase digital crime? Do we really need more hackers running around out there?"

It was a familiar argument. Chad Davis had defended himself against it more times than he or the media cared to count. This was one of the more courteous phrasings he had recently heard. Over the past several years he had been likened to a digital arms dealer, called reckless, labeled an anarchist and a threat to national security. Most of the heat had come from the publication of his first book, *How to Hack Software*, which essentially showed how one could exploit common security flaws such as buffer overflows. One New York Times columnist went so far as to say that he was "handing the technical recluse and techno-social deviant the power to measurably inflict harm on some of the largest corporations and nations." Davis made sure that the quote made it to the back cover of the book for its second printing.

The book, the roasting from the software community that followed, and Davis's reputation for committing live "hacks" during talks made him a big draw at conferences. Some audience members admitted their only reason for attending was to see if he would be arrested on stage.

This had become a real possibility. In 2001 Dmitry Sklyarov, a Russian programmer, was arrested immediately after his talk at the world's largest Hacker conference, DEFCON. Dmitry's crime: demonstrating techniques to essentially unprotect and copy electronic books. His company had a legitimate reason for doing so—they made a product to help users organize their digital books and reference them easily. Pre-2000 this would not have been a crime in the United States, but the introduction of the Digital Millennium Copyright Act—a law essentially banning reverse engineering and digital piracy—had turned the digital world upside down. Other countries were beginning to introduce their own versions of the law, and for this reason, audience members enjoyed watching Davis dance around the boundaries of legality on stage. RSA's European Security Conference was one of Davis's favorites since Dutch laws against breaking software were some of the most liberal in the western hemisphere and his antics could proceed further than usual.

"Allow me to ask your question in another way," Davis responded. "The software industry develops techniques to protect software's secrets. Most software contains secrets, and these are different from application to application. Some of them the manufacturer knows about, like encryption keys, but others, like where the big security bugs are, they usually don't. Imagine that you work for a game company that just released an adventure game that cost millions of dollars and thousands of programmer hours to create. You sell the game for $39.95 a copy. What's your security concern? What are this software's secrets?"

The crowd paused, and under an apparent pressure to answer, the woman still holding the microphone broke the silence.

"I'm not sure what you mean. It's just a game, right?"

With apparent delight, Davis answered. "It *is* a game, one that cost a lot of money to make. The biggest secret is probably the game itself; you want only people who paid for it to be able to have it. This is a *secret* you want kept from the nonpaying consumer. There are probably other secrets too; like how you created a particular visual effect or maybe how you render character movement. These are secrets you want to keep from your competition since the game probably cost you a lot to develop, and exposing these secrets would be losing your competitive advantage. Agreed?"

"That's exactly what I'm talking about!" the woman responded, "You're teaching people how to steal this stuff."

Davis paused before rebutting. He *loved* these spontaneous confrontations.

"Ok. Well we can be pretty sure that if the game is popular enough and if its secrets are valuable enough that people are going to target it, right? Any hacker out there worth his or her salt knows *exactly* what to try. They know how to attack the game's copy protection; they know how to analyze the program in detail to extract its secrets. Some of these guys are good, very, very good. If any of them are here in the audience, they would probably fall asleep during my talk, there's nothing new for them here."

Davis knew there was talent out there. Throughout the years he had met many 14-year-olds that could crack software protection schemes in minutes that had taken a team of experts years to create. At the DEFCON conference in 1999 one particularly skilled adolescent handed Davis a slip of paper with Davis's checking account balance after an off-handed remark about the security efforts of the banking industry a few minutes before.

"And that's the problem," he continued, "hackers share and learn information on how to break systems, but that's where the information stays, in their world. To make software stronger, the people who build software need to know what they're up against. They need to know how hackers think and what they do. That's the only way we can protect software."

The woman sat, apparently disarmed by Davis's rebuttal. The truth was unsettling to most people. They didn't understand that the suppression of knowledge was hurting the software security industry. Davis knew corporations had to start embracing the techniques of the hacker. He had already begun to help software vendors set up hacking groups within their ranks to attack their software before it was released. It made sense, not just intuitively, but financially. On average, it costs a software company almost 50 times more to fix a bug and release a patch after an application is released than if they had detected and fixed it before the software shipped. "Ethical hacking" was just good business sense.

Davis's ideals had made strides in the ivory-towered world of academia too. Last year he launched the first university-level course on hacking. The media frenzy that followed would have certainly resulted in dismissal if not for the massive amounts of money he brought into the university through his research contracts. A new road was being paved. In 2003 the University of Calgary launched a course on virus writing. Shortly after, degrees in computer security began to sprout at universities across the United States.

Some saw it as the lock to Pandora's Box being "hacked" off. Davis knew that the security revolution was a long time in coming and the momentum was larger than the alarmists could withstand.

"It seems as though we have time for one more question," the moderator announced. Davis watched the usher make his way to a small Asian man seated near the back of the room.

The man began to speak in a heavy Chinese accent, "Dr. Davis, you mention buffer overflow in talk. Can you please describe and how we can stop."

Ah, the buffer overflow! This had been the topic of many of Davis's lectures and the source of most of his on-stage antics. He was hoping someone would ask him this question so he could put on a good show. He felt his grin grow with every passing second.

Trying to maintain his serious composure he replied, "Buffer overflows account for nearly 70 percent of the security vulnerabilities in software. They are dangerous because sometimes they can allow an attacker to replace some of the application's instructions with some of their own."

Davis could see the moderator take off his wristwatch and place it on a table in front of him. This was a pre-arranged signal to let Davis know that time was up and that he needed to shut up and get the hell off the stage. Davis abhorred moderators' power trips and always hoped for a lengthy and entertaining talk. Last year, toward the end of his presentation at the SECWORLD conference in London, the moderator not only placed his wristwatch on the table, but without warning, turned Davis' microphone off and ended his presentation for him. An argument ensued, which quickly lead to an escort and a permanent ban from the conference after an offhanded remark about the Queen.

Despite *this* moderator's assertion of power Davis continued; how could he not with a standing question on his favorite topic?

"Buffer overflows happen when we make bad assumptions about the length of user data. Here's an example. Imagine that you're a programmer for some company that needs to collect mailing address information from clients through the Internet. You create a web page, and it has little boxes for the user's name, city, state, and everything else you need. Let's say that you make an assumption about the zip code field. You assume that a user won't enter more than ten characters into that box: five numbers, a dash, and four more numbers. So you set aside a small amount of space for this data in your software that is going to process this information on some server. What would happen if a user put a thousand characters into that zip code field?" Davis was on a roll. He paused for a moment not knowing exactly how technical to make his explanation.

"Maybe everything works okay, but chances are, the server is going to crash. Voilà: a buffer overflow!"

Davis could see the puzzled looks in the faces of some of the crowd. The Chinese man spoke out once more, "Dr. Davis, buffer overflow can do more than crash?"

Davis realized that he needed to delve further into the belly of the beast, "That's exactly right; a software crash is the *least* harmful outcome of a buffer overflow. To understand why a buffer overflow can be so dangerous we need to look at how a computer's memory works. We've all bought computers, and one of the key statistics a salesperson will quote you is how much memory a computer has, usually referred to as random access memory, or RAM. This usually is given either in megabytes, MB; or gigabytes, GB. Before a computer can execute any instructions or manipulate any data it usually has to load that information into memory. That's all a program is, a series of instructions that tell a computer what to do, and some data that the program is going to do something with. When a program gets data from a user, that data usually is put into a structure in memory called the data stack."

He could sense the crowd drifting, but he had to press on. "Think of the data stack as a series of numbered post office boxes and assume that I have boxes 0001 thru 9999 for my computer program. Going back to the zip code example, let's say that I've allocated boxes 1 through 10 to store the zip code, one character per box. There is a special set of boxes, say

numbers 15, 16, 17, and 18 that are used to store the number of the box
I'm supposed to go to for instructions on what to do when I've finished
getting the zip code. In computing terms this is called a return address—
the place in the main program to go back to when we are done with the
current task. We reserved four boxes for this since each box holds only
one digit and we have boxes 0001 through 9999 available."

Davis surveyed the blank expressions. Fortunately he always carried an
extra set of slides to explain his favorite type of security vulnerability. He
fumbled around on his laptop for a few seconds before finally locating
the file *Buffer_Overflow.ppt*.

Buffer Overflow Slide 1

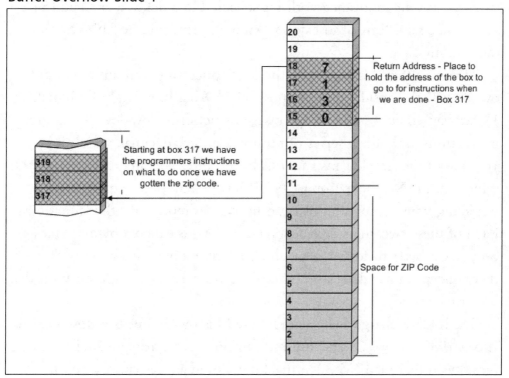

"Here we have a picture of what the data stack might look like. Starting
in box 0317 we have the instructions on what to with the zip code once
it's been collected from the user. Now imagine that the programmer did

not constrain the length of the zip code field. What if the user were to enter 20 characters instead of 10? Let's say we entered 20 1's. This would result in the number 1 being stored in boxes 0001 through 0020, and the return address, boxes 15 thru 18, would now be 1111, the number of a command box that contains who knows what. The computer would then go to box 1111 instead of 0317 looking for instructions and likely find garbage, which would force our application to crash."

Davis realized that he had not yet answered the man's question. He paused for a moment wondering if this was all a wasted exercise given the obvious language barrier. But with one slide already invested, Davis decided to continue. From the corner of his eye he caught the moderator's increasing annoyance with his speech. He quickly turned and in a stern voice said, "I'm almost done," knowing it would buy him a few more minutes.

"I've said that this would be the *least* concerning outcome of a buffer overflow. Let's consider another possibility. What if, instead of a bunch of 1's, we had entered some of our own instructions? Low-level computer instructions look like a series of numbers in hexadecimal, which is base 16. One of the simplest instructions in the Intel x86 architecture is 0x90, which means No Operation or NOP. It's the computer equivalent of twiddling your thumbs. Similarly, other values represent other functions. Each of these two-digit hexadecimal numbers is called a byte. It takes only seven bytes to format a machine in some operating systems. With that concept in mind, let's take a look at what else we could do with that buffer overflow."

Davis felt a charge as he remembered his first buffer overflow exploit. It was 1988; he was 24 and finishing his Ph.D. at Carnegie Mellon when he noticed that his IBM 8086 machine would always crash when he opened a particular file. Back then, little was known about buffer overflows. Software vendors considered crashes resulting from long strings a user error. In fact, software testers routinely were chastised for reporting crashes from long strings. They were quick to be dismissed by managers as unlikely user scenarios, given extremely low priority, and often not fixed at all.

Davis was intrigued by his crashing file. At a time when the Internet was just beginning to emerge, he searched news groups and dial-in Bulletin Boards (BBS) for information on how these crashes could be exploited. Then in November of that year, arguably the first computer virus or worm struck: the Morris worm, named after its creator, Robert Morris, then a graduate student at Cornell. Davis was captivated by the worm and studied it thoroughly when it was released. The idea behind one of the many exploits it used to spread was simple but powerful; use the return address to point back to the beginning of the string you entered. What a phenomenal insight! Once you knew which characters in the string you entered over-wrote the return address, and you knew the location of the beginning of that string on the stack, you could force an application to change its execu-tion path; you could force an application to execute anything you wanted! This is the essence of a buffer overflow and this is its true power and promise: complete control of another person's computer.

Many other viruses and worms that followed the Morris Worm exploited buffer overflows in software. In 2001, the Code Red virus sur-faced, taking advantage of a buffer overflow in Microsoft's Internet Information Server (IIS). At the time, IIS was the most popular web server and the worm spread quickly, defacing countless web pages and grinding Internet traffic to a near standstill. Corporations were inundated with net-work packets as the worm attempted to spread. It's estimated that Code Red and its variants cost consumers more than $2 billion in lost produc-tivity, but Davis knew that the true figure was much higher.

Writing buffer overflow exploits was both an art and a skill and Davis's passion for the flaw had made him a digital Michelangelo.

Flashing back to the present, Davis continued, "Now what if we fill our string with instructions and then change the return address to point to the boxes that store our string? Here's a simplified view of how the stack might look now."

He advanced his PowerPoint slide.

Buffer Overflow Slide 2

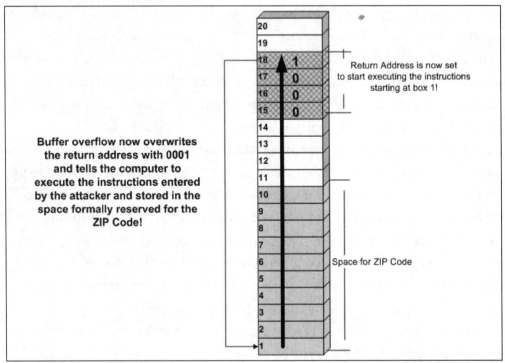

"One option is that we overwrite the return address with the address of the beginning of our data. The server will then execute the instructions we entered as a part of our data. Since we can essentially put any data into the zip code field, we can force the application to execute anything we want! Now we *own* that software, we *own* that server, we *own* that company!"

An approving round of applause broke out and Davis could see a mixed crowd of cheering groupies and a few techno–prude detractors shaking their heads in disgust.

Fully annoyed by the extra time Davis had used up, the moderator interrupted before he could go any further, "Thank you Dr. Davis for your always enlightening and entertaining remarks."

Unsure if this was the end of his speech the crowd slowly began to clap, followed by a prolonged applause. Davis packed up his laptop and made his way down the steps along the side of the stage. As usual, a small crowd stayed behind to greet him there. This was one of Davis's favorite parts of the conference, one-on-one exchanges with real software people who had real problems.

The first person to approach the side of the podium was a tall slim man with black hair. The man had a kind face, and spoke with a thick accent. "Dr. Davis, I enjoyed your talk. My name is Goran Petrovic, and I work for a fuel cell company in San Francisco. We have been experiencing some most unusual software failures that I believe a man of your talents could help us with." Goran pulled a business card from a small silver case and handed it to Davis. He glanced at it, catching the name and title:

Goran Petrovic
Chief Technology Officer
Advanced Hydrogen Systems, Inc.

Davis reciprocated. "San Francisco, I'll be there in a month for another conference. I'd be happy to help in any way I can; please e-mail me and we'll meet up while I'm there."

He knew the fuel cell industry was fast growing yet still relatively young in their commercial product development. *Possibly a great future opportunity.* Davis was usually inundated by e-mail after a conference appearance. Most of them he ignored, but some eventually led to lucrative consulting deals.

The next person to approach was a tall, well-dressed man carrying a large laptop bag. Davis recognized the man from the front row of his talk.

"So you think these kinds of bugs are a big problem, huh?" the man began, with a confrontational tone.

"Don't you?" Davis replied.

The man wore a condescending smirk on his face. "My name is Mike Snell, perhaps you've heard of me?"

Davis had heard of him. Several months ago Dr. Dobbs Journal, a leading magazine for software developers, had run an article on Snell and his company's new authentication software for web applications. The article had stuck out in Davis's mind because of some of the quotes from Snell himself. In one particularly memorable one, Davis recalled Snell dismissing the CEO of one of his competitors as "clueless and childlike." Davis was not about to stroke this guy's ego.

"Can't say that I have," Davis replied abruptly, hoping that this would terminate the conversation.

"You really should keep up with the industry more," Snell replied with the smirk still on his face, "I'm giving a talk in 20 minutes in Salon B. I think you'd benefit from being there."

I'd benefit? What a prick.

"I'll try my very best to make it." Davis had no intention of going. The thought of listening to Snell speak for one more second was excruciating. He just wanted the guy to leave.

Suddenly, Davis noticed a small man pushing his way in front of the crowd with a small object in his hand, trying to gain Davis's attention. Davis recognized him immediately but showed no signs of it. *Never admit to knowing a hacker.*

"Sir, if you could just wait a moment I'll be right with you," he said to the man, trying to suppress any outward signs of recognition, turning even further away from Snell. Not used to being treated so perfunctorily, Snell quickly turned on his heels and left without a word. Davis barely registered his departure because in front of him stood Baff Lexicon, one of Europe's most notorious hackers.

Davis made an attempt at dismissing the rest of the crowd.

"Thank you all for attending and listening to my talk. Enjoy the rest of the conference."

Davis eased away from the crowd that was now beginning to faction into smaller and smaller groups with their own conversations. He moved discretely next to the stage near the curtains where he and Baff could talk in private.

Dispensing with pleasantries, Baff spoke with concern. "I have information about Advice Software's new product. Of course this is not the place or time. We must meet tonight!"

His manner was unusually assertive; Davis could tell this was something big, something disturbing. Davis's stomach dropped. For the past several months he had been investigating Advice's products for the U.S. government. The biggest expert witness appearance of his career was a few days away and Advice was the principal topic.

"What information?" Davis asked.

"Meet me tonight, Hard Rock Café, midnight. There are things they don't want you to know."

Baff handed Davis a card and walked into the crowd. The past few months filled Davis's mind. Given Davis's failure to find any major security problems with Advice's software and the stakes involved, he knew tonight's meeting was mandatory.

A secret meeting? At midnight? What the hell is this guy into now?

This in-person meeting was very unlike Baff. It had been years of e-mail correspondence before the mysterious hacker had approached Davis in person at a DEFCON conference. Despite the questionable ways Baff practiced his "art," Davis and Baff shared many common interests and had corresponded through e-mail for the past several years, though this was only the second time they had met face-to-face.

After a quick glance at the card he realized it was a business card CD, popular in the tech world with many companies. It was an ideal medium to include a product catalog, company information, and contact info. Davis's uneasiness grew as he read the card's text:

David Feller

Lead Developer, Special Projects

Advice Software

Chapter 4:
Amsterdam, the Netherlands

Schiphol International Airport

The Boeing 747 eased to a stop at Schiphol Airport's Gate 15. As the doors opened there was the usual flurry of hurried activity as passengers grabbed their bags from overhead compartments and stumbled out into the terminal.

One man remained, unmoving and apparently lifeless at a window seat in row nine.

"Sir? Pardon me, sir?" the hostess said with an increasingly aggravated tone. The flight from Hong Kong had been 11 long hours and she was in no mood to stay on it any longer than she was paid to.

"Sir. The flight has arrived. Sir?"

The large man slowly opened his eyes and began to move. An 11-hour flight had meant a few drinks and a heavy nap. Without speaking, Danko slowly stood, running his hand across his short military haircut. He turned to face the seats and removed a large bag from the compartment above.

He walked purposefully off the plane and into the crowded terminal. He always felt like a forgotten star as he stepped out of the gate ramp and into the terminal. He would notice people looking at him, searching for their loved ones. Countless times he'd seen husbands, wives, and children run to greet someone who had been absent. He had never experienced that. No one ever eagerly awaited his arrival. No one ran to him desperate for a hug.

As he made his way through the terminal he fondly remembered his first trip to Amsterdam, and a brief but memorable encounter with a prostitute there. Her name was Yuki, but in his Western European accent he called her "Yucky." From a distance, Danko had thought she was an angel, but as he approached he realized how rough the streets had been to her. She wore a spandex top, jean shorts, and a pair of dirty sneakers. Her face showed signs of aging even though she was only 24. Her empty eyes sagged, surrounded by wrinkles. Her arms and legs were bruised from the constant search for a needle entry. Her heroin addiction had led her to Amsterdam, where drugs were more easily available and their use was openly accepted. Danko had enabled her to feed her addiction by providing her with business. He had offered her one-quarter of her asking price. She countered, meeting him half-way, where he agreed. He remembered pulling his rental car to a back street where she joined him for a quick service, only to be interrupted by the police. She jumped out of the car as Danko dropped into first gear and sped off…unfulfilled.

Pausing at a kiosk with tourist brochures, he turned his back to the bustling airport lobby, and discreetly removed a large manila envelope from inside his jacket. There were several sheets inside. The first had a picture of a man along with detailed statistics: height, weight, and distinguishing marks. The second was a map with an address hand-written on the top. Danko surveyed the second page as he walked out of the airport exit to an old Citroen idling near the curb. After tossing his bag into the trunk, he opened the passenger door, and without a word handed the paper to the driver.

Danko recognized the driver, "Johnny," from previous jobs. Johnny was as different from Danko as one could imagine. Danko's childhood was hard, poor, and abusive. Johnny grew up in the mid-seventies in middle-class America. Danko grew up on the streets, resorting to a life of crime to survive. Johnny attended college where he experimented in recreational drugs, never completing his degree. After a few rehab attempts, he decided to move to Europe, eventually falling on Amsterdam. He'd worked with Danko a number of times and he knew tonight would go smoothly if Danko was in charge. He respected him but would never want to do his job; being the clean-up guy was good enough to pay the bills.

"Looks like you got some rest on that flight, man," Johnny said, welcoming Danko. He noticed the papers in Danko's hands and knew he had already reviewed their assignment. "I've already checked it out. He should be there now."

"Then we do it now," Danko replied with a thick accent. Without answering, Johnny pulled out slowly onto the street and the odd-looking pair began their journey to the city center.

Danko unzipped the bag that lay at his feet and inspected its contents: plastic sheets, gloves, a syringe, a knife, and a small plastic bag with two vials of liquid. Johnny had brought this *equipment*, as many of the items would never have made it past security at an airport. Satisfied that everything he needed was present, he sat back in his seat with a slight smile.

Someone is about to have a very bad night.

Chapter 5:
Amsterdam, the Netherlands

RSA Conference

A shadowed corner of the RAI Convention Center offered the perfect refuge for Davis from the mob of hacker wannabees and government IT managers that traditionally stalked him after a talk. Although the conference did not offer free wireless Internet access, Davis had previously walked the halls and knew the spots where he could hijack a wireless connection from a nearby unsecured wireless access point. In this particular corner, wireless access courteously—albeit unintentionally—was provided by a small coffee shop across the street. He was repeatedly amazed by how most companies and homes left themselves open to the casual passerby with a laptop or handheld equipped with a wireless Internet card.

A few years ago, Davis was involved in a study sponsored by the U.S. National Science Foundation on the "pervasiveness of unfettered Internet access." The goal was to see how society was adopting wireless technologies, including the setting up of wireless Internet access networks within the home or business. At the time, access points—the small devices that serve as a base station for the wireless connections—had fallen so much in price that it had become cheaper for many homes to distribute Internet access wirelessly across multiple rooms rather than run wires. He knew that most home users would buy just the access point, hook it up to their cable or DSL modem, turn on their laptop with a wireless card, and hope to God that it connected. If the connection was successful, he knew that most people would never play with the settings, lest they screw something up and suddenly their daughter can't get her e-mail any more. The default for most of these access points was to allow anyone with a wireless card to connect through that access point to the Internet without needing to login or know any passwords and encryption keys.

This practice led to the cult phenomenon of WarDriving—getting in a car with a wireless-ready laptop and looking for someone's house or business to park in front of to sponge free, anonymous Internet access. For some this was a passing hobby, for others, WarDriving was a more targeted affair. It enables an attacker to access sensitive information from within the home or business and also allows the driver to launch an attack against some remote system anonymously. When the victim checks his or her logs, the attack is traced to the unsuspecting home or business owner with the open wireless connection.

What started as a casual hobby soon evolved into a national phenomenon. Instructions were posted widely on the Net for building high-powered directional antennas and making hardware modifications to wireless cards to improve their sensitivity. The practice of WarDriving had become so popular in parts of California and a few other states that WarDrivers devised a method to communicate to each other which homes, businesses, and general locations had open wireless Internet access. WarDrivers would make marks near or on buildings with known open Internet connections. The practice became known as *warchalking* and it quickly gained national media attention. Fortunately, it also caught the eyes of the NSF. Part of Davis's grant was to determine how widespread the practice really was, and to determine the exposure of the average homeowner when deploying wireless.

This was one of the most interesting projects Chad Davis had worked on. Two hours a day for three weeks he and two graduate students cruised suburban neighborhoods in Seattle, Redmond, and Bellevue with directional antennas made out of Pringles cans attached to two laptop computers. The results were stunning. Two-thirds of the homes they found with wireless access points had left their access completely unsecured. Davis's students were able to intercept credit card transactions, account information, and were in a position to use those connections to launch completely anonymous attacks on remote victims.

Today's Internet connectivity at the conference was provided by Café du Laurent. Davis resisted the temptation to browse the company's internal systems and focused on the task at hand: finding out what the hell Baff Lexicon was up to. He knew that Baff valued his privacy too much to approach him in the open unless he absolutely had to. Advice Software's e-vote system was about to play a critical role in deciding the U.S. Presidency and Davis knew that his testimony was possibly the most influential technical piece of information that Congress would have. The decision on whether or not to adopt, like it or not, rested with him.

"So, Mr. Davis, are you coming to my talk?"

The voice came from behind a large artificial plant next to Davis's chair. A man emerged from behind the plant but Davis already knew who it was, the voice carried with it the tone of unabashed arrogance that he had heard just minutes earlier.

"Actually it's *Dr.* Davis, and I'm sorry, Mike was it? It looks like I have some e-mail here that needs to be turned around pretty quick. I would have loved to come, though."

He had planned on avoiding Mike Snell's talk like the plague. The two minutes he had spent with the man after his own talk were enough to determine that Snell was an unrepentant jackass.

"Perfect! I've arranged for network access during my talk and I have a wireless router set up for the audience to try my new authentication system. You can sit in the back and work on your mail, although I doubt you'll want to be distracted."

Dammit.

There was one more possibility for a polite escape.

"Looks like you've got it covered. I'll meet you there," replied Davis. *This guy will never know who was in the room.*

"It's about to start, I'll walk you there so you don't get lost," Mike replied.

Dammit!!!

The two men walked silently to the Salon B conference room. On a stand near the door Davis saw a printed poster board with the title of his captor's talk:

Recent Advances in Authentication Techniques

Presented by: Mike Snell

Davis took an aisle seat near the back of the room to facilitate an easy escape.

"Let me know if I go too fast for you," Mike said in what he perceived as a sincere tone, but came off as arrogant and patronizing.

Davis gave him an obligatory smile and opened his laptop.

Even this guy's family must hate him.

Davis resumed his search into Baff's activities over the past few months. He remembered speaking to him about a fringe warez group that Baff was a member of.

Starting around the time that the Commodore 64 became popular, computer users with the technical talent to manipulate software binaries turned their attention to removing copy protection from software. The movement originally was inspired by game software. In the late 1980s, tech-savvy kids would go to their neighborhood electronics store and buy a copy of the latest video game to be released on the then-popular Commodore 64 personal computer. The Commodore 64 was arguably the first home computing platform that was affordable enough to get broad market penetration, and it made the mass production of commodity software like games a viable business model for several companies. Initially, computer enthusiasts would spend large amounts of money on the latest game released on a particular platform. Often, the boxes that held the game's floppy disc would have sensationalistic titles with pictures of a hero dressed in futuristic armor and alien monsters that meshed with comic books of the time like *Superman* or *Justice League*. The buyer would race home to insert the disk into their system to embrace the rich adventure promised by the game manufacturer on the box; only when they did insert the disk, the game turned out to be two dots on a screen with a maze of lines. Fifty bucks down the drain.

This left quite a few users jaded. They wanted a way to "preview" or just completely pirate games. Around that same time, modems were becoming popular among hard-core home computer users. Soon, bulletin boards—repositories of software and games that a user could "dial" into with the appropriate password—became a popular place where users essentially could steal software and install it on their own machines. The pirated software itself became known as *warez*, derived from soft-wares.

The response to this by the game industry was to add copy-protection technology to their software and lock it to a specific machine. Those individuals who were skilled in low-level programming techniques soon found ways to "unlock" this software, which then forced software vendors to invent new protection schemes, and the cycle would begin again. This escalation of arms between protection technologies and breaking or *cracking* techniques still continues today.

Although some of the software could be cracked by an individual working alone, more advanced protection schemes may have required a team of experts to break. Also, the people with the skills to break software may not have been those with the resources to distribute the cracked software effectively in the community. These factors led to the formation of *warez groups*, people with a common goal and the combined resources to achieve it. In the early days, warez groups distributed software either in trade—so that they could grow their collections—or simply to satisfy their desire to set software free. As groups became more organized, they realized the potential for profit in selling the stolen software cheaply in the United States and overseas.

Many of the large, modern warez groups operated in basically the same way. Usually people had very specific and assigned roles. Some would be responsible for obtaining a copy of the original software, perhaps by stealing it from a vendor before its official release. The more technical members would then take delivery of the software and "reverse engineer" their protection schemes with the intent to remove them. These people were known as *crackers*. Once the software was cracked, another group would verify that it still worked like the original program; these were the *testers*. Yet another group was responsible for packaging the software for distribution and burning the CDs or DVDs for sale; these were the *packers*. Yet another group, known as the *distributors*, was responsible for getting the software out on the street for sale. Their most common distribution channels were Asia and Europe. It's not uncommon today to be able to purchase a $30 DVD with collections of software from multiple vendors with a retail value of thousands of dollars.

Davis knew that Baff Lexicon was a cracker, one of the best in the industry. He also knew that some of Baff's associates could no longer set foot in the United States due to the passing of the Digital Millennium Copyright Act in 2000, which meant that Baff guarded his anonymity now more than ever before.

Why would he risk an in-person meeting? He could have just sent me an e-mail, given me a phone call...

Davis suddenly became aware of his surroundings as he heard his name over the loudspeaker.

"People like Chad Davis love to give these sensationalized pictures of what they think security really is. You want to know the truth? The truth is guys like him are just after fame. They don't have any idea what really happens. The truth is that systems *can* be made secure. Systems like my Cyber Sentinel are virtually unhackable. No hard feelings Chad!"

NO HARD FEELINGS? Who the hell does this guy think he is!?

He felt a dull but worsening pain in his right thigh and realized that it was caused by his own fingers gripping down like eagle talons on his leg.

This had been a setup, one designed to make Mike Snell's talk more palatable by attacking Davis to make an obviously flawed point.

This guy has the balls to invite me here for this and calls ME sensationalistic!

Obviously the situation had to be remedied. Davis quickly turned his attention away from Baff and opened an Internet browser pointed to the demonstration web site that Mike had set up for attendees to play with. The web site was also being shown on a digital projector in back of the podium behind Mike.

Mike proudly announced, "Feel free to access the site on your laptops and play with it as I give my talk. The URL is on the bottom of the slides."

Davis recalled reading about Snell's software before. It didn't sound fundamentally different from any other reasonable solution out there: ask a user for their login information, encrypt it, and send it back to a server for verification. The only discriminator between these sorts of systems was how difficult the encryption was to break and how they managed user credentials.

Chad Davis was no cryptographer but he knew that trying to decrypt something that had been encrypted with a provably strong algorithm was like trying to chisel through a foot-thick steel door with a butter knife: you eventually may get there but by the time you do it probably doesn't matter any more. He knew from experience though, that one usually did not have to attack cryptography directly to break it. Most "secure" systems that use cryptography usually are made weak because of incorrect or poor implementation. Usually these systems can be broken at the seams and Davis was determined to break Mike Snell's in a very public way before the end of this talk.

The home page of Snell's system was similar to many e-commerce sites, asking for a username and password. This was obviously a contrived web application created to demonstrate Snell's latest implementation of his authentication software.

Snell's Login Page

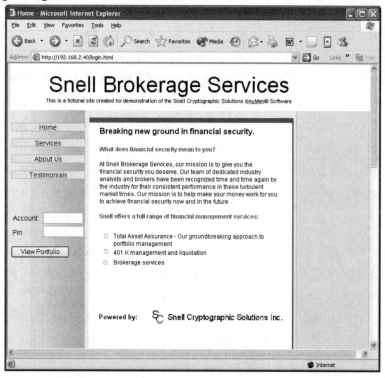

Most web applications that process user authentication information compare the credentials supplied by the user against those stored in a database somewhere on the server. This meant that, on the server, the web application would have to query the database and ask it for the information it needed to conduct the comparison. The standard language for writing such queries is SQL, the Structured Query Language. Specifically, a web application may want to know what the password is that's stored in the user database for the login name "JohnDoe." To do this, one might execute a SELECT query, which selects the record for JohnDoe, and later compare the password stored for that user against the one supplied by the user trying to login as JohnDoe on the web page.

Using the language of SQL, the web developer may construct the query:

```
SELECT * FROM User_Table WHERE Username = 'Request.Form("Username")' AND
Password = 'Request.Form("Password")'
```

The Request.Form commands would retrieve the user input from the web form, and if the query found a match it would conclude that a valid username/password combination is entered and the application could then proceed to permit access to that user. The fatal flaw is that if the web page doesn't check the username and password entered by the user for special characters like single quotes ('), dashes (-), and semicolons (;) a user could actually change the SQL query.

In this query example for instance, a user could enter the username:

```
JohnDoe' —
```

Most web developers would consider this as a strange, but simply invalid, username. Davis knew that it was this ignorance that often led to many "secure" web sites being compromised.

The double dash tells the database server to treat everything following it as a comment. Processing such input would result in the query

```
SELECT * FROM User_Table WHERE Username = 'JohnDoe'—' AND Password =
'Request.Form("Password")'
```

Since everything after the double dash is treated as a comment, the actual query reduces to

```
SELECT * FROM User_Table WHERE Username = 'JohnDoe'
```

This means that JohnDoe's account could be authenticated without needing that account's password! Davis knew that he could do much worse things to the site if he could successfully launch such SQL Injection attacks.

Many web developers don't bother to strip user data of any characters that might allow a user to alter SQL commands. Davis had consistently resisted the temptation to run unsolicited "tests" on web sites for these types of problems. Snell had thrown down the gauntlet, though, and Davis knew he deserved what was about to be done to him.

Davis's first move was to put in some SQL commands that were likely to screw up a query that might take place on the server. His first attempt was a Login name of

```
'  and
```

Not very creative, but if Snell wasn't checking the data, it should result in an error screen equivalent to an open electronic invitation to completely control that server. When he submitted the information, though, a small error message appeared:

Error Message

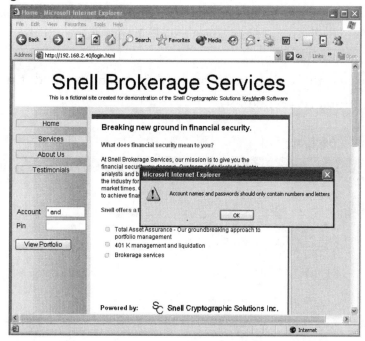

Snell's page was checking, but Davis was not beaten. The little popup error indicated that this page was protecting against those characters on the client: possibly good news.

Davis knew that there were two places to scan user input: on the client and on the server. Protection on the client means that some code running on the web page itself—usually JavaScript—screens user input and either changes it or reports an error, all before any user data is sent back to the server. Protection on the server means that user data is checked after it is sent back to the server but before it is used, in a SQL query for instance.

Many developers consider the two equivalent: once data is scanned on one it would be redundant to scan it on the other. Under this supremely incorrect assumption, many developers opt to check data on the client since more processing is done on the user's machine, which means less work for the server.

Davis knew the facts. *He* controlled any code running in *his* web browser. The fact that Snell's amateurish web page was checking data on the client probably meant no checks were being done on the server. It was time to test his theory.

Davis saved the web page to his hard drive and opened it up in the Microsoft Notepad text editor.

Page Opened on Notepad

```
Home.htm - Notepad
File  Edit  Format  View  Help
<SCRIPT>
checkval=new RegExp("[\-\'\;]");
function validate(){
        if (checkval.test(form0.Acct.value)){
                alert("Account_names_and passwords should only contain numbers and letters");
                event.returnValue=false;
        }
        if (checkval.test(form0.Pin.value)){
                alert("Account_names_and passwords should only contain numbers and letters");
                event.returnValue=false;
        }
}
</SCRIPT>

<FORM name=form0 onsubmit=validate(); action=loginprocess.asp method=post>
```

He scrolled down to the code that was checking user input. The `onsubmit` event of the form containing the Username and Password data called the `validate` JavaScript function. The function did pretty much what Davis expected: search for special characters and then raise an error message if they appeared in any of the fields. All he needed to do was to delete the call to that function and validation would never take place! Since the web page would then be opened from Davis's machine and not the server he also had to tell his web browser where to find the page loginprocess.asp, the page set to process the user data and authenticate.

loginprocess.asp

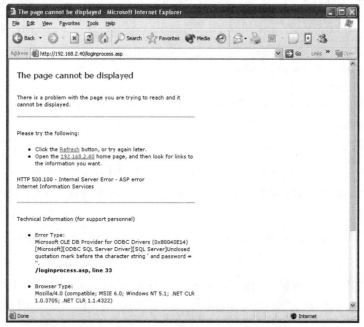

Davis saved the file and then opened it in his web browser. He tried the same input string as before:

```
' and
```

this time, getting a much different result.

Same Page, New Result

Success! The server returned an error message indicating that a SQL query was executed on the server with incorrect syntax.

I've got him! This arrogant bastard is going down!

Davis knew that this could mean only one thing: there were no checks being done on the server, he could ultimately control Snell's machine! Although he had seen error messages like this often it still amazed him how much information they disclose to an attacker. They were essentially a roadmap to control the server. It told him which database server was running on Snell's machine: Microsoft SQL Server. He could infer what version of SQL Server it was by the error message. It disclosed some of the SQL query string to him. It was a welcome mat.

Now, what should I do to this guy?

Davis contemplated his options. By default, Microsoft SQL Server allowed users to execute *stored procedures*, which are powerful functions on the server. Davis knew he needed only one `xp_cmdshell`. The `xp_cmd-shell` stored procedure allowed users to execute arbitrary commands on the server under some common configurations. One thing he could do was to overwrite the home page of Snell's web application. He hit the back button on his browser and started to again type in the username field:

```
'; EXEC master..xp_cmdshell 'echo I am an Idiot! >
c:\inetpub\wwwroot\home.html'
```

Not very subtle but it would certainly make his point. Davis's finger hovered over the enter key.

I can do better than this…

For the next three minutes, he typed feverishly on his laptop. After a final stroke of the enter key a faint but perceptible smile came over his face.

It took almost five minutes before he heard the first muffled laugh from someone in the audience that apparently uncovered the speaker's new presentation homepage on their laptops. Mike Snell was now deep into his talk on security and how it related to his HTML code that he had on the big screen. Slowly, snickers began to spread as people browsed Snell's web site from their laptops.

There was an obvious annoyance in Snell's voice as he continued to talk about his site over a now obviously distracted and amused audience.

Snell seemed to regain composure as a solitary hand was raised from a young man seated two rows in front of Davis.

"Ah yes, a question," Snell announced.

Davis could see that the young man about to speak was trying to regain composure from a near convulsive fit of laughter a few minutes earlier. He waited for an usher to make his way to his seat with a microphone.

This should be good... Davis thought with the excitement of a mischievous school boy.

"Mr. Snell," the young man began. "I've enjoyed your talk so far. I wonder if you would mind walking us through the security mechanisms implemented on the home page in a bit more detail."

"Well I do tend to go over things a bit fast for most people. Let's take another look at it," Snell responded, clicking on the "Home" link of his web page on the laptop connected to the projector.

The unsuppressed laughter of the audience that erupted when Mike Snell navigated to the home page of his web site was the perfect opportunity for Davis to make his exit.

On the white screen in front of the auditorium was the new default page for Snell's unhackable web application:

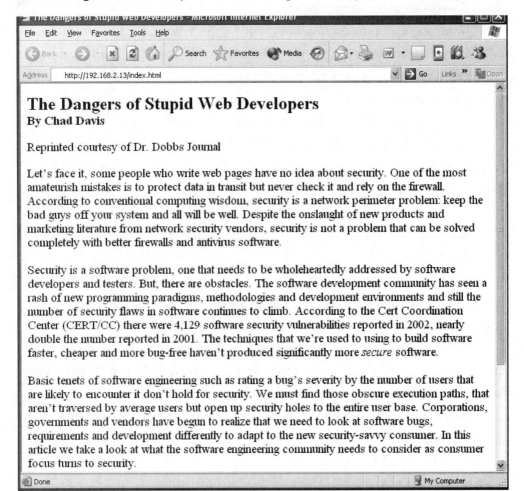

The Dangers of Stupid Web Developers
By Chad Davis

Reprinted courtesy of Dr. Dobbs Journal

Let's face it, some people who write web pages have no idea about security. One of the most amateurish mistakes is to protect data in transit but never check it and rely on the firewall. According to conventional computing wisdom, security is a network perimeter problem: keep the bad guys off your system and all will be well. Despite the onslaught of new products and marketing literature from network security vendors, security is not a problem that can be solved completely with better firewalls and antivirus software.

Security is a software problem, one that needs to be wholeheartedly addressed by software developers and testers. But, there are obstacles. The software development community has seen a rash of new programming paradigms, methodologies and development environments and still the number of security flaws in software continues to climb. According to the Cert Coordination Center (CERT/CC) there were 4,129 software security vulnerabilities reported in 2002, nearly double the number reported in 2001. The techniques that we're used to using to build software faster, cheaper and more bug-free haven't produced significantly more *secure* software.

Basic tenets of software engineering such as rating a bug's severity by the number of users that are likely to encounter it don't hold for security. We must find those obscure execution paths, that aren't traversed by average users but open up security holes to the entire user base. Corporations, governments and vendors have begun to realize that we need to look at software bugs, requirements and development differently to adapt to the new security-savvy consumer. In this article we take a look at what the software engineering community needs to consider as consumer focus turns to security.

Chapter 6:
Amsterdam, the Netherlands

Baff Lexicon's Apartment

Sipping from his Pepsi can, Baff flipped through a five-month old copy of *Wired Magazine*. It was his *New York Times*, and it was the one that described *Han Solo* as "a subversive gang of hackers distributing cracked software on the black market." Baff didn't mind the article treading into the underground software piracy world. Although it exposed how much money companies lost from hackers like him, it unofficially knighted *Han Solo* as present-day Robin Hoods, bringing overpriced software to the common man. Back in 1998 they featured an article about hackers, spammers, and phreakers. The article mentioned Baff's group *Han Solo* but did not "praise" them like the more recent article.

He loved it. *Wired mentioned us!*

They even referenced him directly for his most recent crack. It was Microsoft's latest version of Windows that he conquered under the code name "fox the spookie" and sold off to a distribution group in Asia. He was an enabler: giving others the ability to burn software copies onto CDs with a key to unlock hundred-dollar applications for a fraction of the price. It would then end up in New York's China Town and in Asia, where pirated software is sold on practically every street corner.

This stuff isn't even any good. Selling hundred-dollar software that crashes, loses data, and has bugs that will probably never be fixed. And they call me a criminal!

Baff clearly understood that no software was perfect. But he also thought a company investing hundreds of millions of dollars into developing a software package could do a much better job at keeping guys like him out. *Easy money.*

Downstairs, Danko was finishing off his second pack of unfiltered Camels. Minutes earlier he had asked Johnny to disappear for an hour and come back with another carton of cigarettes. He did not like company during his jobs, but he had to tolerate it when necessary. The car, like the stallions of old carrying their knights in shinning armor, idled roughly to keep him warm. Only this stallion was old and ready to be shot, but it didn't matter, as Johnny would probably dump the car once this job was complete.

As he finished the last drag on his third cigarette, he reached and turned the ignition key to the off position. The car gave out a sigh of relief as he opened the door and headed for the trunk. Danko wore his usual "work" clothes, black on black with an appropriate trench coat for the weather.

"One more and I celebrate," he mumbled in a Yugoslav accent.

He never spoke his native tongue during work. He did not want to bring his language, his culture, into the dark world that fate had immersed him in.

The trunk creaked open and four bags (including his travel bag from the flight) came to sight under the soft yellow glow of the parking lot lights. Danko assessed the collection of the other three bags and reached for a small pistol, adding a silencer that doubled the gun's size. He tucked it inside his coat and looked for identification.

Who will I be tonight?

Through unfortunate personal experience Danko had learned everything there is to know about Europe's police, Interpol, and private investigators. His résumé spanned France, England, Spain, and Great Britain. His picture hung in numerous offices throughout Europe with a different name underneath each one. He owned fake badges, nametags, and passports from almost every country and law enforcement office imaginable. He knew his accent would give him away to anyone paying enough attention, but most people see a badge and assume trust. Sometimes he wished it was more challenging. He wanted them to resist. Challenge his authority. Make him work for it. But how could he complain about easy money.

"Amsterdam," he said quietly, fumbling for the proper identification.

"Jonas Borgstad," he mumbled as he found the right badge and identification.

He closed the trunk and reached for the small bag in the back seat he would need for the staging and clean-up.

This job would require at least one more cigarette.

Taking the last sips from his soda, Baff reached for a cigarette. He had a highly regimented diet of cigarettes, bread, and Pepsi, sometimes going a week without deviating. Baff had become obsessed with the soft drink in 1996 when the Pepsi bottling company ran a promotion in the United States called Pepsi points. Points came on 2 liter bottles, and on 12- and 24-can boxes. The points could be redeemed by mail for "fabulous" prizes like branded Frisbees, hats, and of course, more Pepsi. The marketing wizards at Pepsi touched Baff in a personal and compulsive way. He became obsessed with gathering points, and would not be beneath ripping "proof of purchase" labels off boxes on the shelves of food stores. By the time the promotion ended, Baff had lost all interest in the points and they remained unclaimed in a small shoebox under a mound of comic books, POGS, and other paraphernalia from obsessions past. He was left, however, with an addiction to Pepsi, and a distaste for any other cola. If he missed one of his 10 daily cans, he would get horrible headaches. He felt one approaching and grabbed another can out of a small white fridge next to his chair.

Stabilized with another caffeine infusion he worked on his laptop, preparing for tonight's meeting. He rarely interacted with people outside the digital world, but when he needed to, David Feller was his nom de outré. Several years earlier, he had attended one of Davis's talks at the DEFCON conference, but recently, his reclusiveness made him stop looking forward to attending DEFCON; it had become too popular. Nostalgia kept him coming back, though; remembrances of conferences past when small groups would get together to hack into clueless government agencies and software giants. In fact, it was at DEFCON that one of Baff's more famous handles, "fox the spookie," was born and began his romp through the back alleys of cyberspace.

Davis'ss talk at DEFCON was the highlight of Baff's trip. Among the jungle of lamers and feds, here was a guy who had mastered an obscure but especially profitable branch of computer science known as reverse engineering. Baff had dedicated his short life to these techniques and had elevated them to an art that was worshiped by his hacking brethren. Baff and Davis had been communicating for years through e-mail and ICQ under one of his aliases. When they met in person at DEFCON, he and Davis hit it off almost immediately. They spoke about the new push for "digital signatures" to replace paper signatures as irrefutable proof that a document was created by its signatory. Baff felt conflicted about Davis'ss work. On one hand, he respected Davis'ss disregard for authority during his lectures. On the other, he felt Davis gave away too many secrets. He was making light of Baff's work; of Baff's *profession.*

He remembered Davis saying, "Bits are bits. If I have your software on my machine, I own those bits. I can manipulate them to do anything I want!"

This was the philosophy that Baff lived by. Since DEFCON he'd spent an inhuman amount of time tampering with the new Advice digital paper product. The software claimed to be completely tamper-proof and signed documents unalterable. Two days ago, Baff was about ready to believe their marketing propaganda until he made a breakthrough. Even the best hackers get lucky.

"My God!" he had exclaimed. *It's up for grabs!*

As intelligent as Baff was though, he fell victim to Advice's anti-debugging traps. Unknown to Baff, his tampering had caused stealth packets to be sent to his adversary, Advice Software.

His train of thought was interrupted by a knock at the door.

The knocks were firm. Baff couldn't distinguish them between those of an angry neighbor or of the police.

"Who is it?" he shouted from his desk.

The man answered in a calm and desperately disguised voice, "Amsterdam Police, please open."

What the hell have I done now? Baff was not on the run. He had not done anything too serious lately. *Was it the file?*

He hesitated but did not think much of it, "Be right there."

As he walked to the door he remembered that his computer was still on. *Never leave it on around strangers.* He lunged back to turn it off before partially opening the door, leaving the dead-bolt latched.

Danko's badge shone in Baff's eyes.

"Are you Baff Lexicon?"

"Yes. Who are you?"

"Jonas Borgstad, Amsterdam Police. Have you seen this man?" Danko asked. He showed him a picture of Chad Davis.

Baff replied, "No, who is he?"

Danko stalled for a minute. In his mind he had already staged the murder scene and prepared his exit strategy.

Chapter 7:
Amsterdam, the Netherlands

Victoria Hotel

The man inserted his card into the door lock, removed it swiftly, and heard a click. The lock light switched from a steady red to a blinking green, signaling that his room door was open. He rushed into room 1413 at the Victoria Hotel. *I've got to get this out.*

The room was scattered with the usual business traveler's attire. Suits, shirts, casual slacks, newspapers, miniature versions of select alcoholic drinks. The traveling man's world. In addition to the usual laptop and other small electronic equipment, this room housed numerous high-end cameras, scoping microphones, and surveillance equipment fit for a private eye or a top law enforcement agency.

He took off his jacket, loosened his tie, and popped his shoes off. The man's laptop was already booting up as he gathered cameras from the day's work. The folder he pulled out of his briefcase contained notes from the lectures he attended as well as an RSA conference schedule. He took his notes out, quickly reviewing them for completeness before transferring them into e-mail.

```
RSA Conference - Feb 12 2004: (part 1 of 2)
Mr. Davis attends morning mixer. Mingles with crowd.
Small talk about casino and conference.

Mr. Davis attends morning presentations. Sits alone, takes notes.
```

Mr. Davis' speech. Questioned on security and e-vote initiative. Refused to answer due to his upcoming testimony.

Mr. Davis talks to unknown man. Man is approximately 6 feet tall, slender, black/graying hair, and bearded. Overheard discussion on possible collaboration in the future. Reference photos 1001-01 through 1001-03. Run identification match on individual.

Mr. Davis is greeted by man. The two discuss his evaluation of Advice's software. Plan to meet tonight. Reference photos 1001-04 through 1001-10 Run identification match on individual.

Part 2 of 2 will follow as final daily information arrives later tonight.

He followed the usual routine of uploading the pictures and note files, and clicked the report away. He would wait for his fellow attendees to return with the rest of today's activity.

Nine time zones away, in an isolated room, a laptop chimed as new mail arrived, awaiting review.

Chapter 8:
Amsterdam, the Netherlands

Red Light District

A normal pulse rate for an adult male is about 72 beats per minute. During exercise and physical exertion the heart beats faster, sometimes approaching 150 beats per minute. At its limits, the heart can beat upwards of 200 beats per minute, a point where the body starts to essentially shut down. During extreme exertion, breathing becomes labored, the muscles begin to burn and the body starts to fail. In peak physical condition, athletes experience this threshold well into a full-out run. The average adult male in the United States can go for about one minute. In an unplanned and unwelcome experiment, Chad Davis discovered that he could last just under 35 seconds.

It wasn't *really* his fault. There weren't any signs, no little boxy camera picture with a red circle around it and a line through it. What healthy male wouldn't want to take home a picture of some cleavage and well-placed fabrics? In the red light district of Amsterdam, a husband could purchase more trouble with €50 than in just about anywhere else on earth. Chad wasn't in the market for trouble, but was not beneath taking a few pictures.

The red light "district" was really one main street with a few side streets branching off. Instead of being separated by a traditional median, the river Amstel ran through its center. One side was connected to the other by a series of miniature bridges, not more than 15 feet long and wide enough for a mid-sized car to travel. When seen from one end, the street itself was beautiful: a series of arched, concrete bridges at about 10 car length intervals, lined with lights on both sides, which, upon closer inspection were actually dozens of florescent framed windows displaying the area's most famous commodity—prostitutes.

Anyone who visited Amsterdam had to stop at the red light district, it was one of the city's biggest attractions—or so Davis told himself. He wasn't looking for trouble but it found him none the less after two "ladies of the night" and their esteemed manager saw the flash from his digital camera. Two minutes after his panicked run from the trio, Davis began to regain control of his breathing.

He looked down at his watch. *9:30 P.M. Damn.*

He gathered his composure and began the long walk to Circus Square, home of countless restaurants, bars, and, most importantly, the Holland Casino.

This was his second trip to the casino in as many days. *I'll just go and watch some of the poker tournament. I don't even have any cash…* Over the past few years he had perfected the art of lying to himself. He had blown €800 the night before on a remarkably bad blackjack streak and was about to tempt fate once more. *I've gotta meet Baff; this is, after all, a business trip.*

Half an hour later, the lights of the Holland Casino interrupted his thoughts. He knew the large glass door held his €800 inside. An outsider would have certainly thought it strange that a statistician would repeatedly return to be tortured by a game he knew he would eventually lose. But Davis was one of the worst kind of gamblers, he didn't do it for money; worse, he didn't even feel bad when he lost. He did it for the camaraderie, a group of strangers united against an insurmountable adversary wielding a deck of embossed plastic cards. He did it for the thrill.

After registering at the front desk and paying his €2 entrance fee, he walked straight to the back of the casino, oblivious to the television cameras and spectacle of the World Poker Championship. He walked up to the cashier cage and laid a Visa card on the desk.

"Two thousand Euro advance, please. I'll take it all in chips."

Chapter 9:
Amsterdam, the Netherlands

Apartment of Baff Lexicon

Danko washed his blood-spattered hands in the sink as Baff's still warm body lay next to the door. He carefully dried his hands and removed the small plastic tips from his fingers. Danko had become hardened to killing. The Serbian army had drained him of remorse and regret, now an asset in his new line of work. He gave little thought to taking a life. It was another task like walking the dog or going grocery shopping. This distance and emotional detachment allowed him to be calculating, unencumbered by the thoughts that cloud the mind of the novice.

He always had a plan, a backup plan, a contingency plan, an escape route, and most important, a well-orchestrated motive and scapegoat. Tonight's selection was heroin.

Although the city was famous for its liberal laws and its lax drug policy, heroin was still a dangerous trade. Danko knew that neighbors and the Dutch police would have no trouble believing the recluse in this apartment was somehow involved. The plastic films on Danko's hands were etched from Interpol records. The resulting prints, now strategically scattered throughout the room, belonged to one of Amsterdam's local dealers.

Danko's current employer was well connected, and had plenty of cash. It made this job much easier, because typically he would spend a month or even more to survey and determine who he would volunteer as his murderer. Prints were not easy to come by. He would either buy them or perform reconnaissance to obtain them himself.

Over the years Danko had become a true master, a storyteller with a captive audience. Like any raconteur, he knew that there were rules to his art. One should never be direct, not too direct at least. He had to create wonderfully opaque layers that the skilled detective would peel away, and with each uncloaked clue, feel some self-congratulatory confidence that he had out-maneuvered his opponent. He took pride in knowing that over half of his victim's cases were considered "solved" by local authorities in seven different countries. The idea that he could create such a compelling scene, and plant evidence so precisely as to lead to the conviction of an "innocent" man gave him a sense of power that few people ever experience.

But none of his scapegoats were ever truly innocent. They were thieves, drug dealers, corrupt officials and sometimes murderers. Danko did not choose these men to shoulder the responsibility of his crimes out of some sense of moral justice or desire to bring balance to the world. He chose them because the public could easily believe they were guilty of *something*, and Danko knew that he could use that to his advantage. If his stooge were an upstanding citizen, police would investigate more thoroughly. There would be those that championed the cause of the accused and evidence could possibly surface leading back to Danko. Tonight's scripted scene likely would give the Dutch police the excuse they needed to put away one of the city's top menaces; Danko was confident that no further inquiries would be made.

He removed a small cell phone from his jacket pocket, summoning Johnny with his bag of goodies from the street below. Johnny promptly climbed the stairs to the third-floor apartment and without a word or alarm, stepped over the corpse and sat at the desk of the late Mr. Lexicon. This man was a different type of assassin, one who destroyed bits instead of bodies. His bag's contents easily could have been the spoils of a Radio Shack robbery. He pulled a cable out from a side compartment of the bag and stuck one end into Baff's machine and the other into his laptop computer, which now sat on the desk.

Danko and Johnny did not speak, they both knew what their roles were in tonight's affair. After a few minutes, he placed his laptop back in the knapsack, stepped over the body and calmly walked downstairs, leaving Danko once again alone with his victim. Danko took one final look at his latest masterpiece. *A scene even Shakespeare would be proud of.* He stepped out into the hallway and eased the door closed. Inside the once peaceful apartment lay Baff's body, a needle, heroin residue, and a local dealer's fingerprints.

Chapter 10:
Amsterdam, the Netherlands

The Holland Casino and Hard Rock Café

"I'd like to cash these in," Chad Davis said as he placed two 5-euro chips on the counter in front of the cage window. His head was throbbing. This was the second night in a row he had felt the sting of the Holland Casino. Most of tonight's losses were at the hands of a beautiful Dutch blackjack croupier named Olga. She was exactly what Davis was looking for in a dealer; tall, blond, gorgeous and careless enough to occasionally expose her hole card. The hour he spent at Olga's table was masochistic. He lost €2000 and had to resort to yet another cash advance for a thousand more.

Davis looked down at the two 5-euro notes that were now being handed to him by the cashier. *I could have had ten prostitutes…at once!*

He walked to the front of the casino still not fully grasping the financial loss he had just suffered. As he stepped out of the front door he could see the entrance to the Hard Rock Café only a few meters away.

The Hard Rock Café Amsterdam was one of the most popular spots for drunken American tourists who had had their fill of weed at Amsterdam's famous coffee shops and were overcome by a case of the "munchies." Davis walked in and was seated at a table facing the entrance. He looked down at his watch. *11:52. This better be good, €2000 good!*

It had been four years since he last sat in this restaurant. His wife, Amanda, had sat next to him with their daughter sitting opposite, facing them. He remembered distinctly Amanda trying to speak Dutch to the waitress as she approached their table. "You want a slippery fork?" the waitress responded, laughing. The ribbing she got from Davis and their daughter Elizabeth made it Amanda's last public attempt at Dutch.

He took out his now-empty wallet from his jacket pocket, and slowly rubbed his thumb over the picture behind the thin plastic sheath. His heart felt heavy as memories of their Amsterdam trip came rushing back.

"Would you like something to drink, sir?" a large waitress asked.

"Whiskey, a lot of whiskey," he said without looking up.

"Right away, sir."

As the woman wobbled to the bar Davis tried to push his memories of Amanda and Elizabeth back into the part of his mind that he had worked hard to seal off a year ago.

He began to think about his upcoming appearance in Washington. Davis was the pivotal expert witness in the Secure Electronic Remote Voting System (SERVS) adoption hearings. Washington State was one of the first to provide the ability for people who are out of state or out of the country to submit absentee votes electronically. The state had committed to implementing this system and it was about to go online as the official voting mechanism for the United States Presidential primary. Based on the results and the testimony of a team of industry experts, the system would potentially be deployed nationwide for the November presidential elections.

When Davis was approached about consulting on this project a year ago he was skeptical. "You know something like this can never be completely secure," he remembered saying to Grace Wilkinson, the Voting System Director at the Federal Elections Commission – a fancy title for "your ass is on the line if the election doesn't go smoothly." Davis knew that Grace was under tremendous pressure. The Florida voting fiasco of 2000 nearly cost her career. He also understood the need for a secure electronic voting mechanism. Tens of thousands of U.S. troops in Afghanistan, Iraq, and in other parts of the world needed to have their say and the country had to be assured that their votes were accounted for, properly.

When the project began, there were a handful of software companies that bid for the contract to develop the secure voting system. The obvious front runners were Microsoft and Adobe, but after extensive testing of the prototypes and Davis'ss own recommendations, a mid-sized firm in Washington, Advice Software Inc., was selected.

Only the mention of Advice could have convinced Davis to agree to such an odd meeting with a hacker at an ungodly hour.

Forty-five minutes and three whiskeys later, Davis gave up all hope of meeting his mysterious acquaintance. He stepped outside and grabbed the first cab in the long line that waited just in front of the casino.

Twelve minutes later Davis slid his key car into the electronic reader of room 1434 at the Victoria hotel. As he lay on the bed, he heard the door of the room next to his slam shut. Exactly 32 seconds later, the three glasses of whiskeys kicked in, and Davis was unconscious.

Chapter 11: Seattle, Washington

Advice Software, Inc.

Greg Troler opened the e-mail and started downloading the attached pictures. He opened the necessary software, compiled the report, and clicked it away to the printer. He then began to survey the pictures. *Who was he? And why was he talking to Davis?* The routine had been the same for the past few months. Davis was to testify. The pilot project was to finish without a hitch. The country's future depended on it.

After a closer look, he realized who it was. "Bartholomew Lexicon," he said out loud. "Not surprising I guess."

They had been tracking him ever since the software alerted them to his hacking attempts. Baff was very careful about what information he left on his computers. He was even more careful in preventing trace attempts to his machine. But they were on to him, and had been for some time now.

With a smirk on his face, the man walked to the elevator and headed for the executive suite. He stared at his reflection as the elevator made its way up. He could tell he was aging. Only 27, but he had been working like a slave since college for one purpose. Greg wanted to climb his way to the top. In the elevator mirror he could see the reflection of his nametag:

After two years of remedial tasks they finally assigned him to a heavier project. Some might have called him a simple errand boy for his boss, but he preferred to think of himself as an individual looking for opportunity just like anyone else. *Maybe after this I can get a promotion...or get a chance to do some real work.* What he had learned over the past several months would certainly give him leverage.

The 45 seconds it took for the elevator to arrive were enough for Greg to reflect on his education and career path. The 30 seconds it took to go from the 8th floor to the 23rd were enough for him to ponder his future with Advice Software. *Finally, some good news for the boss.* He knocked while simultaneously opening the door hoping not to interrupt anything. Once he saw that he wasn't, he briskly strode across the room, handing over the documents to the man sitting behind the large, mahogany desk.

"Sir, today's report is in. You should take a look at this."

"Thank you, Greg. It's been a long day," replied his boss. *A long year.* He had a multibillion dollar company to run while keeping tabs on hackers, politicians, and *now* software security experts. He thumbed through Davis's daily activity and then browsed the printed pictures. It didn't take long for him to recognize Davis's newest fan.

"Greg," he wondered, "is this who I think it is?"

"Yes, Mr. Payne," he replied anxiously, almost proud of his report. Chris Payne dropped the report onto his desk and took a deep breath. Reclining into his leather executive chair, he began to question the effectiveness of his people. There was Baff, openly speaking with Davis in the photos when he wasn't even supposed to be breathing at that point.

"Thanks Greg, I'll take care of it from here." Greg nodded and left the room confident he had made a good impression.

His office transcended the definition of lavish. Growing up in rural Kansas, Chris Payne understood the value of hard work. He deserved every penny he earned for himself and for his company. His office was recently featured in *Forbes Magazine* as one of the top 10 executive "shags" in the country. The mahogany double doors were carved to meticulous detail, matching the ornate desk. And, as one walked toward his desk, a spacious foyer lined with paintings, sculptures, and a distinct September 11 memorial would take the guest through a worldly journey.

He gazed around his office. The silence allowed him to ponder his next move. He opened his right-hand drawer and picked up his cell phone.

"International numbers are such a pain," he mumbled.

Even though the red light district of Amsterdam lives on through the night, Danko lay fast asleep in his hotel room. He had a long day, considering the job he had finished earlier that night. He knew he would have time to celebrate tomorrow, but a ringing cell phone now denied him his much-needed rest.

Turning over to look for his phone in the dark, he knocked the alarm clock off the end table, switching the radio on to one of Amsterdam's most popular techno stations.

Answering with a dry mouth, he had to work to get any sound out, but when he did he managed a "Son of a bitch."

Finally picking up the phone he answered, "Yea."

Danko instantly recognized the voice as it demanded, "I thought you got rid of him."

Chapter 12:
Amsterdam, the Netherlands

Chad Davis's Hotel Room, Victoria Hotel

As he lay in bed, Davis could not remember much from the previous night's casino binge. He recalled the €2000 advance and its quick disappearance on a €25 minimum-bet blackjack table. He had spent the night unconscious, and was now pondering Baff's no-show. *Where can I get some Tylenol?* Now his eyes were open but his body felt like it was tied to the bed. He became conscious of the alarm that had probably been blaring for a half hour or more. As he turned to check the time his mind processed the numbers. Eight, colon, three, zero. His body instantaneously jumped out of bed.

"My flight!"

As he rushed to dress and wash up as best he could, he realized he had not packed the night before. *Ten o'clock departure.* He was not known for his meticulous packing. The only thing working for him this morning was that all of his clothes never made it too far from the suitcase. Considering it had been only a three-day event, he hadn't packed heavy. He took his laptop and papers and shoved them in his laptop case as he shoveled all his clothes toward his suitcase. He sat atop his suitcase suffocating it, begging it to close. A couple of heaves and a creative string of profanities later the suitcase was sealed. *Please don't make me open it.*

Ever since September 11, Davis seemed to be consistently chosen for thorough security checks whenever he traveled. A month ago security opened his bag at check-in on a trip from England and decided to detain him for questioning. Two hours later he had to reschedule his flight for the next day. He was furious. He let the reservation employees have it, bitching about airport security and his lost day. The attendant behind the desk tried her best to explain to him that security delays are not the fault of airlines, nor were they ultimately responsible for his lost time. She rescheduled him for a flight and upgraded him for free. Davis accepted but with the grace and kindness of a waltzing bull.

Today would be different, it *had* to be different. Davis had to make it to the airport faster than he could dress. Once packed, he headed downstairs to hail a cab, bypassing the pleasantries and throwing extra cash at the cab driver to get him to drive faster. At 9:15 A.M., he arrived, jumped out of the cab, grabbed his bags, and rushed to the check-in counter.

"Can you please help me? I'm about to miss my flight!" he asked desperately of a check-in assistant guiding travelers as they waited in line.

In an apparently rehearsed tone the assistant replied, "Sir, please be patient, you will make your flight."

"Miss, please look," said Davis showing her his flight itinerary.

The assistant was obviously annoyed. She constantly had to deal with people arriving late thinking they could just cut in front of everyone to make their flight. How could Davis explain last night's casino escapade and his botched meeting with Baff? Would she understand why he was late this one time? Would she even care?

He didn't want to be one of those people, who are habitually late, no matter how early they get up and are ready to leave. Davis knew lots of people like that; almost all of academia had a "rules don't apply to me" attitude. His colleague back at the university, John Pratt would be up at the crack of dawn no matter what time he went to bed. Even so, with bags packed, showered, dressed, fed, and ready to leave, John would somehow arrive 30 minutes before departure and unbelievably always make his flight without incident.

"We'll need to check your luggage first and then you can come with me," said the assistant in an increasingly agitated tone.

Davis knew she hated doing this, but as she tagged his bag and then led him past the line of tired and frustrated travelers, Davis uttered, "I really appreciate this. You don't know what a night I've had."

"Yes sir, no problem," said the assistant instinctively. She imagined him drunk, wandering the red light district. She imagined him, like so many travelers she'd seen or overheard, indulging in Amsterdam's women and drugs, like the tourists at Disney taking their picture with Mickey—it's just something you have to do when you're there.

She exchanged a few words with security and passed him and his papers on to the man leading travelers through the metal detectors.

"Have a safe flight, sir."

"Thank you so much, miss. Thank you," replied Davis. He tried to be as sincere and innocent as possible. *Please make it through security.*

Knowing why he was brought up to the front of the line the way he was, the guard still made Davis wait for a few minutes. Davis thought this was his punishment. He looked at his watch and realized the gate was only yards away. *Going to make it.*

"Right this way, sir," demanded the guard.

Davis followed orders and walked through the metal detector without a hitch. On the other side, he gathered his belongings and headed for his gate. A sense of relief overcame him as he regained momentum. *Home sweet home.*

"Excuse me, sir."

Davis turned and stopped. The sight of a man with short, spiked hair wearing a deadly dark suit stunned him.

"Jonas Borgstad, Interpol," said the man flashing his badge to Davis.

Chapter 13:
Amsterdam, the Netherlands

Schiphol Airport

Davis studied the badge the Interpol Agent held in front of him and realized he had been chosen for the one thing he had hoped against. *I'm screwed.*

"Are you Mr. Chad Davis?"

"Yes," he replied in a defeated tone. "What's the problem? I'm about to board, I had no problems with security."

"Sir, I need to ask you a few questions. Please come with me."

Davis could not believe it. *I was right there! There's the damn gate! Now what!?*

The tall, weathered man led Davis to a private room past the smoker's lounge. He unlocked the door and showed Davis in. Plain walls with a table and a few chairs decorated the room. *Just like in the movies.*

"Have a seat Mr. Davis. This will not take long."

Davis checked his watch. The room was silent. He would not be able to hear the boarding call for his flight. He started to get nervous, which quickly escalated to anger and frustration.

"I have five minutes to board. Please make this quick," begged Davis.

"Do you know this man?" The agent produced three photos and laid them on the table.

Davis took a good look. At first he wasn't sure what he was looking at. But after a few seconds he realized the gruesome scene he was studying. It was a murder scene, Baff's murder scene. *Holy shit.*

"Yeah," replied Davis, trying to maintain his composure, "He spoke to me after my speech at the RSA conference."

Davis was scared. And not just scared he would miss his flight. *Interpol was following Baff? What did he know? Who killed him? How did they find me? Man, I just want to go home.*

"How did you know he was at the conference?" asked Davis.

"We had surveillance, Mr. Davis. Interpol is everywhere nowadays. Was there anything he may have said? Did he give you anything?"

Davis continued, "No, nothing out of the ordinary. Just how he enjoyed the talk I gave."

The Agent asked, "Was there anything or anyone that seemed strange at the conference?"

"There were a lot of people attending, sir, and I cannot remember any that stood out, except for an Asian man asking me about buffer over-flows. Did you attend the speech?"

"No, I was not there personally, Mr. Davis."

He started to get sick from looking at the pictures. He turned them upside down and slid them toward the agent.

"Is there anything else I can help you with, sir?"

"Yes, can you please state your itinerary starting with your arrival here and your final destination? Please be as specific as possible regarding your arrival and departure times."

What the…? Davis was confused. *What have I done?* He gave the agent the information he needed and hoped there was nothing more than a thank you.

But there was more. "Mr. Davis, where were you last night around 10:30 P.M.?" asked the agent in an accusing tone.

"Do you think I killed him?"

"It is routine that we ask, Mr. Davis. Please do not take offense."

Shamefully Davis replied, "I was at the casino. I got home around one."

"Is there anyone that can verify your whereabouts, Mr. Davis?"

"I'm sure the blackjack dealer could…and the cage attendant."

"Ok, Mr. Davis, thank you for your cooperation. You must understand that security is much stricter now in airports."

"Yes I do," said Davis. "You have an interesting accent, sir, where are you from?"

"Northern Amsterdam," replied the agent. "We have a distinct dialect that still escapes me now and then. Have a safe trip."

Davis got up and hastily made his way to the door. Walking out he checked his watch. *Ten nineteen. Dammit!*

Danko watched him leave; he had gotten little information from Davis, hardly enough to justify his paying the inside connections that had allowed him to conduct the interview in this security office. But, that was the way of the world. It was amazing, though, how little money could convince *dedicated* airline personnel to look the other way and allow him a little leeway, especially in this day and age. Of course, not that they believed they had any reason to doubt he had authority to do it; his job was to impersonate and infiltrate.

Danko picked up his cell phone, punched in a couple of buttons, and waited for the other side to pick up.

"He claims to not know anything," he said when he heard the man answer.

"I'm not surprised. Follow him closely. We cannot take any chances."

Chapter 14:
Amsterdam, the Netherlands

Schiphol Airport

"I'm sorry, sir, we did page you several times."

This can't be happening!

"But it was *your* agent that detained me!"

Davis began to resume normal breathing after his sprint to the gate. His brush with Interpol had caused him to miss his direct flight to Seattle.

"Sir, that is really beyond our control. Let me see… I can accommodate you on our next flight that leaves in two hours with a connection in Newark."

"What time does that get me back in Seattle?"

"10:12 P.M. Pacific."

This was a solid six hours later than his original flight but Davis was too rattled to argue.

"Fine, just book it."

The image of a bludgeoned body and an interrogation by international police was too much to take before breakfast. He surveyed the terminal and spotted a familiar green emblem across the room. *Starbucks! These places really are everywhere.* Living in Seattle, Davis had become spoiled to the instant access of a double mocha cappuccino whenever the emergency arose. Now, all he could think about was walking over there and becoming reacquainted.

"Here are your boarding passes. That will be 127 euros Dr. Davis."

Davis couldn't believe the woman had the nerve to charge him after the morning he'd had, but he figured that this was a battle better fought over a toll free number back at his house in Seattle.

"Aren't these coach seats? My ticket was for first class."

"I'm sorry, sir, first class is completely booked! And we have no flights with first or business availability until tomorrow afternoon."

No! Davis had vowed never to fly coach again across the Atlantic after a particularly uncomfortable excursion, where he had found himself encased in a middle seat between two full-figured women. Although not a medical doctor, by some particularly offensive symptoms Davis privately diagnosed the woman to his left with a moderate case of apnea and the one on his right with irritable bowl syndrome. That was an experience he could not bear repeating.

"But what about the 127 euros? Shouldn't I be receiving the difference in fare between the two tickets?"

"Actually sir, after the change fee, late booking fee, and the last minute rates, you owe us 127 Euros."

This is unbelievable! Someone at KLM is going to get their ass chewed out when I get back! But his spirit had already been broken. Davis begrudgingly handed over his credit card.

"Thank you, sir, and thank you for choosing KLM."

Davis let out a slight laugh, gathered his boarding passes and receipt, and began to walk over to the Starbucks counter. He ordered a double mocha cappuccino and dug in his right pocket for leftover euros. He pulled out a handful of receipts, cards, and coins and laid them on the counter, rifling through the pile for the €2. After paying he reached for the pile when Baff's business card CD caught his attention.

He couldn't believe that just yesterday Baff was standing next to him, in the flesh, and now all he had were images of the crime scene and the CD. He and Baff had not been close, but he seemed a decent enough guy and the fact that he was simply *gone* was more than a little unsettling, especially considering he was murdered. Davis also quickly realized that he had just inadvertently lied to an Interpol officer. He grabbed the CD and coffee and sat down at a small table inside the shop. As he sipped, he stared at the disk. He'd seen these types of disks before, usually with company sales videos or the résumé of some ambitious techie. Davis doubted that this particular disk would hold something so mundane. He reached for his laptop and set the small disk inside the CD-ROM tray. His Windows Explorer automatically popped up, allowing him to view the CD's contents:

```
readme.txt
decryptor.exe
encrypted.dat
```

The text file was common but the decryptor and encrypted file would take some work for him to comprehend. Curious, Davis opened the text file:

Text File

What in the world is this? Perplexed, Davis then moved on to the decryptor. Which, when executed, opened a small DOS window on the screen with a simple request for a key. He instinctively tried "Baff" as a password:

DOS Window

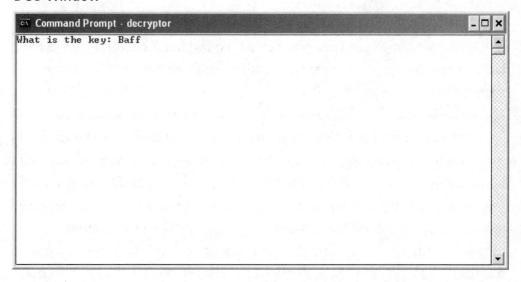

After pressing Enter he gazed at the program's reply:

Access Denied!

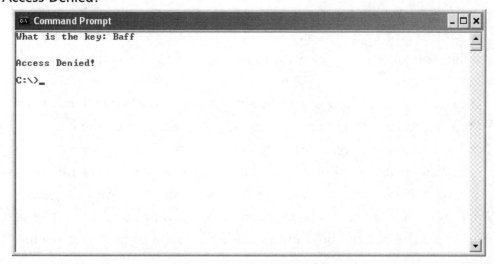

He made a few more attempts at the password thinking of the most obvious possibilities:

Davis

Baff Lexicon

Bartholemew Lexicon

Lexicon

Chad Davis

All of them brought back the same box, the same cursor. Davis then tried entering fragments from the text file, individual words, groups of words, the entire text; all useless.

Screw this, I'm a computer scientist, no password screen can keep me out.

Davis had been up against some tough software before. Some of the most interesting were applications sent to him by the military. Usually all he would get was a binary, some that had an interface similar to the one that now stared him down on his laptop. Davis's first route of attack was always the easiest: guess the password or key. This worked an amazing number of times if he had information about the author or the program's purpose. The next step was a debugger. Davis knew that if an application that wasn't on the network required a password, then that password had to be stored or computed inside the application and then compared with a value entered by the user. He usually was able to exploit this fact by watching the application run under a debugger, a tool that allows developers to watch an application execute instruction by instruction. By watching an application this way, a user is able to see how it works and what data it uses.

Davis fired up a debugger and used it to open the mysterious binary. Within seconds, both the application and the debugger crashed!

Ahh yes…anti-debugging code…this looks like the good stuff, too.

He had encountered problems like this before. Many software companies would rather not have their applications inspected by a debugger. Applications often contain proprietary algorithms or protect sensitive data that would damage an application's market position if they were readily accessible. Some of the best anti-debugging software Davis had run across was in applications that are used to read digital books. Content providers and authors were very reluctant to distribute their works in digital form because of the risk of them being posted on the Internet and swapped for free like music MP3 files. In response, several large software companies developed E-Reader applications that would read encrypted book files that were locked to a particular computer. If a user distributed the book file to a friend, the file would be unreadable. The risk remained, however, of a debugger attaching to the E-Reader application and then siphoning the book contents out of memory while the reader was running.

To make it harder for debuggers to operate, many companies—including those that protect digital content like e-books—include routines whose only purpose is to confuse a debugger and sometimes completely incapacitate it. The response to this by the hacking community has been the creation of anti-anti-debugging tools; tools that slice through anti-debugging code. The result has been an arms race between hackers and developers. Davis was well known for breaking one of the most fortified E-Reader applications, one produced by Advice Software.

For the last year Davis had considered himself at the top of the food chain by developing a tool that circumvented all known commercial anti-debugging techniques. It was this tool that Davis prepared to unleash on the mysterious application.

"Now boarding flight 1278 with service to Newark, New Jersey at Gate D17," a cheerful voice with a slight accent announced over the PA system.

Damn. I guess it'll have to wait a while. Davis closed his laptop, shoved it into his bag, and walked toward the gate.

The plane was packed. As Davis settled into his seat, he casually glanced at the attractive woman sitting to his right in seat 19 F. *Maybe coach isn't as bad as I remember.*

After a few failed attempts at launching into a conversation with her, Davis pulled his laptop out of the bag near his feet. The CD-ROM drive began to whirl as Davis launched the program that had tormented him an hour before. He had had enough, it was time to unleash a tool that had consumed a good portion of the last year to write and that had cost him a marriage—he appropriately named it *Beast*. Beast was a next-generation debugger. It emulated the processor and he who wielded it had complete and absolute power over an application. Davis's goal was to find the encryption key buried somewhere in the application. Davis had developed Beast to help him with some of the more interesting programs he was asked to crack by the government. In a meeting with one of his more clandestine government sponsors, he once casually mentioned his intent to post the tool to his university's web site for public use. Two days later, Beast and all derivative technologies were classified. Davis was heartbroken; he could never discuss the tool with his colleagues again.

The laptop fan spun loudly under the stress of Beast. okay *Mr. Lexicon, let's see what you are hiding.* Beast was the nuclear bomb of hacking. Davis began to think that Baff's little executable was an unworthy target, but he needed to know what it was protecting. Beast lay open on the desktop, awaiting its master's command. Davis typed the location of the target and Beast attacked its victim. Two seconds later, Davis was met with a most unusual error message…

While an application is running, most of the application's instructions and data are stored in computer memory. A memory address identifies a particular location in memory that a machine can reference to both access data and execute instructions. Most of the time, memory addresses are represented as hexadecimal values (base 16). Thus, each digit of a memory address can take the value 0 thru 9 or A, B, C, D, E, and F representing the numbers 10, 11, 12, 13, 14, and 15, respectively. Davis's machine had a 32 bit processor, meaning that every memory address can be represented by 32 binary digits or 8 hexadecimal digits. For readability, all addresses usually are quoted in hexadecimal values. For Windows machines, most applications use addresses that start with 00. A typical memory address therefore could be 0011FB5C, for example. If an application attempts to read a memory address beyond its bounds, the application will crash. There are several reasons why this can happen, the most likely being a programming error, or some crafty anti-debugging code trying to destroy its aggressor.

Davis was dumbstruck as he looked down at the error message. An error while reading a strange memory address. Somehow, this application had gotten the better of Davis and even more concerning was the memory address it crashed on:

Error Message

Two rows back and diagonally across from Davis, a man peered intently, trying to catch another glimpse of the screen. The man pulled out a small notepad from his pocket:

> 13:15 - Davis continues to work on his laptop. Limited conversation with attractive lady seated next to him.

Chapter 15: Seattle, Washington

Chad Davis's Home

Suburban Seattle is much like other suburban neighborhoods across the United States. An escape from the city's traffic, noise, population, and crime, but close enough to the big city to make that often painful commute to work. Metropolitan cities like New York, Miami, and Boston all have frustrating commutes from neighboring towns or even neighboring states. Commuters can expect to be in traffic for at least an hour one way. For Davis, it was an average of 23.8 minutes one way from his subdivision in Redmond to his office at the University of Washington. He had timed it every day for one month, gathering time, route, and mileage data so he could determine the most efficient route.

His house was modest. It blended in well with the others in the neighborhood. The landscape was lacking but with monthly alimony payments and a borderline compulsive gambling habit he watched his expenses carefully. The living room walls inside his two-bedroom house were lined with books on software, computers, world history, and a variety of other subjects. The kitchen had a bachelor feel to it with the few plates, glasses, and silverware he had, bearing no decorative relation. His utensils of choice were plastic, saving clean-up and wash time. His bedroom consisted of a mattress, an end table, and a closet where his clothes were "neatly piled." He used the second bedroom as his office. A couple of clichéd motivational posters decorated the walls where more books were piled on the floor, closet, and his journal-covered desk. Among the clutter covering his desk was a picture of his daughter, Elizabeth, and his ex-wife, Amanda.

Outside, a grey van drove slowly past his house. It came to a soft stop and reversed in front of 3652 Trule Lane. The men inside resembled cable installers, phone repair men, or even Amway salesmen. But the van had a plain appearance with no logos to reveal its true purpose.

"We've got 30 minutes," said the driver glancing at his watch, "let's make it quick, this is big money."

"Joe, take the back and open the front door. Ron and I will ring the bell for you. According to our surveillance he doesn't have an alarm or a dog."

He knew Ron hated dogs. It was almost a year ago when a job in Portland had gone terribly wrong because of an ambitious Doberman. Ron had been the first to go in and the dog—appropriately named Chopper—apparently waited until he was inside the house to attack. What followed could only be described as inhumane. Twenty seven stitches and half his manhood later Ron froze every time he heard a bark.

The men headed for the front door with tool belts and briefcases.

The driver came up to the front door, turned to Ron, and said, "You'd think he'd keep his lawn in a little better shape."

Having scanned the lawn and trees Ron replied, "Does that look like dog shit to you? There better not be any fuckin' mutts in there." The driver couldn't help but crack a smile.

"Remember, we gotta make sure we cover everything. All the phones. Rooms. He cannot make a move without us being able to see or hear him."

Ron nodded and rang the doorbell. Seconds later Joe opened up, welcoming them as if he had lived there all his life. As he checked his watch the driver asserted, "Four minutes down, 26 minutes left."

Chapter 16 Seattle, WA

Chad Davis's Home

It was nearly midnight as Davis pulled into the driveway of his home from the SEA-TAC airport. As he forced the car into park he lowered his forehead onto the steering wheel while the garage door closed behind him. He slowly got out of the car, his neck aching from a failed attempt at sleep on his connecting flight through Newark. He opened the back door and grabbed his laptop case out of the back seat along with a bright yellow piece of paper.

The garage entrance to the house led directly into the kitchen. The oak cabinets, marble kitchen top, and stainless steel appliances that once evoked a slight jealousy from neighbors were now covered with student papers, coffee cups, and a potpourri of empty pizza boxes. The debacle had begun when Davis's wife moved out 13 months ago and only accelerated when his once-a-week maid was deported 10 months later. Davis didn't care, as long as there was a clear path to the microwave and the refrigerator.

As he entered the house he walked by an angrily flashing answering machine. He looked down. *The hell with it.* He picked up the cordless phone from the charging base, and walked into the master bedroom. The room looked like a small typhoon had selectively picked up socks, underwear, and other garments, and distributed them haphazardly throughout the room. To an outsider, the scene would have initiated a robbery report but Davis felt comfortable in disarray.

He let the laptop bag drop and then slumped onto the bed in a space with a perimeter of questionably clean socks. He held a yellow piece of paper up with his left hand and began dialing on the phone handset.

"Welcome to the automated delayed baggage center. Please enter your claim number followed by the pound key."

Davis again referred to the yellow sheet and began pressing buttons.

"There are no updates on your luggage at this time. Thank you for calling. Goodbye."

He let out a sigh and tossed the receiver to the other side of the bed. This had been the third time in the last six months that his luggage had been "delayed." After the fiasco in Amsterdam, Davis assumed that if anything, his luggage would arrive before he did. After waiting for half an hour in Newark to go through U.S. customs and looking at an empty luggage conveyor belt, the yellow claim ticket he was given dissolved all hope.

Davis had anticipated losing consciousness as soon as he touched the bed. Instead, he was restless. His mind was consumed with images of Baff and the mysterious files on his CD. The flight from Amsterdam had been frustrating on two fronts. The first was the complete noninterest from an attractive but now assumed to be lesbian passenger seated in the seat to his right. The second was the utter impenetrability of Baff's odd executable. Davis had made little progress on deciphering the files' contents on the plane. He tried to think about other tools he could use, techniques he could apply, but each road he traveled led only to more frustration.

He pulled the television remote control from on top of an old shirt to the side of him and clicked on the TV situated across the room. He flipped through the news channels, all of which seemed to be running stories on the upcoming Presidential primaries. *Slow news week.*

He paused on one channel that was discussing the outcome of the Iowa caucus that had taken place a few weeks earlier. Davis wondered if he might be on one of these shows in the weeks ahead based on his role in the upcoming Washington primary.

Several months earlier he had received a phone call from Grace Wilkinson. Her team were responsible for making sure that voting at precincts was orderly, secure, and beyond media reproach. Davis had heard about her before the call. She was one of many targets in the media witch hunt in 2000 over voting irregularities in Florida. Apparently, she had managed to keep her job but was now under a political microscope for the upcoming elections.

Grace explained the government's desire to move toward electronic voting. Companies such as Diebold were in the process of deploying e-voting machines in several states, but the government's plan was even more ambitious. Her charter was to allow absentee votes to be cast and then delivered directly to elections offices electronically. As the leading software security expert, Davis was hired as one of the people tasked to evaluate the underlying technology of three large software companies that had bid on the project.

After months of testing, Advice's software sat on top. It was the one solution that Davis was not able to crack the encryption on. Once Advice was selected, a challenge went out to leading researchers in the fields of cryptography, statistics, number theory, and computer science to poke holes in Advice's e-voting architecture. Advice weathered the pounding, and the planets were in alignment for adoption in the 2004 general election. The last hurdle would be faced in two days when it would be used in the Washington state primary and ratified by Congress.

Although several experts were hired, Davis's testimony to Congress was viewed as key. He had been involved in the evaluation from the beginning and would now answer questions from members of the acceptance committee from the House of Representatives and the Senate. Until yesterday, Davis had been pretty confident in his findings. The month before, he wrote a glowing review on Advice's implementation for *Infoweek*. His review, however, was couched with the usual cynicism on software security, but if one *had* to go with electronic voting, Advice was the frontrunner.

Davis's mind returned to Baff. *What the hell is in that file?*

The bar across the bottom of the television screen scrolled with woes of higher gas prices and the fate of candidates in the coming elections. As Davis began to drift off, he was hit with a moment of clarity.

Why was an Interpol agent investigating a crime in Amsterdam? Amsterdam isn't a member country of Interpol...

Several miles away, another passenger from Davis's flight was typing on a laptop at Advice Software's office in Redmond. The man was typing notes into an e-mail that were scrolled on a small pad next to the keyboard. The closing line read:

```
Subject's luggage is being inspected. Scheduled for return to his house
tomorrow morning.
```

The man clicked the Send button and moments later a message appeared on two computers, one on the top floor of that very building and the other in southern China.

Chapter 17: Washington, D.C.

Senator Shift's Home

Behind the conservative public façade of Washington, D.C.'s political elite are lives filled with strippers, alcohol, and drugs. Senator Shift was an exception. He was raised Protestant. His parents worked hard to provide for him and his younger sister in rural West Virginia. He was a leader in the Boy Scouts and held office in both middle and high school. In college he was part of every political organization he could find. He met his future wife, Judy, during his sophomore year at Yale, where they both attended liberal rights sit-ins and protests—and more importantly, dabbled in recreational drugs. Shift had smoked pot on numerous occasions but feared LSD because he had seen what it did to others. *The hallucinations aren't worth it.* When he married Judy they moved to Arlington, Virginia to begin an internship with a prestigious D.C. political firm. He quickly made his way through the ranks and ran for mayor of Arlington. Two years later he battled for a Senate seat where he won amidst controversy over negative campaigning from both sides. He was a changed man after he realized what politics could do to a man's image. He vowed never to attack another opponent's personal life. As Shift painfully discovered, everyone has a past dirty enough for the media to exploit.

He had been serving as Senator for just two years when Chris Payne, the CEO of Advice Software, approached him with a most unusual and unexpected proposal. He was eager, excited. He felt for the *cause*.

"The country is headed in the wrong direction," he had said during their meeting almost half a year ago. "I am honored that you're considering funding my campaign for the U.S. Presidency, Mr. Payne."

Every minute he spent outside D.C. he spent with his wife of seven years and his two daughters. He worried about the new risks and challenges his kids would endure growing up in the 21st century. He cared passionately about the country's economy, its youth, and the international milk it had spilled over the past few years. He believed in Payne and his agenda. He felt for Payne's loss and that of so many Americans eager for a change. Although full of pep rallies, small town meetings, and other fundraisers common to the public and the media, Shift's were not prearranged. Often his camp was unaware where he was headed or what he had planned. He would arrive, gather a crowd, and preach his message of change. In downtown Middletown, Connecticut, he entered a bank and found his way to the roof. As people went about their business, he campaigned through a megaphone stressing change in the White House, the economy, health care, and as he proclaimed, "A change in the United States' international agenda."

Local Wesleyan University students loved him. They thought his method was unique, lacked the political stiffness many have grown to abhor watching local and national candidates debate. He was real, unpredictable, and human enough to make mistakes.

In Washington, D.C., Senator Shift was well liked too. He was a blunt politician. He kept things simple. Hearing him speak was entertaining for most of his coworkers. He would make innocent observations, what many called, "An oversimplification of serious political and social issues." Shift was known to take an issue like the increase in job losses and simplify it to basic, almost childlike reasoning.

"Corporations should not have to sacrifice quality workers to save face," he would argue. "Upper management's only concern is to meet the numbers on the books so their bonuses are guaranteed. What about the engineer who has four mouths to feed and was doing it on a tenth of the CEO's salary?"

"You're advocating Communism!" exclaimed a fellow senator. "This country was and will continue to be built on entrepreneurship."

The issue of unemployment ran deeper than a company's wish to maintain public profit projections and line the pockets of those already living large. But Shift was angered by recent corporate scandals that made the blue-collar worker's life miserable.

His recent Senate resignation was unexpected but most applauded and supported him in his bid for the United States Presidency. One of his most controversial agendas was the attempt to regulate and limit any corporate Chief Executive's salary based on his average employee's salary and the company's performance. The big fish were sweating but controlled far less votes than the blue-collar masses that loved him, especially the younger demographic: fresh college graduates desperate for jobs.

His views on the United States' international agenda were also a hot topic. He openly blamed Saudi Arabia for harboring, funding, and turning a blind eye to terrorist movements in their own country and throughout the Middle East. Shift vowed to "squeeze terrorism-harboring countries and governments to the point of suffocation." He did not stop at Islamic fundamentalists either. He lashed out at Israel for their continuing occupation of disputed land that Shift believed "clearly belonged to Palestine." Advocating in his most recent interview that, "When it comes to our country's domestic and international safety we must trust no one but ourselves. We cannot fall victim to any other country's agenda."

The media tore him apart for his views, labeling him an extremist. Shift was personally offended and emotionally hurt.

For all of this, Shift weathered the storm without hesitation. At the moment, he was laying in bed reading the day's New York Times, when his attention momentarily shifted to the TV, set to the 24-hour news channel, where a respected news station commented, "If Senator Shift were to become President of these United States I predict this world will see conflicts and terror unleashed in the Middle East and beyond yet to be imagined. His international politics mirror those of an angry swarm of bees looking for anyone and anything to sting to defend their hive. We live in a civilized world. Any conflict, no matter how large, whether it be international or between mother and daughter, can, and should, be resolved with dialogue."

"They're bashing my politics again. We have a long road ahead of us."

His wife was preparing for bed, applying moisturizer to her hands, brushing her teeth, and dabbing some anti-wrinkle cream under her eyes.

"You're above that, honey."

"They'll probably dig into our past," Shift apologetically said as his wife tucked herself into bed beside him.

With a kiss and a hug she replied, "If that's what it takes to change our country then so be it."

She leaned over and turned off her light. "Goodnight."

"Goodnight," replied Shift as he clicked off the TV and continued reading the paper. A couple of minutes later he could no longer keep his eyes from closing. He let the paper drop to the floor and turned his light off. As he lay down to sleep, thousands of Americans checked their e-mail, surfed the net, and unknowingly received Shift's message.

"*And in other news tonight, a USA Today poll shows Senator Shift gaining ground on the White House. He is closing in on the President with the latest numbers giving Shift 46 percent of the vote, a 5 point increase from a month ago. The error on the poll is plus or minus one point five percent.*"

Chapter 18: Seattle, Washington

Chad Davis's Home

Chad was not a morning person. He worked best after the sun had set. If he wasn't teaching, he would set his alarm clock for noon and occasionally followed lunch with a mid-afternoon nap. His internal clock was on hacker time. Even though Davis was not a hacker, he found that both his work and his associates were more approachable at 2 A.M. instead of 9 A.M.

Even though he had been on an airplane for half the previous day, Davis could not go to sleep without tinkering with something. Usually it was some new debugger, plowing through e-mail, or reviewing papers, but last night he had more pressing concerns: *What the hell did Baff have on that CD?* It must have lingered in his sleep, because he was up before nine o'clock preparing a meal he was very unfamiliar with: breakfast.

As the eggs scrambled and bread toasted he powered up his laptop ready to attack the CD again. Setting his plate down with eggs, toast, some microwaved bacon, and condiments, he remembered to call Hans Sheridan, one of his best friends, and an FBI agent.

"Good *morning*," Davis proudly said as Hans picked up, making sure to point out his accomplishment.

"Chad? Are you sleepwalking or something? It's not April Fools is it?" Hans replied with characteristic sarcasm.

"I know, I know. Hey, there's a first time for everything. Haven't heard from you in a while. How are things going?"

"Pretty good. We've been busy this past month. I had a couple of trips outside of the field office these past few weeks and now I am back home. How about you? What do I owe this relatively early call to?"

"Well obviously I would not be calling you before noon on a Saturday if I didn't have a favor to ask."

Hans laughed, "As usual. What is it? A parking ticket? Indecent exposure? Hey, you just came from Amsterdam, right? I have some penicillin if you need it."

Chad hesitated for a minute. He quickly thought about what he was about to ask and where he was about to do it from.

"Real funny. Hey Hans let me call you right back. I got breakfast on the stove."

"Wow, not only are you up in time for breakfast, you're actually cooking something! This must be serious. Ok, don't keep me waiting too long."

"Just give me a minute," replied Davis and hung up.

He walked over to his desk, quickly grabbing a bite of his now lukewarm eggs and toast. Among the piles of papers he grabbed his cell phone and called Hans again.

"Sorry about that. My eggs were browning."

Hans smirked, realizing by his caller ID that Chad switched from his land line to his cell phone. "No problem. I hope they still taste good."

"Yeah, as good as I'll ever make them. So, I have a question for you. I was at the airport in Amsterdam and got questioned by Interpol…"

Hans interrupted inquisitively, "Interpol? In Amsterdam? What were they doing there?"

"Yeah, well, hindsight is always 20/20. I guess your bureau-trained paranoia hasn't rubbed off on me. So can you find out any info on the agent that stopped me?"

"I can try. You got his name?" asked Hans.

"Sure, hold on a second."

Davis grabbed his carry-on bag and searched through his papers, pens, and accumulating garbage. He grabbed a card with his scribbled writing and reached for his cell phone, "You still there? Ok, it's Jonas Borgstand. B-o-r-g-s-t-a-n-d."

"Got it. Give me an hour or so and I'll see what I can get. Maybe you should get some sleep."

"Thanks, I owe you one."

Ending the call, Davis's stomach growled at him for ignoring his now cold, and probably tasteless eggs. He sat down and stared at them on his plate, contemplating what else he was going to eat. *Cereal is always a good start to the day.*

After a couple of bowls he decided to plunge into that CD and not come out until he figured out what Baff wanted to show him.

Davis opened his laptop, ready to do battle. Some sleep was all he needed to get a fresh perspective on Baff's little brainteaser. Davis knew that potentially he could spend weeks trying to decipher Baff's cryptic text file. *Maybe it doesn't mean anything, knowing Baff he probably just needed to take a note or something and accidentally saved it to disk.*

Davis didn't believe that, but it was too early in the morning to admit he had intellectual limitations and just couldn't figure it out. It was partially an excuse to try some of his honed reverse engineering skills.

Reverse engineering software is the art and science of understanding and manipulating software after it has been compiled, and during the past three years Davis had become a master. When a person writes a computer program, they tell the computer's hardware what to do by giving it a series of instructions. At their lowest level, computer instructions are represented as bits—binary digits that have two states, on or off, one or zero. Most of the time, when one sees these instructions, they are represented in hexadecimal (base 16). Instructions are usually visible if one opens an executable file in a hexadecimal editor. An executable file is just a collection of these instructions and some data that these instructions will operate with or on.

In the early days of computing, programmers would write complex programs using these instructions directly. Programmers who wrote endless strings of hexadecimal numbers would command absolute power over machines that occupied rooms the size of warehouses. Efforts were made to make the process of writing machine instruction easier by allowing programmers to write short, English-like codes to represent a series of numeric instructions. These mnemonics became known as assembly language. When a programmer was finished writing his or her instructions in assembly, a piece of software known as an assembler would convert these mnemonics into their machine-instruction equivalents. People soon realized that they were writing the same sets of instructions over and over again. A mechanism was needed to both encapsulate these instructions and to make the process of controlling a machine simpler. The result was the development of so-called high-level languages that allowed users to program with English-like constructs. These program files would then be converted into machine code using a compiler. Most modern applications are written by teams of programmers using various high-level languages like C, C++, and Java.

Davis realized that a huge misconception about compilers lingered in the minds of programmers. Most programmers believe that once an application was compiled and in machine-executable form that it was unalterable. Beyond that, many believed that any secrets hidden within the lines of source code like passwords were locked in an impenetrable vault by the compiler, a vault to which no one had the combination.

Reality, he knew, was quite different. People like Baff made their livings by changing the behavior of software. Most of the time, the behavior that they worked to change had to do with the software's restrictions on copying or distributing it. Many companies for example, choose to make users "activate" their products either through the Internet or by a key given over the phone. This activated software would then be fully functional on the machine it was originally installed on but useless on any other machine. Other software vendors had begun to raise the ante by distributing hardware "keys" that needed to be inserted into the machine to run their application. All these methods were created in an effort to stop software pirates from copying and distributing software without paying for it; over the years all had been broken.

Davis's interest today was not in removing copy protection; it was getting that damn decryptor to work. His first step was to use a hex editor to examine the decryption program.

Abstractly, there are two ways to manipulate and inspect software: statically or dynamically. Dynamic analysis is done while the application is running, usually by watching the application execute instruction by instruction with a debugger. Baff obviously had thought hard about protecting against this. On the plane Davis hit a silicone wall. He threw several commercial debuggers at the application, even an advanced one that Davis himself had written—all failed. Baff was good.

It was now time to do some static analysis; dissecting the binary file itself using some inspection tools. Davis's first step was always a hex editor.

To the casual user, the output of a hex editor is a sea of garbage; meaningless characters that somehow must miraculously come together to make a program do what it does when they execute it.

Output of the Hex Editor

WinHex - [decryptor.exe]

File Edit Search Position View Tools Specialist Options File Manager Window Help

decryptor.exe

```
Offset       0  1  2  3  4  5  6  7   8  9 10 11 12 13 14 15
00000000    4D 5A 90 00 03 00 00 00  04 00 00 00 FF FF 00 00   MZ■.........ÿÿ..
00000016    B8 00 00 00 00 00 00 00  40 00 00 00 00 00 00 00   ,.......@.......
00000032    00 00 00 00 00 00 00 00  00 00 00 00 00 00 00 00   ................
00000048    00 00 00 00 00 00 00 00  00 00 00 00 E0 00 00 00   ............à...
00000064    0E 1F BA 0E 00 B4 09 CD  21 B8 01 4C CD 21 54 68   ..º..´.Í!,.LÍ!Th
00000080    69 73 20 70 72 6F 67 72  61 6D 20 63 61 6E 6E 6F   is program canno
00000096    74 20 62 65 20 72 75 6E  20 69 6E 20 44 4F 53 20   t be run in DOS
00000112    6D 6F 64 65 2E 0D 0D 0A  24 00 00 00 00 00 00 00   mode....$.......
00000128    E7 D3 49 86 A3 B2 27 D5  A3 B2 27 D5 A3 B2 27 D5   çÓI†£²'Õ£²'Õ£²'Õ
00000144    B0 BA 4E D5 A1 B2 27 D5  A6 BE 28 D5 BB B2 27 D5   °ºNÕ¡²'Õ¦¾(Õ»²'Õ
00000160    20 BA 7A D5 A0 B2 27 D5  A3 B2 26 D5 F3 B2 27 D5    ºzÕ ²'Õ£²&Õó²'Õ
00000176    A6 BE 78 D5 DD B2 27 D5  A6 BE 47 D5 B4 B2 27 D5   ¦¾xÕÝ²'Õ¦¾GÕ´²'Õ
00000192    A6 BE 7D D5 A2 B2 27 D5  52 69 63 68 A3 B2 27 D5   ¦¾}Õ¢²'ÕRich£²'Õ
00000208    00 00 00 00 00 00 00 00  00 00 00 00 00 00 00 00   ................
00000224    50 45 00 00 4C 01 03 00  E7 42 B6 40 00 00 00 00   PE..L...çB¶@....
00000240    00 00 00 00 E0 00 0F 01  0B 01 07 0A 00 10 01 00   ....à...........
00000256    00 70 00 00 00 00 00 00  CF 5A 00 00 00 10 00 00   .p......ÏZ......
00000272    00 20 01 00 00 00 40 00  00 10 00 00 00 10 00 00   . ....@.........
00000288    04 00 00 00 00 00 00 00  04 00 00 00 00 00 00 00   ................
00000304    00 90 01 00 00 10 00 00  00 00 00 00 03 00 00 00   .■..............
00000320    00 00 10 00 00 10 00 00  00 00 10 00 00 10 00 00   ................
00000336    00 00 00 00 10 00 00 00  00 00 00 00 00 00 00 00   ................
00000352    44 51 01 00 28 00 00 00  00 00 00 00 00 00 00 00   DQ..(...........
00000368    00 00 00 00 00 00 00 00  00 00 00 00 00 00 00 00   ................
00000384    00 00 00 00 00 00 00 00  00 00 00 00 00 00 00 00   ................
00000400    00 00 00 00 00 00 00 00  00 00 00 00 00 00 00 00   ................
00000416    00 00 00 00 00 00 00 00  18 44 01 00 48 00 00 00   .........D..H...
00000432    00 00 00 00 00 00 00 00  00 20 01 00 38 01 00 00   ......... ..8...
00000448    00 00 00 00 00 00 00 00  00 00 00 00 00 00 00 00   ................
00000464    00 00 00 00 00 00 00 00  2E 74 65 78 74 00 00 00   ........text...
00000480    44 02 01 00 00 10 00 00  00 10 01 00 00 10 00 00   D...............
00000496    00 00 00 00 00 00 00 00  00 00 00 00 20 00 00 60   ............ ..`
```

Page 1 of 184   Offset: 0   = 77   Block: n/a Size: n/a

Davis looked at the output and saw much more. He saw an application, baring its secrets, its purpose. He had learned to do some amazing things by editing a program directly in a hex editor over the last few years. He could change how the application behaved, how it responded to input and how it looked. He could also add features and change flawed ones at the lowest possible level.

This skill had made Davis a lot of money in 1999, when many companies were throwing money at anyone who could soothe their Y2K computer fears. Most companies were still running ancient software that used two digits to represent which year a transaction or event was taking place. When the original programmers had developed these applications no one thought that they would still be in use a decade or sometimes two decades later. The fear was that when the year rolled around from 99 to 00 many applications would fail possibly by instantly archiving transactions that took place in 2000 as 100 years old, automatically voiding transactions, dividing by the year 00, or other unimaginable horrors. It was during this period that Davis mastered the art of bending software to his will. He would have to modify old applications for which the source code was either lost or unavailable, and make them work with the new date format. If anyone could make this decryptor give up its secrets, it was Chad Davis.

Davis skimmed the output from the hex editor. Nothing immediately obvious. There were some strings that looked like ASCII art. A few interesting phrases:

```
"Success…the key is yours!"
```

followed by a peculiar 32-character long number. By its length and its placement within the binary Davis assumed it could be only one thing: a password hash!

```
51d2b210d1ad862d781f065eb22d9370
```

Interesting Phrases and Numbers

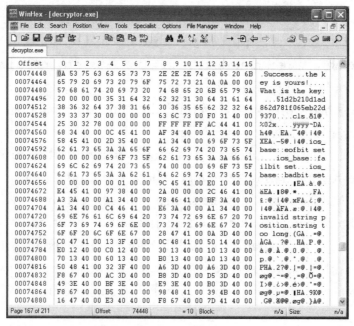

Hashes were a testimony to modern cryptography. Davis had used their power several times in his programming days as a graduate student. A hash function reads a long string or file as input and produces a "digest" of that data. Ideally, the security properties of these functions ensure that the digest looks random and does not leak any information about the data itself, and that other messages cannot be found that produce the same digest. Specifically, what makes these numbers interesting is that they have a few very desirable properties.

First, finding an input that produces a given hash is (hopefully) extremely hard. Second, finding two inputs that hash to the same result is difficult (if not impossible). Third, knowing the hash, you cannot recompute the original data; thus, hash functions are also known as one-way functions. Finally, small changes in the data can cause drastic changes in the value of the computed hash.

One application of hashes is to ensure that files are not tampered with. One can compute the value of a file when it is in a known, "good" state and save that hash value in a safe place. Later, one could compute the hash of that file again and compare the old value with the new: if the two match, the file has not been tampered with. It was doubtful that this was the way Baff was using it. For one, it was stored in the file itself. That means if the user changed the file, or a part of the file, they could also recompute and change the stored hash value. Baff was too clever for that. Another popular use of hashes was to store passwords. Davis figured that this is exactly what Baff was doing.

Baff, you bastard!

The general problem with storing passwords in a program is that an attacker with a hex editor might be able to see that password stored in binary and then use it. Using hashes was a good alternative. Davis knew that this is how most of the widely used operating systems like most flavors of Linux, UNIX, and Windows managed passwords. In most versions of Windows, for instance, when a user logs in, a hash of the password is calculated and then compared with a hash of the original password stored when it was initially set. The result is that nobody's password is actually stored on the machine, only the hashes. This is the reason that a system administrator is often unable to tell you your forgotten password, but they are able to set a new one. Apparently Baff had taken the same approach with his decryptor.

Like any cryptography though, this could be broken. The only question was how long would it take. Davis had used some of the dubbed "password recovery" tools—which usually were used as "password theft" tools—like L0pht Crack for Windows passwords and John the Ripper for UNIX/Linux. For a funded project through the U.S. Navy Davis had also written several of his own tools. Most of these tools worked by "brute-forcing" passwords—trying various combinations of letters, numbers, and special characters, computing their hashes, and then comparing these computed hashes with the one stored. For operating system passwords, many tools can recover a reasonably complex password from a hash in a few hours, likely trying several million combinations in the process. Davis knew that his task was harder. For operating system passwords, there are a few things that make the process easier. For one, usually there is a known maximum length like 8 or 16 characters. Davis had no idea what kind of password Baff was expecting. One character, ten, a hundred; all possibilities. Davis did not have that luxury. His testimony was a couple of days away, and he had to know what Baff had found.

When Davis studied cryptography as a graduate student at Carnegie Mellon he was amazed at how widely these techniques had been used during the two World Wars. Many battles had been won or lost based on how skilled each side was at breaking encoded messages. What amazed Davis at the time was how breakable many of the systems were. The important thing was how long it would take to break it.

Ok Baff, let's do this…

Davis knew that the sledge hammer approach would not work in time. There had to be another way. There were two widely used families of hashing algorithms: the Secure Hash Algorithms (SHA) and the

Message Digest (MD). Baff's hash had 32 hexadecimal characters, which meant it was probably either MD4 or MD5, both of which had a 128bit = 32 hex character hash value. Most of the world had moved from MD4 to MD5, which was more difficult to crack. From what he had seen so far, Davis was pretty sure that Baff would pick the harder one.

MD5 it is.

Again, trying to attack the cryptography directly was not an option. Davis recalled the first try-and-buy software that he cracked. He changed the hard-coded date that helped the software compute its expiry time. In the early days some software developers started to use this method to get around the "setting the system clock back" trick. Looking back, Davis recalled what a horrible scheme that was. He changed the stored date from 1993 to 2013 and the application worked like a charm. *Fifteen bucks saved!* He was about to apply the same principal here.

If I can calculate the hash to a password that I do know, maybe I can replace the stored key with the fake key. Then I enter the password that corresponds to that key! Damn I'm good!

He was good, but so was Baff. Obviously Baff wanted him to crack this thing if anything happened, but why did he have to make it so goddamned difficult? Davis opened a web browser and found a free MD5 hash calculator.

Hmmm…now for a password…ah, why not…

Davis entered the string "advice" and the resulting hash was:

```
fd99cadea9d8ef6a1ffcc52a2e3e8017
```

Davis had a plan. He had his string. He had its hash. It was time for this application to suffer. Davis again opened up his hex editor and faithfully replaced the original hash with the new value he computed and saved the modified file as c:\cracked.exe.

Success!

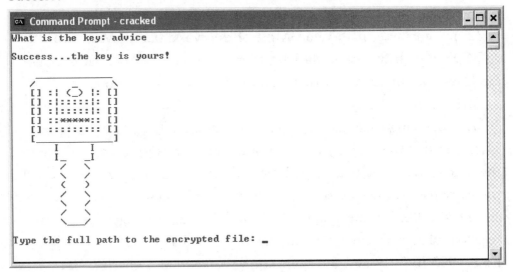

Now, the moment of truth…

Davis ran the modified file and once again was asked for the key. This time things were different, this time he had made his own key. Davis typed "advice," his newly contrived password. With a quick press of the Enter key, success!

He looked with amazement at the screen in front of him; he had done it. He gave the application the location for Baff's mysterious encrypted file and gave it the location to save the decrypted file. Within seconds it had produced its result. Davis quickly opened the decrypted file in his hex editor. He didn't recognize the symbols, characters, and patterns before him. He spent the next several minutes scrolling through it. It wasn't an executable, it didn't have the right headers. It was not a document file, at least it was not in any format that he had ever seen before. He slammed his hands down on the desk.

This is complete garbage. Son of a bitch! I don't have time for this!

A ringing phone interrupted the audible string of profanities now freely flowing from him.

"Hello!"

"Hey; easy. What the hell is the matter with you?"

"Sorry Hans. I am about to take an axe to this CD I'm working on cracking."

"CD? What are you joining the Spice Boys or something? You may not wanna do that just yet. On a more pressing matter that boy of yours, Jonas whatever-the-fuck-his-name-was, is a ghost; Interpol never heard of him."

A cold shiver ran down both of Davis's arms. He was afraid of this, but what did it mean?

"Chad, you still there?"

"Yes, I'm here. Can we meet somewhere? How about Redmond Town Center, Thai restaurant in 20?"

Davis's voice was overtly shaky. He had dealt with criminal elements before but they were hackers, guys who harmed bits, not people.

Had Jonas killed Baff? Is he trying to kill me?

The thought was too much for him to bear.

"I've got a better idea." Hans said in a decidedly different tone. "Remember that place where we met up about a month ago, I'll meet you there in an hour. Ok?"

"Ok. One hour."

Davis hung up the phone. His left hand trembled slightly as it let go of the receiver. Hans's last words had really shaken him:

The place we met last month? Why didn't he just say Starbucks on 45th? Is my phone being tapped? Does Hans know something he's not telling me?

The only explanation for Hans's vagueness that Davis could imagine was that he suspected a wire tap. It was now more important than ever to find out what Baff was trying to tell him.

Davis turned his attention back to the CD and tried to put the failure of the last two hours' efforts behind him. His next step was to use a disassembler to try and find out why he had failed and how he could unlock what Baff had spent so much effort to keep hidden. A disassembler was the opposite of an assembler. Whereas an assembler converts assembly commands into machine instructions, a disassembler attempts to convert machine instructions into assembly instructions that are more easily read by humans rather than machines. Almost every operating system ships with an assembler and a disassembler that are installed by default. As Davis found out early in his professional career though, understanding how a binary works was an art, one that could not be fully captured in a rudimentary disassembly tool. Sometimes the process would take days of staring at complex control flow graphs and looking at hundreds of pages of assembly code. To be successful one had to become a detective, following digital clues and making leaps of deductive reasoning.

The right tools were essential. Davis opened the decryption program in Datarescue's Interactive Diasassembler (IDA Pro). IDA was not a tool for the casual computer user; it was a craftsman's tool, a tool meant to be wielded by software assassins.

Within 25 minutes of staring at IDA Pro Davis realized why his approach was doomed to fail. It appeared as if Baff actually used the characters in the unknown password itself to encrypt the file. The original password was needed if he was to make any sense of the encrypted file in time.

Davis looked down at the clock in the bottom right-hand corner of his computer screen, and began to shut down his laptop and place it in a small carrying case.

I hope Hans has some answers!

A few dozen feet away in a grey van two men stared intently at the black and white video feed from Davis's home. Since listening in on the conversation between Davis and Hans minutes before, they knew one of them had to call Danko. People who knew his identity tended not to live very long; he made sure of it.

"So are you gonna call him?"

"I wouldn't call that man if his sister was the last woman in the world!" replied the first man.

Even with rap sheets neither man wanted to call Danko with the news that Davis and Hans were on to him. After a minute one finally caved in.

"All right, give me the damn phone. Someone's in a load of trouble."

Chapter 19:
Amsterdam, the Netherlands

Red Light District

Danko's eyes were closed. Tonight he had splurged and chosen his companion from one of the finer shops in the red light district. He typically could not afford the better looking ones, and he never really cared much for looks anyway. "As long as it's a woman" was his motto, and even that rule was occasionally flexible. But tonight he would celebrate: two nights, two countries, two successful jobs. As he was being satisfied by his paid participant, his mind was elsewhere. His deepest fantasy would be getting married, having kids, and raising a family back in his native Yugoslovia. But he did not believe in love or in truth, and for that reason true love and raising kids were out of the question. A prostitute's services were ample to fulfill his need for sex and to escape from his secret world.

A ringing cell phone brought his conscious dream to a halt.

"Hold on," he said annoyingly. "Yes?" he answered with the tone anyone on the other line would realize meant, *this better be the most important thing in the fucking world.*

"Davis is onto us," replied the voice.

"What do you mean?"

"He's got some sort of file from Baff. He's been messing with it. We've been listening in on his conversations with some FBI friend of his, and he checked out your airport alias."

Danko angrily replied, "You just watch him and keep track of everything. I take care of rest."

He hung up and turned his attention back to the bed where she lay waiting impatiently. She checked her watch and nonchalantly said, "Fifteen minutes."

"Don't worry honey."

In the shower Danko felt refreshed. He got what he wanted and arrogantly thought he gave her what she needed. But the sudden realization that he had to call his boss to inform him of Davis's newest adventures soured his mood.

Stepping out of the shower he stared at himself in the mirror, trying to catch a glimpse of the father figure he had often dreamt to be. All he saw was a killer. *I've got to make the phone call.*

"We have a problem," Danko said with obvious frustration and feigned contriteness. "Davis is starting to ask questions. He has some file from Baff."

"No names over the phone!" the man replied.

"Yeah, I know, but we have to do something."

"Get on the next plane to Seattle and come see me."

"My flight leaves in an hour."

With that, Danko dropped his towel, assessed his clothes, and determined what he would pack and what he would wear. He'd done his job. He wanted to get paid and move on. The last thing he needed now was a confrontation with Payne.

Chapter 20: Seattle, Washington

Saturday: Starbucks

Davis sat down in a corner of Starbucks Coffee Shop near the window with laptop in hand. Not surprisingly clouds covered up most of Seattle's sun but Davis wasn't interested in the weather. He hadn't seen Hans when he arrived but suddenly noticed his friend walking toward him from the other side of the store with two cups in-hand. Hans placed Davis's favorite, a double mocha cappuccino, down on the table along with his double espresso. He took in the aroma of the espresso and sipped it slowly.

"I can't believe this shit. Two-fifty for an ounce of coffee. I'm in the wrong business."

Chad smirked, "That's why you should get a double mocha cappuccino like me! More volume for the buck."

They sipped their coffees slowly as Chad booted up and logged into his laptop. Hans could easily tell Chad had a look of concern on his face.

"So first you call me way before your wake-up time, you ask me to check out a guy that doesn't exist and now we're out for a cup of coffee. Certainly not the way I'd plan my Saturday."

Chad replied, "Boy, I love your sarcasm. Did I ever tell you that?" He continued, "You know I'm doing that expert witness gig on that new e-voting software that Congress is pushing through?"

"Yeah, I don't think I like the way this is going."

"When I was in Amsterdam, someone I knew gave me this CD and told me that he had some important information about my testimony and about the e-voting software I've been evaluating. I believed him, this guy *was* one of the biggest software hackers in the world; he wouldn't have come to see me in person unless he had something important…or was scared shitless."

Hans's usual laid back demeanor began to change. He leaned forward attentively in his seat. "What do you mean *was*?"

Chad paused and lowered his voice, "The guy is dead! We were supposed to meet a few nights ago after the conference but he never showed. I was on my way to board my plane yesterday when that Interpol agent stopped me on the way in, questioned me, and showed me pictures of the guy's body. He even had crime scene photos. Could you be wrong? Maybe the guy really was from Interpol."

"We've got pretty close ties with those guys, and my contacts say no. Besides, Interpol has no authority in the Netherlands. It doesn't make any sense."

Hans paused for a moment taking another sip from his coffee and asked, "What was on the CD?"

"Don't know. It's encrypted. I've been trying to break it for the last two days."

"I'll do anything I can to help. But the things we would need to do take time. I can get our lab guys to help, but we usually end up calling you anyway, Chad."

"Thanks but I've got to find out what's on this thing immediately…I testify about the software in front of Congress on Monday. I can't postpone it if I don't have something solid or they will have my ass; they might even be able to throw me in jail or something!"

Hans thought for a minute and finished his last sip of the now cold espresso.

"Tell me about the CD, did you find anything?"

Davis proceeded to recount his frustration of the last few days. It was a relief to be able to bounce it off someone like Hans who was much more than a casual computer user. Hans had a Masters degree in Computer Science from Duke. He had worked for years in the FBI as a signals analyst, intercepting and cracking digital communications, mostly from domestic organized crime figures. Davis told Hans about the CD, the anti-debugging code, the hash, and the absolutely miserable problem the whole thing had been.

"So we don't have time to break the decryption software, what about the encrypted file itself?"

Davis had studied and used cryptography on many occasions but was far from an expert. He knew the theoretical strengths and limitation of the codes, though. Protecting data on disk or during communications, was where the science of cryptography shined. Cracking a code that was encrypted by one of the modern encryption standards like the government-adopted Data Encryption Standard (DES) or the Advanced Encryption Standard (AES) was doable but extremely labor intensive. Davis's experience had repeatedly convinced him that crypto was weakest at the software level. He'd read academic papers about clusters of computers working together to break a particular implementation of a modern algorithm. He had no time for that.

"What do you mean? Wouldn't the encrypted file take even longer to break?"

"You said that it looks like the guy had encrypted based on the text of the password, and you said it looked like something simple, maybe an XOR. So what about frequency analysis?"

Hans may have had a point.

Modern cryptography has its roots in early Rome. One of the first known applications was a substitution cipher used by Julius Caesar, which became known as the Caesar cipher. Messages were encoded by substituting every letter in the text by one that is three positions to the right. This meant that A became D, V became Y, and so on. There was also the

Atabash cipher, used in the Bible, where a letter was represented by its corresponding letter if the alphabet were written in reverse. In this scheme, A became Z, B became Y, and so on. Both of these are dubbed monoalphabetic substitution ciphers because a single character is represented by one and only one symbol. Most modern cryptographic schemes use alternate encoding methods such as encrypting in groups or blocks and then using values from the previous block to encrypt the next block. These became known as block ciphers.

One of the easiest ways to crack a substitution cipher was through frequency analysis. When Davis first had learned about the technique in college he was awed by both its simplicity and its power.

He recalled the lesson vividly. It was his first year in the doctoral program at Carnegie Mellon. For the first time a special topics class was being taught on cryptanalysis, the art and science of breaking codes. When Davis and the 12 other students walked into the class they met an odd series of characters written on the blackboard:

```
53++!305))6*;4826)4+.)4+);806*;48!8`60))85;]8*:+*8!83(88)5*!;
46(;88*96*?;8)*+(;485);5*!2:*+(;4956*2(5*-4)8`8*; 4069285);)6
!8)4++;1(+9;48081;8:8+1;48!85;4)485!528806*81(+9;48;(88;4(+?3
4;48)4+;161;:188;+?;
```

The professor began:

"Good morning, and welcome to Cryptanalysis. In this class we are going to learn how to break things; how to uncover secrets that people have tried to hide. This will not be an easy class, so for those looking for a free elective, drop/add forms are on my desk."

After that statement Davis had planned on dropping immediately, he was already taking more than the normal course load.

"We are going to begin by breaking something right away. The rest of this class is dedicated to cracking the message on the board, and you are going to break it with no help from me. I will tell you two things, though: one, its encrypted with a monoalphabetic substitution cipher; and for those of you who slept through your intro to computer science class, the monoalphabetic substitution cipher is where we replace one letter with another. So for example, all B's are represented by F's and all E's are represented by Q's, which would mean that the English word BEE would look like FQQ. All letters are thus replaced by one and only one other letter. Second clue: the original message was written in English. Go to it."

This guy must be insane! These clues are useless, "the original message was written in English," thanks for the "help," Davis remembered thinking.

The professor paced the room for five minutes while the class stared blankly at the front of the room.

"Anybody have any thoughts?"

The silence was persistent.

"Ok, let's think about this. We don't have a clue what the message says but we do know it was written in English. Anybody here a "Wheel of Fortune" fan or play "Hangman"?

A few hands were tentatively raised.

"What are the five consonants and one vowel that people usually ask Pat Sajak for when they're trying to solve the final puzzle?"

A thin man in his early thirties raised his hand. Davis recognized this guy, he had been in at least two of Davis's other courses. Nice enough but loved to suck up to the professor.

"R, S, T, L, N, and E?" the man responded after the professor motioned toward him.

"Exactly! Why though? Why those same letters over and over again? Why not start off by asking Pat, 'Can I have a Q please?'"

"That would be kind of stupid, right? How many words have a Q in them compared to the number of words that have an E?" The comment was offered by a student sitting to Davis's immediate left who appeared to have been reading a comic book until the outburst.

"You got it! So people on Wheel of Fortune pick letters by how often they appear in words in the English language. So how does that relate to our current dilemma?"

Once again silence swept the class. This time it was Davis who broke it.

"What if you counted how many times a character appeared on the board. If it's there quite a few times then it probably represents one of the more popular letters, like R-S-T-L-N-E, if it's there only a couple of times then it's probably like a Q or Z."

"You've got it! Mr.?"

"Davis, Chad Davis," he replied with a slightly proud tone.

"Mr. Davis has just made a critical insight. We can start by reasoning about what certain characters represent by how many times they appear in the encrypted text, or their frequency. This technique is part of something we call frequency analysis."

The professor placed a transparency onto the class projector.

Transparency Showing Frequency Analysis

Letter	Frequency (%)	Letter	Frequency (%)	Letter	Frequency (%)
E	12.31	L	4.03	B	1.62
T	9.59	D	3.65	G	1.61
A	8.05	C	3.20	V	0.93
O	7.94	U	3.10	K	0.52
N	7.19	P	2.29	Q	0.20
I	7.18	F	2.28	X	0.20
S	6.59	M	2.25	J	0.10
R	6.03	W	2.03	Z	0.09
H	5.14	Y	1.88		

"A recent study yielded these frequencies for letters in the English language. If you look at a single document, the frequencies are likely to be different, but still close. Of course, the larger the message, the closer the frequencies are likely to be to the global averages shown on this slide."

Davis recalled being impressed that gibberish could be interpreted based just on the frequency of letters it contained.

"Now to the problem at hand: breaking the message on the board. Go to it."

For the rest of the lecture the class worked on the problem as a group. The professor stood at the board with chalk-in-hand writing down their assumptions and values for letters but offered no further help. Eventually, the class had decided on a partial key:

```
8 -> e
5 -> a
! -> d
3 -> g
4 -> h
6 -> i
* -> n
+ -> o
( -> r
; -> t
```

The frequencies did not match exactly with the ones for the English language but they were close enough to narrow a character down to a set of two or three letters. Sometimes they had to make leaps of logic based on adjacent letters, words that they hypothesized, and character position. In 45 minutes they had decrypted the message:

'A good glass in the bishop's hostel in the devil's seat twenty-one degrees and thirteen minutes northeast and by north main branch seventh limb east side shoot from the left eye of the death's-head a bee line from the tree through the shot fifty feet out.'

Davis was amazed. They had broken a type of encryption that had been used for centuries just by letter frequencies. The message was now in English but appeared to make no sense. The message's *meaning* was now encrypted. The professor did not elaborate further but he set, at least what appeared to be at the time, a highly unusual homework assignment:

"For those of you who decide to continue with this course, your assignment before next class is to find and read a copy of Edgar Allen

Poe's essay *The Gold-Bug*. For the rest, I still have withdrawal forms on my desk."

Davis did not drop the class. He went immediately to the library to read *The Gold-Bug*, which walked the reader through the frequency analysis of the very puzzle they had solved in class!

English literature would have been much more interesting if we had gone through this stuff. Poe's essay went on to further unravel the riddle as it related to his story. Davis was intrigued. Over the next several months the class explored more historical instances of substitution ciphers, in places as diverse as a Sherlock Holmes mystery and the Bible. It gave Davis an appreciation for the art and a rounded view of the subject. But it was that understanding that now left him somewhat puzzled at Hans' suggestion.

Davis looked across the table at Hans who was apparently waiting for a reply.

"You've probably done more frequency analysis than me; but won't it screw things up since we don't have a straight substitution? It looks like we are doing an XOR on the file one character at a time, but the key we are XORing with is rotating."

"What do you mean?"

"Imagine I have a text message, 30 characters long. I tell you that I have encrypted that message by XORing it with the word *chair*."

"Go on," Hans replied, apparently not understanding what Davis was getting at.

"The message is longer than the encryption key, right? So what do I do? I encrypt it with the key chairchairchair etcetera until my key is 30 characters too, the same length as the message. Right? If all the letters in the password were the same, then we would have a monoalphabetic substitution cipher: each character in the message would be replaced by one and only one character and then we could do some frequency analysis."

Hans continued to sip his coffee and Davis interpreted his nonresponsiveness as confusion, so he continued.

"It's like if the whole message was only five letters, say the word happy, and we encrypted it by XORing it with the key chair. The first "p" in happy is in the third position, which means it would be XORed with the letter "a," the third character in the key chair. The second "p" in happy, though, is in the fourth position, which means *it* would be XORed with the letter "i," the third character in the key chair. The same letter in the message has two different encrypted values! Therefore it's not a straight monoalphabetic substitution cipher."

"I get it, I get it. But it easily can be made into one."

Davis was confused. He started to question what Hans had been sipping from that now-empty cup in his hand. Sensing his confusion, Hans continued.

"We used to run into problems like this all the time. With a repeating key of five characters we can break the message up into five monoalphabetic substitution ciphers."

Hans grabbed a napkin and began to write.

Hans' Five Monoalphabetic Substitution Ciphers

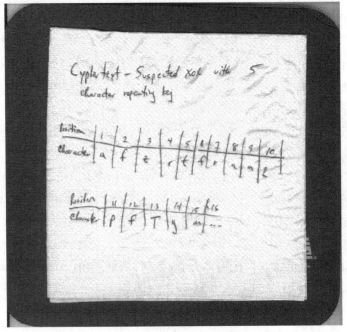

"Ok, let's say that we have a long message that we think has been decrypted with a five-character key. You're right; we could not just do frequency analysis on this as-is and hope to get anything useful. But, imagine if we wrote it this way…"

Hans once again put pen to napkin:

Alternative Cipher Text

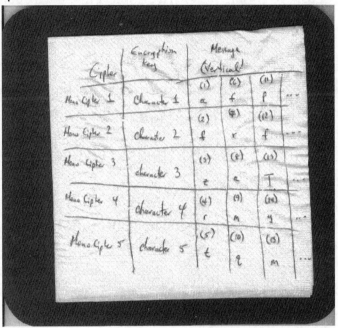

"Starting at the first letter, every fifth letter is on the first row. Starting at the second letter, every fifth letter is on the second row, and so on. Each row was encrypted with one and only one character. Now we've got five different cipher texts, each with a one-to-one mapping with its replacement character. We can do frequency analysis on each of these, then recombine the results to make the message. You loose some of the ability to infer words because each cipher will just look like a jumble of letters, but if the message is long enough, statistically speaking, we are almost sure to hit on the right values for the 20 most common letters and then the rest should be easy enough to find once we put it all back together."

The idea was simple but brilliant. Davis was impressed. A wave of excitement passed over him, which quickly subsided as he spoke his next words.

"This is great, but the thing is we don't know how long the key is."

Hans paused. "No problem, we have some software that will make determinations based on a range of key sizes. It will spit us out best-guess analysis for keys of length 1 to 100 in about an hour depending on how long the message is. The longer the better."

The message was long; Davis had no doubt about that. The encrypted file that Baff sent was almost a megabyte, a million characters! Davis had hope. It sounded painful but at least the message could be decrypted in time.

A megabyte? That can't be right...

Davis quickly checked the properties of the encrypted file on Baff's disk. Sure enough, Davis had remembered correctly. He sagged back in his chair, the frustration on his face was apparent.

"What's the matter, Chad? You look like someone just sat on your cat. This will work, man."

Davis was slow to reply. "I don't have a cat."

He took a sip of his cappuccino to focus.

"The file is roughly a megabyte long." Davis said with disappoint-ment.

"That's great, more stuff to refine our analysis. That will make things quick."

Again Davis paused before answering.

"You don't get it. This whole time we've been assuming that we had a message written in English, and we could count how many times a char-acter appeared in order to break it. This file is about a Meg. It's sure as hell not going to be a text file. It's probably an application, or a zip file, or a picture, or whatever. Hell, it may even be in Dutch. Frequency analysis is probably going to be just a huge waste of time."

Hans knew that Davis was right. They didn't know what the hell that file was. Trying frequency analysis would not be the quick-fix solution they were hoping for.

Hans slumped back in his chair as a Starbuck's employee brushed past him to clean off the now vacant tables next to them. Her humming of what sounded like a hymn was somewhat unsettling.

It was a full minute before either man spoke. Hans broke the silence.

"Let's look at that weird text file again. What did it say?"

Davis opened Baff's text file and began to read:

"For the vision is yet for an appointed time, but at the end it shall speak, and not lie…"

The woman wiping tables jumped in, "…though it tarry, wait for it; because it will surely come, it will not tarry. Sorry for eavesdropping, it's just that it's one of my favorites."

The woman began to walk away, back toward the counter. The two men stared at each other in disbelief. Davis excitedly jumped to his feet, knocking over his chair.

"Excuse me, miss? Do you have a second?"

"Sure." The Starbucks employee walked back to Davis's table. She was young, not more than 25 and spoke in a deep southern accent.

"Umm. You mentioned that this poem was one of your favorites."

"Poem? Oh, you mean the verse. Why it surely is, me and my momma used to learn a verse every day. It's from Habakkuk."

"Habakkuk?" Davis replied.

"You know the book of Habakkuk in the old testament. Chapter 2 verse 3 if I remember rightly."

Davis glared over at Hans and then back at the woman.

"Thank you, miss. You've been really helpful."

"Alright," the woman responded with a puzzled look. She turned her back to the men and continued toward the counter.

"Goddammit! I knew I should have gone to church more often!" Davis could hardly contain his excitement. He had been wrestling with that quote for the past two days.

"Amen!" Hans replied.

Hans pulled his chair to the same side of the small table as Davis.

Davis spoke out loud and began typing on the keyboard.

"H–a–b–a–k–k–u–k."

Password Habakkuk – Denied!

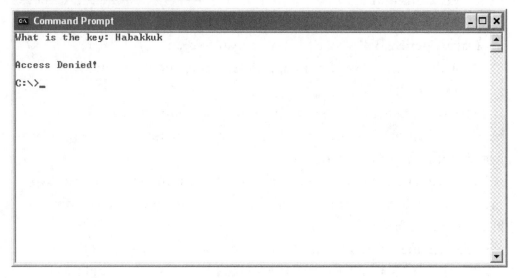

Access denied! ACCESS DENIED! Davis was about to snap.

Hans spoke. "Try it with the chapter and verse…what did she say…chapter 2, verse 3?"

Davis made one more attempt:

"Ok. H–a–b–a–k–k–u–k–2–colon–3."

Access!

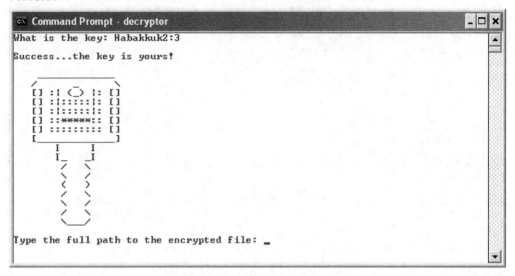

```
Command Prompt - decryptor                                    _ □ ×
What is the key: Habakkuk2:3

Success...the key is yours!

        /            \
     [] :! <  > !: []
     [] :!:::::!: []
     [] :!::::::!: []
     [] ::*****:: []
     [] :::::::::: []
     [_____]
          I    I
         I_  _I
         /    \
        \    /
        <    >
        /    \
       \    /
        /    \
        \___/
Type the full path to the encrypted file: _
```

"Ho-ly shit!" Davis could hardly believe it! He quickly typed the path to Baff's encrypted file. Next it asked him for the destination of the decrypted file.

"What the hell extension should I give it? .DOC, .TXT, .EXE?"

"Just call it stuff.txt and then we'll check it out in a hex editor." Hans replied. Davis did and the two men looked anxiously at the screen as Davis loaded it into the editor.

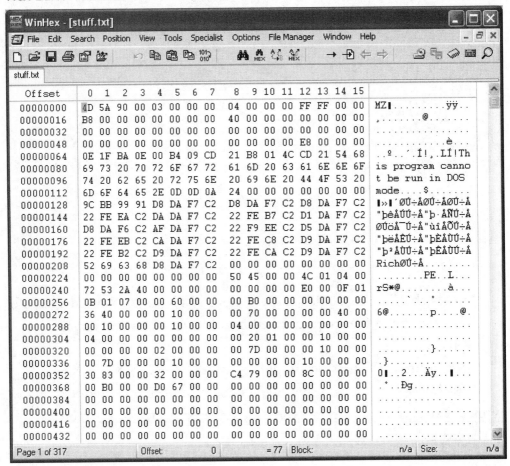

All Davis needed was to see the first two letters of the file, MZ, and he knew instantly what he was looking at...

Chapter 21: Seattle, WA

Starbucks

"It's definitely a Windows executable."

Davis spoke with confidence. The two had entered his world now; a land of executable code, machine instructions, and hexadecimal; the domain of the reverse engineer.

"How can you be so sure?" Hans asked.

"*MZ*," answered Davis. The blank stare he received from Hans was not the reaction he was expecting and so he continued, "MZ is the beginning of the DOS header. All Windows executables have it, too. See that PE half-way down the page? That's where the Windows header information starts; the information that tells the operating system where to find the right instructions in the file. We are definitely looking at some sort of program here, and by the filler information it looks like it was compiled with a Microsoft compiler."

Hans was impressed. He had seen Davis in action before, usually dissecting computer viruses or exploiting buffer overflows, but it still impressed him how the man could extract such precise information from what appeared to be a jumble of nonsensical characters.

Davis was surprised but not shocked at Hans's confusion. Even though Hans had a Masters degree in computer science, low-level program analysis had become a lost art. Every year top-tier universities were graduating computer science students who could recite obscure theoretical concepts in algorithm theory or discrete mathematics, but many of them couldn't write a simple program. Even worse were their skills at the lowest levels, like assembly language: the series of short words that represent low–level machine instructions. Applicability and practicality had been shunned in most curriculums in favor of abstract concepts and arcane facts. He had met several Ph.D. students during his travels that couldn't write more than two lines of C code without looking at a reference or getting help from compiler error messages.

"Well, then what are you waiting for? Let's run the damn thing!" Hans said excitedly.

Davis closed the file and renamed it from stuff.txt to stuff.exe. He hated to execute programs without checking them out first, and had dissected too many viruses to run suspect code on his machine. But this was no ordinary situation, and whatever the program was, Baff had gone through a lot of trouble to make sure it got into Davis's hands.

"Here goes…" Davis clicked on the file, and with a whirl of the laptop's cooling fan, a familiar screen appeared.

WinZip Self-Extracting File from Baff's CD

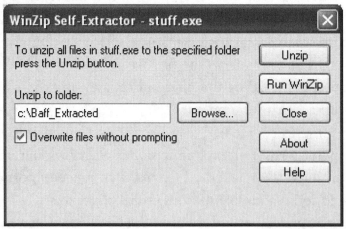

"It's a zip file!" Hans exclaimed. He was right, Baff's encrypted file had actually been an executable ZIP file; a compressed collection of other files, and it had been created to self-extract when double-clicked. Davis began the extraction then looked at the compressed file listing.

Compressed File Listing

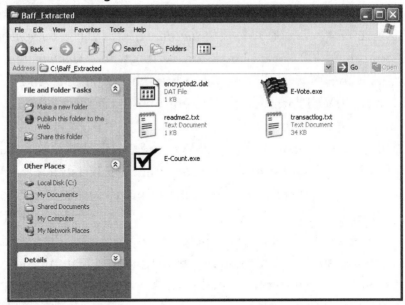

The two looked silently at the screen, trying to understand what Baff had laid out before them.

"Another readme file!?" Davis exclaimed, "I hope it's not another biblical egg-hunt."

He opened the text file, readme2.txt:

Mr. Davis, there is a flaw in the software that your country is about to use in its Presidential election of MMIV. This flaw, I believe, was created on purpose.

I believe that there are people who know what I have discovered. If this is true, you must bring these things to light.

I warn you, these are powerful people who have been giving me visions, manipulating my very mind and yours. Do not give these files to anyone, I fear what may happen if some of my associates gain access to them.

I cannot say more here, the risk is still too great. Do not try and contact me. I will lay underground for some time. It is the safest thing for me and you until this matter is resolved.

B.L.

Hans turned toward Davis, "That guy was a complete whack job!"

For a moment, he couldn't help but think that Hans was right. Had Baff gone insane? *"giving me visions,"* what the hell was Baff talking about?

Hans continued, "Do you believe any of this stuff? '*Manipulating my very mind,*' Is it me or was this guy just a little too paranoid? And what's up with the MMIV? That poor bastard got one thing right though. He's laying underground alright…only permanently."

Baff had been eccentric, Davis couldn't argue with that. Over the past several years, Baff had sent him some pretty unbelievable stuff. He talked about a digital Armageddon and how some of his associates were working on a "super" virus—one that could be tailored to cripple the critical infrastructure of a country. None of these things were ever disproved, but Davis had learned to pad Baff's statements with a little realism, and realistically, Baff *must* have been on to something.

"Let's not forget that the guy was *killed* hours after giving me this disk. He found something, something big."

Hans nodded in acknowledgement, "So what are all of those other files?"

Davis first looked at the two executables: E-Vote.exe and E-Count.exe. "These are the same files I've been messing with for the last few months. They're Advice's voting program and the application that the central server in D.C. is going to use to count the absentee ballots. They look to be about the same size as the files I already have; I'll check it out when I get home."

Davis shifted his attention to the transactlog.txt. He opened the file and displayed it on the screen:

transactlog.txt File

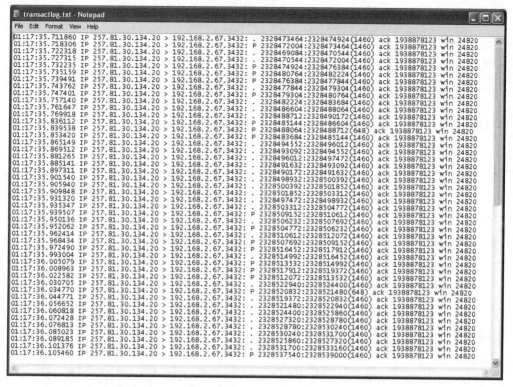

"Looks like a bunch of packet headers to me," Hans said. Davis nodded his head in agreement.

Davis wasn't an expert on networking, but he knew a packed header when he saw one. He remembered having to explain the concept to his most recent freshman class. As he stood in front of the class, he was prepared to go through a set of mind-numbing slides on token ring networks and the OSI 7-layer model of networking when, to the class's surprise, he walked over to his laptop and deleted the PowerPoint presentation file. "This is too boring for me to teach today," he had said. It was obvious that Davis had no respect for protocol or classroom decorum, and it would have been the worst mistake the university had ever made to grant him tenure, if not for his brilliant work. Still, it amused him to know he couldn't get fired no matter how much theatrical bullshit he pulled off in class.

He began his lecture completely off-the-cuff. "Today we are going to talk about how networks *really* work." Davis turned to one of the students that had come in late and was now seated in the front row. "Mr. Boswell, right?"

"Yes sir," the apparently dazed young man replied.

"Say you needed to send 200 pounds of stuff to a friend and it absolutely, positively has to get there. But, there's a problem—UPS won't ship any one box over 50 pounds. Obviously you've got to break that stuff up into at least four boxes, each weighing less than 50 pounds. For each box of stuff you need to create a label that will tell the delivery people some critical information, like who the sender is, who the recipient is, the delivery address, that this is box 2 of 4, stuff like that."

Boswell nervously nodded his head in agreement.

Davis continued, "Now let's say that you wanted to send me some data, over the network. The same process happens; the data is broken up into small chunks and then packaged into structures called packets. Each packet contains information on where the packet has come from and where it's headed. Information like the sender IP address, recipient IP address, the sequence number of the packet so that the recipient knows in what order to piece the data back together or if some data got lost along the way. All this information makes up the IP header..."

Snapping back to the present, Davis surveyed what seemed to be an endless sequence of packets that Baff had captured.

"What do you think they are?" Hans asked.

"No idea. Looks like a bunch of Internet traffic to me, I'll check it out when I get home. This other encrypted file...I wonder if we can just run it through that original decryption program."

Davis once again launched decryptor.exe, using the same password, Habakkuk2:3, and pointed it to the new encrypted file. They opened the output file produced by decryptor.exe in a hex editor, hoping to again get some meaningful information.

decryptor.exe with Habakkuk2:3

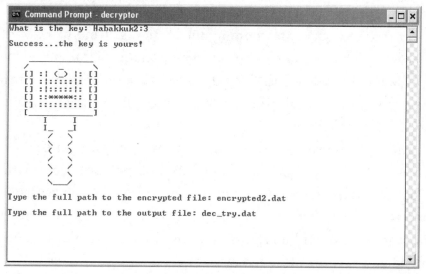

Output File

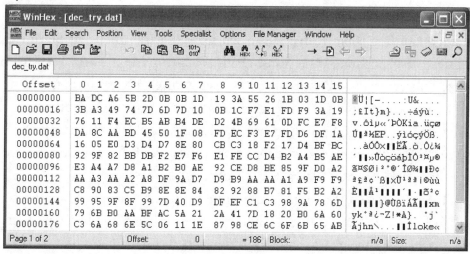

Instead, they found what seemed to be a nonsensical sequence of hexadecimal values.

"This looks like complete garbage. What do you make of it Hans?"

Hans leaned forward in his chair, "I'm getting too old for this stuff. It seems like this Baff guy was a real character. I had a feeling that the second encryption wouldn't be the same as the first…but there's no other decryptor, is there?"

"I don't know, but we're running out of time. Let me work on this more at home." He began closing out the programs before remembering what he wanted to ask Hans. "Hey, if I give you a description of the Interpol guy, do you think you can run it through that fancy equipment you guys have at the Bureau?"

"I can't promise we'll find anything, but we can give it a try."

Davis nodded and began describing the Interpol agent in exacting detail as Hans took notes. Over the past few years of doing reverse engineering work, Davis had developed an eye for nuance. It was a necessity when pouring through line after line of machine instructions, hoping to put together a million-piece jigsaw puzzle.

Having finished their coffee and discussion, the two men left Starbucks and headed in separate directions, Davis toward his home and Hans to his office. This created a dilemma for the man sitting in the van parked only a few car lengths down the street. He couldn't follow them both, and feared that choosing the wrong one could unleash Danko's wrath. Danko was not a people person and it was oftentimes painfully obvious that he hated to work, or even interact, with others.

The man started the engine and pulled onto the street two cars behind Davis. "If Danko doesn't like it I'll tell him to kiss my ass!" The threat held little weight though; he knew Danko had made men disappear for less.

Chapter 22: Seattle, WA

Chris Payne's Home

Danko's assignments never led him to the posh neighborhoods like the one he just entered. He usually met his business contacts in bars or out-of-the-way streets. Deals and money were exchanged in specific steps, rarely calling for a face-to-face meeting of Danko with his current "employer."

"You are to follow the steps exactly," he would say. "If you mess up, I'm watching you."

Danko knew that law enforcement could be following him at any moment, and over time, he had devised the best ways to meet his contacts and get paid with the least chance of being noticed while maintaining near complete anonymity. This time around was a little different though, and it made Danko slightly uncomfortable.

He pulled up to the mansion, and waited for the gates to open. He slowly drove his obviously out-of-place rented Ford Taurus up the driveway and parked outside the front door.

The butler welcomed Danko, showing him in. For a butler he was a rather large man and in good physical condition, leading Danko to believe he did more than just serve drinks and walk the dogs. He quickly assessed the butler's physique and muscle tone in case of an emergency. *It would be a difficult hands-on battle.*

"May I take your coat, sir?" asked the butler.

Danko nodded and slipped his coat off, handing it to him.

"Mr. Payne is in his office. Please follow me."

As they walked toward the stairs, Danko could not help but notice the lavishness that Chris Payne chose to surrounded himself with. Paintings, sculptures, furniture. As many clients as Danko had served, he had never been inside any of their homes, and the lavishness of this one amazed him.

From behind his desk, Payne immediately noticed Danko's awe as he entered his office.

"I've earned every penny Mr. Danko, just like you earn yours."

"I think you earn more pennies than I do," replied Danko.

Payne smirked, "Have a seat Mr. Danko, can I get you something to drink?"

"Coffee, strong," replied Danko. He saw Payne nod to the butler who silently left the room, but Danko doubted he'd receive what he truly requested. The coffee in America was never strong enough for him. Espressos were adequate but he grew up sipping Turkish-style coffee with the grounds in the cup. One shot could keep him going for hours. *Not like this weak American brew.* To Danko's surprise, the butler quickly returned with what could only be a small espresso-like cup filled with what he had hoped for.

Payne acknowledged Danko's surprise with a knowing smile, "I had a feeling you would prefer a taste from home."

Danko picked up the cup and took in the aroma, "Yes, it is good. Thank you."

Payne motioned again to the butler and like any well-trained servant, he quickly exited, closing the office door behind him.

"So, Mr. Danko, how has business been so far?"

"So far, so good," replied Danko, sipping on the hot coffee. He set it down to cool and to allow the grounds to settle.

"How is Dr. Davis doing?"

Danko defensively replied, "I am dealing with him. Do not worry."

"We need him, do you understand? This is a serious business matter, and he must be there to testify in D.C. I solicited your services because of your ability to get the job done. Don't let me down, Mr. Danko."

Although Payne's tone was not harsh it was spoken with commanding resolve. It made Danko respect Payne.

"Find out everything you can about him, anything that we haven't already found out," continued Payne, "how he lives, breathes, eats, works. Find out about his family, friends, sexual preferences, pets, everything."

Danko nodded and finished off the coffee.

"I will complete my tasks Mr. Payne; just make sure you follow my payment instructions once my business is finished."

"Payment won't be a problem. The butler will give you keys for the car I'd like you to use for your stay here in Seattle. When you're finished I will instruct you on where to return the vehicle. We'll keep the other for you in the meantime."

Danko stood up, "Thank you for the coffee, I will be in contact to update you."

Danko walked toward the ornate study door. He knew Davis was starting to become a problem and babysitting was not something Danko enjoyed. His specialty, his calling, was death. Reports that Davis was starting to ask questions about Danko's identity would have already put Davis in a coffin if it weren't for Payne's insistence.

I give this one more day. If he keeps asking questions…Payne can keep his fucking money.

Chapter 23:   Seattle, WA

Chad Davis's Home

Davis pulled into the driveway of his home. It was only the early afternoon but he felt completely drained. As he opened his car door, a grey van pulled to a stop several houses away.

Davis opened the front door to his house, walked in, and set his laptop bag on the couch. He slumped down next to it and glanced over resentfully at the bag. He loathed the thought of opening the laptop again. He was so sick of the CD, Baff, the elections, all of it.

His thoughts turned to Amanda. Times like this, when his life was chaotic, he could turn to her for comfort and reassurance that all would work out for the best. The problem was, those were the *only* times he turned to her. He never had time to spend with her and Elizabeth, to listen to their problems, to comfort *them*. Deadlines always loomed, grant proposals were always due, journal papers had to be submitted; there was never enough time. He felt that if he wasn't working, taking every opportunity, that he was missing out on something; that the world would pass him by. Davis budgeted his time on deadlines, but he never thought there would be a deadline on family. Amanda proved him wrong.

The divorce had ripped his world apart. To keep his sanity, he had buried himself even deeper in his work. The courts granted him the weekends with their daughter Elizabeth. But it had now been three months since he'd seen her due to his travels and other commitments. Even then, at their last visit, she treated him almost like a stranger and he felt powerless to change that. Remembering Amanda and Elizabeth was like acid to his mind, the thought of what he lost was too much to bear. And so, once again, he drew on a skill he had perfected over the last ten years: drowning personal problems in work.

He turned his attentions back to Baff and the CD, opening his laptop and powering it on. As the computer fan whirled and the screen came to life his thoughts drifted toward Amanda's smile, a sight he hadn't seen for some time. *Snap out of it! She's gone, just accept it!* But he couldn't accept it, it took him a month and a half to sign the divorce papers but even then he thought it was something that could be fixed, if only he could get past his next grant deadline. Letting out a deep sigh he looked at the text file full of network traffic information on the screen in front of him. He painstakingly began to wade through it.

Source, destination, timestamp, sequence number, looks like normal network stuff.

He tried to imagine the time it must have taken Baff to go through all these precautions, the decryptor, the files, and how purposely enigmatic he had left things.

"Would it have killed him to write me a note explaining all this stuff?"

He paused as he realized the irony and gravity of what he had just said, before starting to inspect the packet information more carefully. The source IP address was the same for each packet, as was the destination IP address. *That's a start.*

Davis knew there were several easy ways to find out who an IP address belongs to. One is to ask a Domain Name Server, or DNS, that maps domain names like www.yahoo.com to IP addresses. In Windows, Linux, and UNIX, typically you can use the *nslookup* command to map a particular domain name back to its IP address or an IP address to its domain.

He began to scrutinize the destination address, 192.168.2.67. *Well that sucks.* Even with Davis's minimal networking skills he recognized the address as part of a range of IP addresses allocated for private networks. IP addresses in the range 192.168.0.0 through 192.168.255.255 were not addressable on the Internet. Instead, these addresses usually are assigned to individuals inside a particular home or corporate network. A home user, for example, could have a single IP address that points to their home and then buy a cheap router so that any computer inside their personal network would get assigned a 192.168.x.y address, which meant that multiple machines could share the same outward-facing IP address. When packets are returned from a machine on the Internet back to one of the machines inside the home, the router receives the packet and then readdresses it to the appropriate private address internally.

The packets in Baff's file were obviously captured inside one of these private networks: the destination address would not help.

Davis then turned his attention to the source IP address. He ran NSLookup hoping to find out who was hosting this web site. The source seemed to be a web site hosted by servers at Yahoo. He then typed the IP address into his web browser. He was more puzzled than ever when he saw the site loading in his browser: www.mezonic.com. He glanced at the header lining the top of the page next to the Company's logo,

The Mezonic Corporation. Leading manufacturer of video chips...

What the hell is this? This can't be what Baff wanted me to find, there must be more information in these packet headers.

Davis spent the next two hours meticulously reading through the file, even digging up some of his old network reference books. He sat at his desk, in the corner of the room, making notes, trying to find patterns in the data. Soon, both his will and his body began to fail. By 10 P.M., he was asleep at his desk with his cheek stuck to a page of TCP/IP Illustrated, Volume II.

Danko spent many nights alone in cars or hotels watching others, hunting them. Some would end up as victims, others merely were watched for information.

Tonight Danko was in the van, alone. Closed circuit television monitors, audio recorders, and infrared displays were laid out in the back. At the end of the road, a streetlight glowed while a characteristically light Seattle drizzle sheathed the evening in a grey mist.

As he opened his second pack of cigarettes for the evening, he laid his gaze on the monitor that showed Davis, seemingly fast asleep.

In Serbia, Danko had mastered the art of observation. He could easily discern a person's most minute physical traits, their strengths and weaknesses both mental and physical. After a brief encounter he could, with uncanny accuracy, predict a person's instinctive behavior to just about any extreme situation. His primary subject now was Chad Davis, and from his questioning at Schiphol Airport, Danko knew his subject would not cave in easily.

Tonight he would sit and observe…and smoke. The night was young and Danko had plenty of cigarettes to get him through until morning.

Chapter 24: Washington, D.C.

Senator Shift's Home

Senator Shift's days were hectic. The campaign, the interviews, rallies, and commercials all wore on him. Next week he would embark on a three-month nationwide tour to spread his message of government reform and the role of the U.S. abroad, and campaign in the remaining primaries for the Presidential nomination.

Tonight he was home, barely awake at 1:30 A.M., going over demographics and speech notes when he decided to call Chris Payne. He pulled out a small brass key from his pocket and unlocked the bottom desk drawer. The Senator slid the drawer open and picked up the small cellular phone that sat inside. He pulled a battery from a charger that lay on the desk and brought the phone to life. With the press of a few buttons, he scrolled to the only number saved in the phone's memory—a private line—and hit Send. It rang only twice before being answered.

"Mr. Payne, how are you this evening?"

"Just fine. You're up late, Senator. Working hard?"

"Yes. It just doesn't seem to end, you know."

Payne sensed the fatigue in Senator Shift's voice. "I hope this campaign is not wearing you out, Senator, there's still much to do and this is only the beginning." There was a pause before Payne continued, "We are on the secure line as agreed, yes?"

Senator Shift laughed lightly, "Well it's definitely not a vacation Mr. Payne, and yes, please be assured, I am calling from our secure line. I'd like to hear how we're progressing."

Shift's reassurance eased Payne, and the concern quickly disappeared from his voice. "As you know, Dr. Davis will testify at the congressional hearings in a couple of days about our electronic voting software."

The senator quickly asked, "And how do you expect the testimony to go?"

Payne paused again. A week ago, he was certain that Advice's software would be implemented by the Federal Election Commission and that it would then be given the go-ahead by the U.S. government. The software had received stellar reviews from various independent and not-so-independent evaluators. Most importantly, he knew Chad Davis had been satisfied with the software during his own in-depth evaluation. But now, after the RSA conference and what he knew about Davis and Baff Lexicon, Payne wasn't so sure. Baff had attempted to hack into the software, and he knew Baff met Davis at the RSA conference. What he didn't know was what Baff may or may not have figured out about the software, or what he may have told Davis.

"Senator, as you know the testimony will decide the fate of the implementation of our software for the electronic vote initiative. I know Dr. Davis's evaluation so far has been positive. We are seeing to it that it stays that way."

The Senator reluctantly asked, "And the chip? Is that working?"

Chris Payne sighed silently.

He reluctantly replied, "Mezonic has secured contracts to supply their rendering chips to just about every video card manufacturer we know of. When we met six months ago, 70 percent of new computers had our chip installed. Today that number is at about 90 percent. That is a lot of free advertising."

"Excellent," replied the Senator, "That's good news. You know the White House has already started smearing my campaign and my name.

We are still eight or nine months out and it's already starting to get ugly. Any help we can get would be great."

"Just stay the course Senator. We have heavy guns of our own."

Senator Shift felt more at ease, "Thank you Mr. Payne. I don't need to tell you how dedicated I am to this cause. Our country is being taken away from the people. We cannot fail."

Payne's voice grew with passion, "We *will not* fail. There *is* no other option."

"Seems like we're full steam ahead, then. I'll be in D.C. on Tuesday. Will you still be there after the testimony?"

"Definitely, Senator. I'll make sure we have some time to talk in person. Get some sleep."

The Senator smiled and said, "Thanks! It's a pleasure talking to you, as always."

"Goodnight, Senator."

Chapter 25:   Seattle, WA

Chad Davis's Home

Davis was not sure if he was dreaming or if the phone was actually ringing. His eyes resisted all attempts at opening them. His alarm clock glowed a dim 8:45 A.M.

"Who in the hell?"

It took him a second to get his bearings. *Sunday. Early morning. Back to sleep!*

He heard his answering machine pick up and after a couple of seconds his phone/fax began to spit out pages from an incoming fax. Early Sunday morning faxes were completely uncommon—downright nonexistent. He lay back down and closed his eyes. Trying to fall back asleep was not as easy as he thought given his cloudy state of consciousness. His mind reflected on the previous day's events. He had yet to decrypt Baff's files, and Hans couldn't find any records of the Interpol agent.

"Hans!"

He jumped out of bed and stumbled toward the fax machine. The fax was indeed from Hans.

The first page was as he expected, a quick note from Hans asking him to check out the attached documents. Davis's eyes widened and his heartbeat increased to a nerving pace.

What followed was a series of mug shots, one per page. The first three men fit the description he had given Hans but none were the mysterious Interpol agent. A sudden nauseous feeling overcame him as he flipped to the fourth picture. It was the face of *his* Interpol agent, *Jonas Borgstad*, glaring at him with numerous aliases and an unsettlingly impressive rap sheet. His agent's true identity was Danko Vulcic.

Davis was on the phone immediately, "Hans, how'd you find this?"

Hans barely had a chance to pick up and put the phone to his ear. He quickly replied, "It was a long shot but I did a search with the name you had and your description. I also have some good friends across the pond. I assume he's in there?"

He anxiously answered, "Yeah. Number four, Danko voo-something. Who is this guy?"

Hans was eager to give his friend all the details he had found, but decided to keep it short while on the phone, "He's a rather experienced… how would you say…*consultant*. Without getting into too much detail his services usually are solicited by high-powered figures all over the world."

Why was this guy asking me questions? He knew the CD was part of it and Jonas was linked to Baff, but the whole thing just didn't make sense. Davis's stomach sunk and his heart filled with terror.

"Chad, you still there?"

"I'm here. What can I do about this?"

"Stay put, I'll be over in an hour." Hans responded.

"Alright, but what about the…"

Hans interrupted in a commanding tone, "I'll see you in an hour."

With that, Hans's voice was replaced with the hum of an empty line. Hans's abruptness made Davis even more concerned. He had known the man for years but had never heard such a sharp tone in his voice. There were obviously things he didn't want said over the phone.

Davis slumped to the couch, holding Danko's picture in his hand. He studied it intently and began to read through Danko's morbid accomplishments. "Wanted in connection with seven murders internationally. Former covert operations specialist for the Yugoslavian army. Suspected involvement with a bombing in Lima, Peru." Although it was early, Davis needed a drink.

As he reached to place the papers on the coffee table in front of him, something at the top of the page caught his eye:

`03/08/04 8:46 AM FROM:FBI TR1274 TO:Davis,C  PAGE:005 0f 009`

He quickly flipped to the last page, and again focused on the header atop the page:

`03/08/04 8:47 AM FROM:FBI TR1274 TO:Davis,C  PAGE:009 0f 009`

That's it! Davis lay back on the couch; he knew he had found what he was looking for.

Chapter 26: Seattle, WA

Chad Davis's Home

It was almost 10 o'clock when Davis heard the knock on his front door. It startled him. He had been so engrossed in calculations for the past hour that he completely forgot Hans was on his way. He walked toward the door, reached for the handle, and paused, deciding to look through the peephole. The morning's events had made him suspicious of everything, everyone. He wasn't sure what to expect anymore. His simple short-term goal now was to make it to the testimony in one piece. Through the peephole he saw Hans. A flood of relief washed over him and he immediately opened the door.

"You're not going to believe this," Davis exclaimed as Hans entered the house.

Hans saw the excitement in his eyes, recognizing the look of a detective who just cracked an impossible case wide open. Hans had experienced that feeling before and could sense it in Davis. He knew how good it felt and he knew how exciting it was to be a part of it.

"Hold your horses! I just walked in. You're not going to offer me a drink?"

Davis was too excited to appreciate Hans's humor.

"We don't have time for a drink, I need to show you something."

Davis made a beeline toward his laptop, which was sitting on a table in the living room. Hans did not follow. Instead he seemed to take a casual stroll around the foyer, apparently admiring some of the art that

Davis's wife deemed too "ugly" to take in the divorce settlement. Davis looked back and spoke in a raised voice toward the front door.

"I've got everything set up in here!" he exclaimed.

"I've always admired this painting, but the house, the house has really gone to hell since Amanda left, huh?" Hans casually remarked.

Davis was not amused. Hans was wasting time and Davis didn't have much left to waste. *What has this guy been smoking?*

"Screw you. Look, do you want to check out this program or do you want to fondle my art?" Davis responded in a half-joking voice.

"Hey, Chad, remember that CD I loaned you three months ago and you never returned? It turns out that my cousin played drums in the background for track 12. You still got it? Can you put it on?"

Davis was at his snapping point. Hans was acting strangely, like he didn't even care about Baff's murder, the encrypted files, the election, the trained assassin who was stalking him, none of it. He jumped up from his chair and stormed into the foyer. He began to rant before reaching the entrance way. "Dammit Hans, what the…"

Davis stopped mid-sentence. It took him a few seconds to realize what he was looking at. Hans was crouched on the floor over one of the paintings that had been hanging on the wall only a few moments before. He had apparently unhinged the painting and placed it face down on the tile. Hans looked up at him with one finger placed over his lips.

Davis kept silent. Hans removed the finger sitting on his lips and pointed to what appeared to be a small stain on the back of the painting's canvas. Leaning in for a closer look he noticed the stain was raised and it had a pattern, what appeared to be circuitry. *A bug!?*

Hans began to speak again, still in a relaxed tone. "You know, the CD, do you still have it? Put it on the intercom system, you have got to hear my cousin, the guy rocks."

"Sure," Davis said in a voice that he hoped sounded calm and natural.

He walked over to a small cabinet in the living room near the wall-mounted CD player that was attached to the house intercom system. The intercoms had been Amanda's idea. She knew that Chad obsessed over his work and she wanted to be able to call him in his study, or anywhere in the house where his sessions might bring him. Eventually, though, she stopped calling and stopped listening.

Davis reached for the second CD in the stack of disks that he had been too lazy to put back in their cases. He inserted it into the player and advanced to the twelfth track. A screech erupted through the house, followed by drums and an electric guitar. Davis walked back into the foyer where Hans now held the listening device between his index finger and thumb, studying it intently. On seeing Chad approach, Hans stood up, walked the bug into the living room and rested it on a table near the intercom where music was blaring.

Hans whispered in Chad's ear, "Bring the laptop into the foyer."

Chad was frozen. He had heard some pretty unbelievable stories of the cases that Hans had worked on. Kidnappings, bombings, hijackings, stealth surveillance, but never imagined he would be part of one. The bug meant that his paranoia over the last two days had now been validated. Somebody *was* watching him, probably the same people who had killed Baff...maybe Danko.

Hans nudged him slightly and pointed toward the desk where his laptop sat open. Chad staggered toward it. He picked it up and unplugged its power supply, as Hans motioned him to the foyer.

There was an ornate standing table in the foyer with one chair to the side of it. Davis shoveled some junk mail and random papers aside, placed the laptop on the desk, and sat on the chair. Meanwhile, Hans pulled a small stool in from the living room.

Davis spoke in a low but alarmed voice "Hans, what the hell is going on?"

Hans grabbed him by the shoulders and pulled him close. He spoke quietly into his ear, "I don't know who bugged you but they've got better stuff than us! This must have cost a fortune, very cutting edge."

Hans's guarded tone seemed to change to one of admiration, like a craftsman admiring the work of a master.

"Are we safe here? Are people listening to us right now?" Davis whispered.

"Trust me, this room is clean; the chances of them putting two bugs in one room is very slim, and with that music in the background, they'd have to be standing right next to us to hear anything. The best thing we can do is not tip our hand. We can't let them know that we know."

Hans paused briefly; he could see that Chad was scared and might do something irrational. He continued speaking, "These guys are pros, if they know we're on to them they'll either disappear or we may put your life in danger. Don't worry. I'll have a team of guys around this neighborhood within the hour. I'll drive straight back to the field office. A call is too risky; if they've got this type of equipment we have to assume your phone is tapped and that they have cell phone scanners."

Hans's words were anything but reassuring. Chad became aware of his own heart beating. He felt dizzy and became noticeably pale. Hans immediately recognized the signs of panic and spoke with a trained tone of calmness.

"Chad? Everything is going to be fine. This is what I do, remember? Just sit tight."

There was a thought that passed through Davis's mind but he was too distressed to bring it into focus. *Plane? Plane!*

"I'm supposed to be on a plane to D.C. in three hours."

"Damn." There was a long pause where neither man spoke. With a deep breath, Hans continued, "Ok, here's what's going to happen. You'll go to the airport as planned. I'll make sure some of our guys are watching. You'll never even know they're there. Then, I'll have some of our guys meet your plane in D.C. This is the congressional testimony, right?"

"Yes. I'm supposed to testify about this goddamned software and now I don't even know what to say. Do you think that's what all this is about? The testimony?"

"I'd say there's a good chance. But right now, the best thing you can do is to act normal until we find out more. At least normal for you." Hans broke his chiseled façade of control with a slight grin.

Normal? Somebody is watching me, maybe even trying to kill me. Normal! Chad was way out of his element. He was lost and had to trust that Hans knew the way, but there was something else gnawing at his mind. *The fax. The packets!*

"Hans, there's something I have to show you, something I've found out about one of Baff's files."

Davis reached into his front pocket and pulled out two folded sheets of paper. They were two of the faxed sheets that Hans had sent over that morning.

Davis continued, "Take a look at these and tell me what you see."

Hans held the two sheets and stared at them, "These are two of the mug shots I sent, so what?"

"Take a look at the fax headers," Davis replied, hoping that Hans would make the same leap that he had.

Hans studied the headers intently:

```
03/08/04 8:46 AM FROM:FBI TR1274 TO:Davis,C  PAGE:005 0f 009


03/08/04 8:47 AM FROM:FBI TR1274 TO:Davis,C  PAGE:009 0f 009
```

"I don't see what you're getting at. It's standard fax stuff, right?"

Davis responded excitedly, "Suppose that I wanted to send you a message, a secret message that only you could read, and that only you knew was there. But there was a catch, I had to send it through a public channel, where everyone could read the actual data I sent."

Hans was familiar with this problem. There were several kidnapping cases he had worked where the police could contact the kidnapper only by taking out personals ads with some keywords or numbers that conveyed a message by rules laid out by the kidnapper. Anyone who picked up the newspaper the next day would get the message, but only one would find the hidden meaning in it. The first time he had worked a case like this, the kidnapper had a note delivered that said that all future communication would be conducted through the newspaper. The drop point for the money would be included as the address of a personals add with the title, "Exuberant male stud seeks hot lovin'."

"We've had to deal with this stuff before in kidnapping cases, but I still don't understand how that relates to the fax. None of it is stuff a sender can control: the from machine, the name, the page number."

"Remember that quote from the Bible that was in Baff's file; *time*, it was all about *time*!"

Hans's confusion lingered. He was beginning to think that the stress was starting to get to Chad.

Chad continued, "Look at the time stamps. Suppose I wanted to send you some information out in the open. What if I wanted to be absolutely sure that no one would suspect the message? One thing I could do is to send one bit of information per page: a single binary piece of information, off or on. I tell you that an even number as the last digit of the time stamp means *on* and an odd number means *off*. Then, if I use standard ASCII character representation—eight bits to represent a single character—I could send you a single character with eight faxes!"

Chad picked up a pen from the table and began to write on the back of one of the faxes.

"Imagine you received eight faxes with these timestamps."

```
8:41        = odd     = 0
8:42        = even    = 1
8:44        = even    = 1
8:45        = odd     = 0
8:47        = odd     = 0
8:49        = odd     = 0
8:51        = odd     = 0
8:52        = even    = 1


01100001 binary = 61 hex -> 'a'
```

"If we write this binary number out, it is equal to 61 in hexadecimal. ASCII, the American Standard Code for Information Interchange, assigns numeric representations for all the letters, numbers, and punctuation marks in the English language. In ASCII, 61 hex represents the letter 'a'. After 200 faxes or so, one could send a short message."

"That's a hell of a lot of faxes, but I get your point. I sent you those faxes though, so where are secret messages coming from?" Hans responded.

Davis responded excitedly, raising his voice momentarily and then quickly lowering it, remembering their current situation.

"Not the faxes, the packets! Baff's file of packet headers. I spent most of the night looking at those things, checking the IP addresses and analyzing the data. The only thing I was able to find out is that they seem to have been sent from some microchip manufacturer in China. Then this morning when I got your faxes, I realized what I was missing. It's network steganography!"

"Steganography, that's the picture stuff, right? Like hiding one picture inside another one?"

"Exactly! Except it doesn't have to be a picture. Steganography just means hiding things in plain sight. Your kidnapping cases, you were using steganography to communicate with the kidnapper—it was there for everybody to see, but only one person knew what to look for."

"What does this have to do with the packets?"

"It wasn't anything *in* the packets, it was *how* the packets arrived. They were out of order." Davis cracked a slight smile. He felt a deep satisfaction as he spoke.

"It's been a while since I've done any network programming, but packets arrive out of sequence all the time, don't they?" Hans replied.

"The Transmission Control Protocol stack resequences packets once they arrive so that the application can piece together the data. The way the receiver knows which order to put packets in is the *sequence number*. The sender picks a starting sequence number, then each packet afterward has a subsequent number. For example, if the starting sequence number is 1, the next packet may be assigned the number 18, then the next possibly 38, and so on. Sometimes, delays through the Internet cause packets to arrive out of order, but sequence numbers allow the data to be pieced back together in the right order."

Hans was beginning to get frustrated, "Ok, so you've just told me that order doesn't matter and is unpredictable. Then who cares about order?"

"Usually, though, packets arrive in the order that they are sent. If they are sent with brief pauses, and assuming no weird firewall is in the middle, this is almost a guarantee. I started by running some statistical analysis on the packets, and they seemed really strange—they are out of order too often to be a coincidence and their patterns are too repetitive to be random!"

"What are you saying, that somebody is trying to send a message through packet sequencing?"

"Exactly! Think about it, it's perfect. You don't change anything in the packet at all; the data stays exactly the same. The message is in the timing! I've found that the patterns repeat in series of five."

"Ok, I am completely lost."

"Take five packets, say with sequence numbers 100, 200, 300, 400, and 500. Think about how many ways those packets could arrive. We expect them to arrive in the sequence (100, 200, 300, 400, 500), but they could just as plausibly arrive in sequence (300, 200, 500, 400, 100) or (100, 200, 500, 300, 400). In fact there are five factorial ways they could arrive, 5 times 4 times 3 times 2, that's 120 different possibilities!"

Hans did not respond, he needed to let the possibility sink in. After a moment he began to speak. "Ok, let's assume that you're right and someone *is* sending messages through the packets. They would be coming from that Chinese company, Mezonic, right?"

"That's what it looks like."

"Why would they bother? I mean, these are probably some driver updates or something, why not just embed any information you want to send in the data of the packet itself? Hell, if you're worried about someone accessing it, just encrypt the damn data."

"You FBI guys; always making assumptions. If a message was in the packet data, a lot of people at Mezonic would need to know about it. The software people, support people, the people who implement the hardware, and so on. Also, if someone started asking questions, or decrypted the data, it would be hard to deny that the company was up to something. Using the packet sequencing stuff, it's almost impossible to detect, and there's no trail in the data itself. I figure, doing it this way, you only need to bring in two people at the company: an administrator of the server that sends updates and controls how the packets are sent and one of the chip design guys who's included some routines to interpret the data once it arrives."

For the first time since they had sat down, Hans started to think that Davis may actually have found something. "Did you crack the code?"

"It was really simple actually. If you assign the packets numbers like 1, 2, 3, 4, 5 you can list all 120 possible permutations of those digits to make 120 five-digit numbers."

"Yeah, but how do you know what the different numbers *mean*?"

"If you order the five-digit numbers numerically, you can make a one-to-one mapping with the position of the five-digit number in the sequence with the ASCII values of characters."

The look of confusion on Hans's face was apparent. Davis continued, "Check this out." He pulled a spreadsheet up on his screen:

Spreadsheet

Item	Hex	ASCII	1st Packet to Arrive	2nd Packet to Arrive	3rd Packet to Arrive	4th Packet to Arrive	5th Packet to Arrive	Value (from position digits of the packet)
60	3C	<	3	4	1	2	5	34125
61	3D	=	3	4	1	5	2	34152
62	3E	>	3	4	2	1	5	34215
63	3F	?	3	4	2	5	1	34251
64	40	@	3	4	5	1	2	34512
65	41	A	3	4	5	2	1	34521
66	42	B	3	5	1	2	4	35124
67	43	C	3	5	1	4	2	35142
68	44	D	3	5	2	1	4	35214
69	45	E	3	5	2	4	1	35241
70	46	F	3	5	4	1	2	35412
71	47	G	3	5	4	2	1	35421
72	48	H	4	1	2	3	5	41235
73	49	I	4	1	2	5	3	41253
74	50	J	4	1	3	2	5	41325

Davis continued, "Now take a look at these packets."

He opened Baff's packet header file. He scrolled down and high-lighted a group of five packets.

```
01:17:35.761647 IP 257.81.30.134.20 > 192.168.2.67.3432: .
2328486604:2328488064(1460) ack 1938878123 win 24820

01:17:35.769918 IP 257.81.30.134.20 > 192.168.2.67.3432: .
2328488712:2328490172(1460) ack 1938878123 win 24820

01:17:35.836112 IP 257.81.30.134.20 > 192.168.2.67.3432: P
2328485144:2328486604(1460) ack 1938878123 win 24820

01:17:35.839538 IP 257.81.30.134.20 > 192.168.2.67.3432: P
2328488064:2328488712(648) ack 1938878123 win 24820

01:17:35.853420 IP 257.81.30.134.20 > 192.168.2.67.3432: P
2328483684:2328485144(1460) ack 1938878123 win 24820
```

"These packets are out of order. Look at the sequence numbers. If we replace the first packet number in sequence, 2328485144, with 1; the second, 2328486604, with 2; the third, 2328488064, with 3; the fourth, 2328488712, with 4; and the fifth, 2328490172, with 5; we see that the packets arrive in the sequence 3, 5, 2, 4, 1. Looking the number 35241 up in our table shows that these five packets represent the letter E. Since I spoke to you this morning I did this for each five-packet group and deciphered the message."

Packets Reordered

Timestamp	Sequence number		
01:17:35.761647	2328488064	⟶	3
01:17:35.769918	2328490172	⟶	5
01:17:35.836112	2328486604	⟶	2
01:17:35.839538	2328488712	⟶	4
01:17:35.853420	2328485144	⟶	1

Davis paused. Hans was now leaning forward. He was oblivious to the loud rock music consuming the house. "Well, what did it say?"

"It's not so much *what it said*, it's what the video card does with it! It looks like every three weeks, the video driver launches a maintenance application that connects through the internet to Mezonic to look for software updates. It receives the updates but also looks for these messages. I replayed Baff's sequence to my machine and then put the video driver in a debugger. Remember Baff's note about people giving him visions? Now I know what he meant. Once every three minutes, for a fraction of a second, the machine shows the message on the screen. It's so fast, you wouldn't even notice it, like a flicker but even more subtle. It's like the subliminal message stuff that's been done with music, but this one is visual; see it enough, and I wouldn't be surprised if it started to change the way you thought. It's mind control on a huge scale!"

Hans leaned back slightly. He had heard of mind "programming" techniques that were used during the second World War where victims would be put to sleep with music that had subliminal messages and then watch movies that had images designed to invoke a specific response. But mind control through a computer?

"You can't be serious."

"Maybe 'mind control' is a little harsh," Chad continued, "but it's certainly an attempt to influence people. Think about it. When we stare at a computer screen our mind is open, we are in a mode of acceptance, of susceptibility."

Hans wasn't convinced. Years of working for the FBI had taught him to rely on hard evidence. Up until now all Chad had given him was theory, possibilities, and potential. In short, a paranoia-induced conspiracy theory.

"Ok, assume this is true, and the flickers aren't just random. What does the message in Baff's packets say?"

"When I feed Baff's packets into my machine, this is the message I get."

Davis opened a debugger on the screen and then advanced to the instructions just before the screen flicker. He advanced the debugger once more and the screen went dark with large text displayed in the center of the screen:

THEY OWN OUR MINDS

"Jesus!" Hans exclaimed.

Hans leaned backward and almost fell off the unstable stool.

"Now that you know where to look, what did it say before you ran Baff's packets?" Hans said.

"Nothing. But I think it's because I've never allowed it to do an update. I always have all the network stuff on my machine locked down."

"Let it run, let's see what happens."

With a few clicks, Davis disabled the personal firewall on his machine, the guard that protected him from unwanted communications over the Internet. He then manually launched the video driver update tool.

He watched the lights on his cable modem flicker as data was exchanged between his machine and a server at Mezonic. Moments later the activity stopped.

"Let's see what we got," Hans said excitedly.

Davis again fired up his debugger and forced the process to freeze the message once it appeared on the screen. This time, it was indeed different. This was a message that was being sent to millions of computer screens, a message that neither of them ever could have imagined. The two stared at the screen in silence; neither of them could fathom the implications. Chad couldn't imagine the number of users who were unknowingly receiving these updates and being swayed by Mezonic's messages. Most home users didn't have a firewall; they clicked "OK" on every screen that popped up and hoped to God that their system just worked. These were the people that Mezonic was reaching…the majority of the population of the United States.

Hans spoke first. "Chad, I'm going to get five of my best men. They will be watching your every move. Go to the airport. Don't tell anyone about this until I know who we can trust."

Hans stood, reached for Chad's shoulder and squeezed hard "I don't know what's going on here but we are damn sure going to find out."

Chad said nothing. He didn't hear a word that Hans said. His eyes were fixated on the computer screen. His mind was racing. *My god!*

The computer screen showed four words in a large but soft font superimposed over his Windows Desktop:

VOTE SHIFT FOR PRESIDENT

Hans had been right—in order for anyone to hear them over the music, they would have had to be right next to where he and Chad sat. But he was wrong in thinking the room was clean. A small listening device embedded in the wood of Davis's foyer table had been faithfully transmitting the conversation between the two men to the grey van parked just down the street. Danko also had been watching them from a small camera in a light fixture just inside Davis's front door.

Danko leaned back in his chair surrounded by electronic equipment; in a few minutes one of his helpers was scheduled to drop off Danko's car and take over surveillance in the van while Danko took care of Hans. Seeing Hans remove the bug behind the painting angered him. His men had worked hard to get Davis's place "fixed."

Don't worry Mr. Davis, you will *be met at the airport.*

Chapter 27:   Seattle, WA

Chris Payne's Home

Chris Payne's wealth did not come as easily as most imagined. Stories of wealthy people were usually romanticized; the path to wealth was made to look easy, even accidental. It was usually a dreamer story of starting a small business in a garage, and as fast as one could spell IPO, it was Leer jets and caviar. Chris knew that it was anything but. Twelve hour days were the norm for Chris Payne, even now. Although he had stopped going to the office on weekends he spent most of his Saturdays and Sundays at his home office going over e-mail, reviewing papers, and reading up on his competition or the industry in general.

This Sunday morning, Payne was going over a pile of new client contracts at his home office. On top of the pile was a proposal to custom-develop a secure digital order form for a large e-commerce store. To the left, sitting on its own, was a document that Payne and his lawyers had meticulously been preparing over the last four months. It was a multi-state, multiphase contract to deploy e-voting systems at a total cost of $49.6 million. For this project though, Payne cared little about the money.

Each system consisted of a ballot program and a national database server to process and count precinct results. The system was versatile; it could be adapted for both national elections as well as elections at the state and county levels.

The phone interrupted his reading but Chris let it ring, expecting his butler to pick up. The ringing abruptly stopped and shortly afterward, there was a knock at his office door.

"Mr. Payne?"

"Yes, come in," replied Chris.

"A Mr. Steve Watts is on the phone."

"Thanks, I'll take it in here."

The butler transferred the phone call to Chris' office.

"Steve, how's life in Macau?"

"Well, we're pumping out chips faster than ever. Get this, I had our new controller run the numbers, we are going to loose only about half the money we thought. Hell, when this is all over, we may be able to turn this thing into a legitimate business!"

Payne paused before replying. "We don't measure Mezonic's success in dollars, we measure it in votes."

When Chris had first conceived of Mezonic, it seemed so distant, so unreachable. "We are close Steve, so close! I'm getting ready to head out to Washington D.C. for tomorrow's testimony. I'm just going over a couple of contracts. Somebody's gotta keep the lights on."

Steve thought about their cause and about why he was in this. He knew it wasn't about money or a winter home in the Bahamas.

"I know, Chris. We've made some good progress over the past year. I think we are just now starting to see the results."

"You've done a great job at Mezonic, Steve. The latest sales figures show that you pretty much own the video card market. That's great, although your numbers are starting to raise some eyebrows with our auditors. I don't know how much longer I can legitimately justify investing company money in Mezonic. We may need to start thinking about raising prices. We don't need to show a profit, just a bounded loss."

Steve sighed, "Yeah, I know, Chris. We're looking at different options and I plan on making some changes over the next month." Steve's mind reflected on a change he had just been forced to make. A man, a friend that had been silenced.

Eric Tang's face had haunted Steve since he had made the call to Danko. Eric's family had asked him to speak at the funeral which had taken place earlier that morning. As he approached the lectern at the old Catholic church in Macau, he felt empty. No sadness, no guilt, no joy, just numbness. Steve's ability to feel had been lost four years ago, when his wife and daughter were killed in an embassy bombing in Kenya. The family had been on vacation when their passports were stolen. At the embassy, the line was long; hours separated the Watts family from the front counter. Steve had gone back to the hotel to pick up his wife's forgotten driver's license when he felt the earth shake. By the time he made it back to the embassy, it was a billowing cloud of ash. The pain was too much for his mind to bear, and so he not only denied himself grief, he denied himself all feeling.

"What's our market share these days?" Chris asked.

Steve took a minute to process the question. His mind was far away, with his wife and daughter, "Ninety-two percent."

"Excellent, up another percentage point. Every little bit helps. So where are we in information? What are we advertising?"

Steve leaned back in his chair, preparing to give a lengthy answer, "We are on schedule. I think the early campaign push was successful. We ran basic suggestive messaging, associating Shift's name with icons, like the flag. The latest polls show that the race for the party nomination is tight, but he's showing a slight lead. We've increased the frequency and started to run negative imagery for his opponent."

Chris acknowledged, "Good. I still think we're on the right course. Shift's climb in the polls proves it. The Senator has moved from unranked to dead even with the old frontrunner."

"That's just what we want. We're at full throttle on our side. I think Advice can handle it from there," Steve said.

Chris jokingly replied, "Passing the buck are we?"

"Right!" laughed Steve, "I'm a manager now, I'm supposed to delegate! Seriously though, from your side, where do we stand?"

"Well, the race is close, and that's exactly how we want it to be. I'm flying out to D.C. later today; tomorrow we hear Dr. Davis' testimony. Everything is on track there, I have people taking care of it."

"And the system? Is it ready?"

"Of course. The primary looks like it will come down to the absentee votes. We had some issues with a hacker, but our associate took care of it."

"I see our Serbian friend has been busy. I know we still have hurdles to overcome but we are close. I can feel it," Steve responded.

"Me too, Steve. Hey, I'll be on CNN tomorrow. We're doing a big splash for the Washington State primaries with our e-vote system. I'll let you know how it goes."

"Let me know? I'll be glued to the television. It's not all rickshaws and fried rice here you know; we *do* get satellite T.V."

"Okay, Steve," Chris said with a smile, "it was good to catch up. I'll be in touch."

"Good luck tomorrow, the world and I will be watching."

Chapter 28:   Seattle, WA

Chad Davis's Home

In 1870, Luke McRedmond laid claim to a large piece of land roughly 17 miles southwest of present-day Seattle, Washington. This area, now known as Redmond, is nestled within King County, and is home to companies like Nintendo of America, AT&T Wireless, Eddie Bauer, and the international software giant, Microsoft.

Before fur trappers and homesteaders settled the area, Native Americans thrived off of the Sammamish Valley. Salmon were so abundant in the Sammamish River that when the pioneers arrived they called their settlement Salmonberg. The word "Sammamish" comes from the Indian term *Samena*, meaning "hunter." The lake was once a gathering place for Native American tribes where, at the south end of the lake, tribes would celebrate their winter festival—"potlatch"—hunting, fishing, and collecting berries in preparation for winter. Today, the outer rim of the lake remains lined with magnificent redwoods, sprinkled with houses and parks. Although winter had come and gone, Danko would honor those local natives and their hunting traditions as he awaited Hans's departure.

He didn't have to wait long. Hans walked slowly out of Chad Davis's house, scanned his surroundings, and got into the driver's seat of his parked car. Under the cover of trees a block away, Danko watched the grey Toyota Camry back out of the driveway. He started his car but did not put the car in drive. Instead he reached for his pack of Camels and lit a much-needed cigarette. Danko had learned to be patient, to move only when necessary. He loved the hunt.

As Hans began to make his way north up the East Lake Sammamish Parkway, Danko followed a couple cars behind.

Sunday afternoon traffic was light. The parkway was not a highway, rather a two-lane road running up the east side of the lake. A mix of lavish and quaint homes scattered the waterfront; on the east side of the parkway more developed neighborhoods and apartment communities flourished. Spring had arrived, leaves were blooming, and surprisingly the sun smiled down on the state of Washington, causing the lake to shimmer.

Hans's mind raced as he drove. He planned what needed to be done; form a team, stake out Davis's house, cover him at the airport, collect him in D.C. His mind drifted back as he noticed the number of cars that had sporting equipment strapped to their roofs. Canoes, camping gear, mountain bikes, and fishing poles were the norm. He noticed the occasional model airplane wing hanging out a car window as he made his way north toward Marymoor Park, where a large field allowed techie hobbyists to try their luck at flying their "birds."

Danko knew they were still about half-way up the lake and it would be a few more miles before the trees and surrounding landscape replaced homes, and more importantly, potential witnesses. He was patient. As the car in front of him slowed to turn he kept his eyes ahead on Hans. He was now only one car behind.

Hans noticed the car behind him was trying to position itself for a pass. He slowed as they drove down a straight section of the parkway and allowed the car with a couple of mid-twenties college students to pass him. *Ah, to be young again.* He looked back through his rearview mirror and noticed a man with a cigarette hanging from the side of his mouth tailgating him.

Danko could smoke a cigarette without ever having to use his hands. He would inhale and exhale while keeping the butt perfectly placed between his lips, reaching up only occasionally to tap off the extinguished ash. As he inched closer to Hans he tightened his lips down and took an extended puff from his cigarette. Easing the grip on the cigarette's filter he exhaled through his nose and mouth, squinting his eyes as he planned his attack.

Police officers around the country practice what is known as the Tactical Vehicle Intervention Method, or the Pursuit Intervention Technique. This technique is simple but effective. A police officer in pursuit of a vehicle at high speeds comes up to the right side of the suspect car's rear bumper, and with one swift move, causes the vehicle to spin out and come to a stop, allowing police officers to demobilize and arrest the fleeing suspects. Danko had mastered the technique but realized he needed something a bit more…final. He wasn't out to spin Hans's car out of control; he wanted to take Hans and his car out, permanently.

Danko peered ahead and saw no other cars on the stretch of road they were now traveling. *It's time.* They had finally made it past the heavy residential area and now were surrounded by a dense collection of trees. Danko pressed on the gas and rode close to Hans' bumper for a couple of seconds. This was one of the learned skills in his profession, and at 60 miles per hour, he knew a vehicle was covering roughly 88 feet per second. A break in concentration, debris in the road, anything, and Danko could very well be joining Hans's fate. Danko pressed hard on the gas and hit straight into Hans's rear bumper.

"What the hell!" exclaimed Hans as he struggled to maintain control. He looked up behind him. Danko's cigarette had shrunk in size but had not budged.

Hans's mindset immediately switched. He was no longer a civilian, but an FBI agent. A hunted agent. He sped up, quickly assessing his location and situation. *A drop on the left and woods on the right, shit!*

Danko demanded more power from his car and slowly gained ground on Hans again. His foot was now hard-pressed against the floor mat.

Another collision. This time the impact was harsher. Hans's rear bumper was now dragging, hanging on only by shreds of steel and plastic.

"Who is this son of a bitch?" yelled Hans.

He leaned over and reached for his pistol. With one hand on the steering wheel and the other on his gun Hans looked back to eye his attacker. This time he realized the driver was the one man he didn't want to see: *Danko!* In that split second, Danko struck again, this time forcing Hans off the road and into the trees that lined the east side of the Parkway.

Danko screeched to a stop and looked over at the crash. Hans's car had hit a tree head on, wrapped around it in a twisted pile of metal and glass. Danko could just make out the airbag that was now covered with streaks of blood.

Mission accomplished.

Chapter 29:   Seattle, WA

Chad Davis's Home

Closing the door on Hans's departure, Chad Davis's mind was now racing. His heart was pounding. *What did I get myself into?* He now knew he was being watched, but he had to put that out of his mind. He had already uncovered part of what Baff had wanted him to see, but he still had to find out what else Baff had. All senses were now focused on one thing and one thing only, the software on that CD.

Davis had a flight to catch and, as usual, was nowhere near ready. At least this time he had an excuse. Fortunately, it was a short drive to the airport, but ironically it would feel like one of the longest he had ever taken. He grabbed the cleanest and darkest looking suit he could find in his closet and threw it into a suit-bag. A couple of shirts and ties followed.

Tomorrow Davis would testify before Congress on what he now felt was not just Advice Software's e-vote system but something much bigger. The nation's Presidential election could very well be compromised and without the message he now carried, no one would ever know. It was David versus Goliath—and he didn't even have a stone to sling.

Would they believe me? I don't even know what to tell them.

He wrapped his dress shoes in a couple of plastic bags and haphazardly threw them in with his clothes. He then randomly grabbed some toiletries off the bathroom counter and tossed them into one of the suit bag's compartments.

Walking back in to the living room, Davis turned his attention to his laptop still on the desk in the foyer. Without question it was going with him, along with Baff's CD. He placed them in his briefcase along with a mound of papers—both technical and editorial—on electronic voting. His final report to the Congressional Election Committee on his analysis of Advice Software's e-vote system had to go with him as well.

Before heading out he decided to call Grace Wilkinson; he needed to talk to her about tomorrow's testimony. The phone rang. And rang. He knew that getting her to pick up on a Sunday evening was a stretch and after several rings, her voicemail picked up.

"Grace, this is Chad Davis. It's Sunday evening and I am on my way to the airport. We need to talk about Monday's testimony. This is urgent. Please give me a call back as soon as you get this message. You have my hotel and cell numbers. Thanks."

A sudden sickening feeling overwhelmed him. *God, the bugs! How could I be that stupid!* Davis couldn't believe what he had just done. Hans had told him not to do anything suspicious, anything out of the ordinary and not 10 minutes later he used both the word "urgent" and "testimony" in a phone call to a federal official!

Can't worry about that now, I'm already late for my flight!

At times Davis would arrive home from work or from a long trip on the highway and not remember at all how he got there. He couldn't believe that he consciously was in control of the car and was able to get himself safely to his destination. The drive to the airport this evening was such a trip. He parked in the long-term lot and as his car came to a stop he snapped back into reality. *What did I miss in that system?*

He wasn't the only one to analyze Advice's software. One major voice against it was rogue software expert Michelle Lovine. Although Michelle's intelligence and expertise was of the highest caliber, the industry and public generally paid little attention to his extremist analyses and remarks. His favorite conspiracy theory was that Microsoft was now capable of influencing people's decision-making through their most commonly used software packages. *If only he knew about Mezonic.*

"That damn paperclip is controlling more than you think!" Michelle would exclaim at conferences. His opinion on electronic voting was no less extreme. He claimed that electronic voting was open to tampering on a wide scale and that a few major national and international groups might be able to control the outcome of not only the U.S. Elections but any other country's elections that followed the United States's lead.

Various newspaper op-eds carried Michelle's rhetoric: "…these machines don't offer any traceability. No paper trail. We must be able to audit votes while maintaining voter privacy. That just cannot be done electronically. Voting should be done the old-fashioned way: paper, paper, and more paper. Then hand-count and recount and recount and recount the hell out of them."

Another e-vote software evaluator was an independent testing authority (ITA) called Computer Technologies, Ltd. Their evaluation returned similar runtime bugs to those Davis found, but nothing out of the ordinary. *Maybe nobody's found the secret. Maybe there is no damned secret!* He was at a loss; frustrated because he couldn't find anything in the software; frustrated because Baff left him secrets that were only part of the puzzle.

While these thoughts churned nonstop through his head, he had checked in and was now already clear of security and boarding the plane. As he walked through the plane's doorway, he greeted the stewardess with a faint, "Hi," before walking up the aisle to find his seat. When he got to row 38, Davis assessed his flight neighbor and although he was unfortunate to have someone seated next to him, at least the man was slender. The man looked up at Davis as he stood in the aisle.

"You coming or going son?" asked the man in a deep southern accent.

"What? Oh, I'm going," replied Davis, "to D.C."

"Well that's a good sign, because that's where this flight is going." The older man smiled, disarming Davis.

Davis realized how his tussled appearance might appear to the man and tried to regain his composure as he took his seat. He felt the man's stare follow his movements before the man asked, "So, if you don't mind me asking, what business leads you there?"

Davis hesitated. *Relax, you're on the plane, Hans's guys will be watching you once you step off it, you're golden. Stop being paranoid and just try to be civil to the nice old man who just wants to pass the flight with conversation.* "I'm a computer science professor from U.W."

"Ah, computers and what-not? I'm generations behind when it comes to that stuff. So what do you do with them?"

"Most of my work is on software security."

"Boy, you're way out of my league. I'm just a simple accountant."

Simple accountant? Does he know how many people can't add in this country?

"Sir, accounting is not simple," replied Davis jokingly.

"Well I guess, whatever floats your boat, huh? I think it's easy but couldn't tell you a thing about software security. I just use my computer for the spreadsheets, the Internet, and the digital camera my grandkids bought me. So what are you doing up in D.C.?"

Davis didn't know how to reply. He wanted to vent. He wanted to tell this strange man everything that had happened to him. He had to get it off his chest.

"Well I'm actually testifying before Congress on electronic voting."

"Testifying? You in trouble?" asked the man jokingly.

"No," replied Davis, managing a nervous laugh.

He paused to regroup his thoughts and continued, "I'm going to give a report on an electronic voting system that might be used for the Presidential election in November. The system is going to be used in the Washington State primaries tomorrow."

"Sounds interesting," replied the man, "I noticed that one of the candidates, Shaft or Shift or something, is pushing for that electronic voting. I say stick with the paper stuff. Those boys in Florida may not know how to count but we do in Washington." The man chuckled, "So as an expert what do you think?"

What do I tell this guy? Is he just an old man?

Davis answered guardedly, "Well as you can imagine I can't say too much about it, but generally speaking there are pros and cons both ways."

The man smirked, realizing Davis' answer was overly sanitized, "I understand, son. In my opinion, machines shouldn't be the official counting record for anything! Spreadsheets have made my life much easier but I still go over the numbers the good old-fashioned way."

Davis was intrigued by the man's comment, "So you think votes should be hand-counted? That's millions and millions of votes. Think of how many mistakes people could make counting them."

The old man smiled, "Well let me give you an example. Let's say I work in a bakery as a cashier."

"Ok, go on," replied Davis.

"So as a cashier I have customers walk in and buy coffee, doughnuts, cakes, muffins, you name it."

"Right, and you take their money."

"Easy son, I'm getting there," continued the man, "let's say the bakery is an all-cash business. At the end of the day that register should be balanced: 'Cash In' minus 'Starting Cash' equals 'Receipt Totals'."

Davis again jumped in, "That's a pretty simple system. I'm still not…"

The man interrupted, "I told you I'm getting there. I tell you, you computer guys have no attention span for a real discussion."

They both laughed. Davis blushed slightly, "Sorry, it's a bad habit of mine to butt in."

"No problem. Where was I? Oh yeah, so at the end of the day that register will be balanced or someone's in a world of trouble. That bakery owner's life blood is that register. It can't be off balance. He cares about that cash just like the elections guys care about those votes."

"I don't get it," replied Davis.

"Well at the end of the day that cash is hand-counted. The baker would never assume that the cash totals on those receipts are equal to what he actually has in the register. If there's a discrepancy you can be damn sure he's gonna find out why. Maybe a coffee was sold as a soda or a muffin as a cookie."

"I see what you're saying," replied Davis, "but voting needs to be done anonymously, and it's on a much bigger scale than one bakery's worth of cash."

"Well then, let me give you another example." The man paused for a second, "I'm sorry I don't know your name. I'm Lars Johnson."

"Lars? Chad Davis. A pleasure."

They uncomfortably reached across the airplane seats and shook hands. Before Lars could continue a voice interrupted, "Sir, something to drink?" The discussion had taken them past the plane's taxiing and take-off, and the in-flight beverage service had already begun.

"Coffee my dear, if you would," replied Lars.

The stewardess filled a small cup with coffee and served it to her passenger.

"Thank you," replied Lars.

The stewardess turned her attention to Chad, "And for you, sir?"

Though he was only slightly more at ease, he still felt the same array of emotions as he did before leaving his house: he was tired, nervous, and nauseous. He asked for the only thing he thought would help, "Whiskey. On the rocks, please."

"Yes, sir. That will be six dollars."

Davis fumbled through his pockets and carry on bag, managing to scrape together seven one-dollar bills.

"Thank you, sir. Enjoy!"

Davis grabbed his drink and turned to Lars, "Cheers!"

"Cheers Mr. Davis. Good luck to you tomorrow."

"Thank you. So what example were you about to give me?"

"Oh yeah! See now I forgot what I was talking about. Trust me son, old age is a bitch and a half! So let's see, what was I thinking ...oh yeah! If you thought a bakery is too small an operation to compare to a voting center then think about how casinos collect their cash."

Davis took a chug of his whiskey. *Aaaaah, pure ambrosia.* He looked down at the plastic cup in his hand. *Six bucks for two gulps?* He thought back to his recent visit to the Holland Casino. He remembered the cart full of money being picked up by large men in dark suits with ear pieces and security escorts. He thought about the boxes of cash they removed from the slot machines, placing them in slots on a larger cart that looked like a big array of mail boxes.

"Ok, I see, a casino does have some similarities, maybe."

Lars adjusted himself in his seat, "Well, okay, we're talking about serious amounts of money here. And although the money is usually machine-counted, they've still got some sanity checks. For one, the security and scrutiny applied to the transfer of the cash from the machines to a central counting office. Apply that to ballot boxes at elections. Now, think about the number of employees that witness the money being counted. You don't leave that type of job to one or two people with a machine. And you do not leave it to people working for the same side. Casino employees and security are there, at least. You also have a bunch of individual counts, small amounts that then get totaled. No one count could throw the big count off too much."

Davis knew the issue was more complicated. The tampering of a vote count at the state or local level was just as dire as a global manipulation when the election was close.

Davis's attention was fading and a sudden wave of drowsiness washed over him. He could barely keep his eyes open, but he kept up with Lars, "I see what you're saying."

What did I get myself into? All he could think of was tomorrow's testimony. *What will I say now?* Even though he had submitted his report and his conclusions were positive, he now had more and more doubt.

"You've given me some good things to think about." Davis paused. "I hate to be rude Lars but if you don't mind I would love to try and get some sleep. Believe me I'd love to continue this conversation but my eyelids feel like they each weigh a ton."

"Sure thing, son. I've got some papers to go over myself. I'll keep an eye out for you on the news," replied Lars.

"Please do! And if you're ever in Seattle again, you can find me at the University of Washington. Just look me up."

Chad turned to face the seat in front of him and reclined his seat as far back as possible. Lars turned his attention to his carry-on, pulling a folder out and dropping his tray down in front of him. Except for the loudly snoring man a couple of seats behind him, the rest of the flight was fairly uneventful. The usual chit-chat among some passengers and the usual drink offerings. Although his body was willing, his mind and his thoughts would not let him drift off to sleep. With eyes closed he continued to think about the files. *I've got to figure this out.*

One row back and across a man was intently watching Chad, noting his every move.

Boarded plane

Talked with passenger next to him for 30 minutes

Took nap

Chapter 30:   Seattle, WA

Outside of Elizabeth Davis's Middle School

Danko pulled to a stop near the curb a few blocks away from Kent Middle School. He usually had at least a few hours to rest in between jobs but it wasn't 30 minutes ago that he had left the scene of that fatal "accident" on Lake Sammamish Parkway. Danko grabbed a lone folder laying on the passenger seat and began to study an enclosed dossier intently. Having removed Hans from the picture, he was now ready to concentrate on a more direct attack: Davis's family.

Amanda Davis, not a bad-looking wife. Amanda was five feet, four inches tall with mid-length brunette hair. She was slender but not overly trim. Danko categorized her as having "the right curves in all the right places." She had dark brown eyes, trimmed eyebrows and soft lips. He had also inspected her car in detail, a 1998 Honda Accord. It was dark green and had a worn rear bumper with a bumper sticker saying, "Support your Troops," covering the biggest scrape.

Danko grabbed his cell phone. After a few seconds the line picked up.

"What time do we leave?" asked Danko

"Be here by two. That should give us enough time."

"Ok, I am still in the middle of job. I will arrive by one."

Danko couldn't recall a job where he had to pick up a wife and a daughter. He had no problem with women, but children were not his specialty. If it were up to him, the kid would stay, but Payne was specific.

His uneasiness with children ran deep. A couple of years ago in Serbia he was eating lunch at a local tavern when a mother and her child sat down next to him. The child must have been eight or nine years old and seemed well behaved. As Danko got up to leave, the kid was awed by Danko's size and demeanor, spilling his drink all over Danko's shoes. The child began to laugh. His mother told him to apologize to the man. He did it with a smile, trying to save the rolling glass before it also fell onto the floor. Danko's reaction was surprisingly restrained but he was furious inside.

He felt the cold drink soaking through his canvas shoes to his bare feet. He looked at the kid with menacing eyes, "What will you do about this now?" he asked the child.

The mother repeated the apology, "I am sorry sir. It was an accident."

The child's smile quickly disappeared from his face as he sensed his mother's concern and growing fear of what this man may do. His eyes began to water and he slowly began to cry, trying to hold back any audible sobbing. If any enemy of Danko would have been watching him that day, they would have determined that his weakness was crying children.

"It is ok. Do not cry. It will dry in some time. Stop crying!"

Danko looked at the mother whose face had turned from concern to fear. He repeated a quick, "It is fine," and hurried off.

The sound of cars starting and the rush of kids exiting the school brought Danko back to his job at hand.

Sundays usually meant school doors were locked and the sounds of schoolchildren were silenced. This Sunday, though, a recital practice had filled the school with students. Danko had parked far enough away to be able to scope the area without being part of the school-zone traffic.

The green Accord he was tracking slowly made its way up to the front of the school. Although she was wearing sunglasses, Danko quickly identified Amanda as the driver. He watched her as she waited for her daughter, Elizabeth, to come out. *She'd better not be the crying kind*. After a few minutes a petite girl, not more than ten years old, carrying a clarinet, walked out the front door of the school.

Danko noted her opening the back car door, throwing her instrument in, and getting in the front passenger seat of the car. Amanda took off her sunglasses and greeted her daughter with a hug and a kiss. Both mother and daughter now smiled and began talking. As the row of cars inched forward, Amanda slowly pulled out of the school driveway and into the main street.

Eventually they passed by Danko's parked car without notice. He started his car and slowly made the u-turn. Amanda and Elizabeth were a few cars ahead of him.

Danko would follow.

Amanda had met Chad Davis when he first started teaching computer science courses at Carnegie Melon. It was his first year after he'd completed his doctorate degree. He was a shy, timid man—nothing like the professor and speaker he eventually grew into. Amanda was completing her Master's degree in English Literature and decided to break the "monotony" of her literature courses with a semester of Independent Study: Computer Evolution. She had made a few rounds through the Computer Science department looking for someone to ask a few questions. What better choice, she thought, than the young, cute Chad Davis. He was, of course, happy to help as he had felt an instant attraction. He was amazed a woman in the English department would be interested in computer history. He loved telling her stories about the ENIAC and the days when a single computer took up an entire room. It was almost like a grandfather telling his grandchildren stories of walking to school uphill both ways in the snow without a coat. Davis's passion for computers and their history were almost comical to Amanda, but she let him babble on, inflating his ego. After Chad's computer history lesson, they started to talk more casually. By the end of the semester they were spending more and more time off-campus together—dinner, movies, weekends in Amish country.

As their relationship grew, Davis talked about moving to Seattle where he had received a tenure-track associate professorship offer at the University of Washington. He'd hoped that their relationship was strong enough for her to instantly volunteer to move with him. Being a Pennsylvania native she wasn't keen on moving away from family and friends, but his marriage proposal sealed the deal and after some job hunting she found an editing position with a small publishing company in Seattle.

Their daughter, Elizabeth, was conceived soon after their move to Seattle. Amanda took a leave of absence that eventually led to her being a full-time mom, working part-time from home for the publishing company. Between her work and his teaching and research contracts it was more than enough for the family to live on.

Success at the university, though, meant long hours at the office and time away from home for travel and conferences. He loved his wife and was crazy about his daughter, but his inability to prioritize his family and obsessive work ethic deteriorated the relationship. Amanda had been left feeling like nothing more than a distraction to Chad, and when problems started, Chad found he wasn't able to deal with the issues, instead directing even more attention to his work. His work he understood, codes could be cracked, scripts could be written, but his personal life didn't boil down to 0's and 1's.

In 2000, Amanda filed for divorce on grounds of neglect and irreconcilable differences. She received full custody of Elizabeth and moved out of their home into a two-bedroom apartment. Davis was heartbroken but he continued on at work and freed up the majority of his weekends to see his daughter. As time passed, his weekends turned from days off with Elizabeth, to 12-hour software analysis marathons. She saw her father every other week, then every month; more recently she spoke to him on the phone weekly but barely saw him or spent time with him. It was tough on Amanda and even worse on Elizabeth. The past few months had been especially difficult for him. His focus on the e-vote software system made him miss his family even more.

Last time they spoke, Chad had told Elizabeth, "I miss you honey. Why don't we hang out after my trip to D.C.?"

"Ok dad, you promise?"

"Of course. There's nothing that would make me happier. It's been too long."

Danko tailed Amanda from school to the grocery store and now they were approaching their apartment complex. He took a deep breath as they pulled into the entrance and slowly made their way around the parking lot to their space.

As they got out of their car, Danko pulled in across from them, opened his car door and stepped out.

"Excuse me, miss. Are you Amanda Davis?"

Amanda looked up at the large man with the short military haircut. Elizabeth turned around and also noticed Danko walking toward them.

As Danko made his way to his subjects he slowly pulled out a wallet with the fake badge he would use. He quickly assessed his surroundings and what he would do in case of an emergency.

It's time to go to work.

Chapter 31: Seattle, WA

En route to Airport

Amanda and Elizabeth quickly packed a couple of carry-on bags with some clothes and toiletries before following Danko to his car.

"Mom, where are we going?"

"We're going to see your father, honey. We're flying to Washington D.C.," replied Amanda.

Danko was at the wheel heading toward the executive airport. He was ahead of schedule, just how he liked it. Amanda Davis sat next to him while Elizabeth sat in the backseat.

"Do you work for my dad?" asked Elizabeth.

"No," Danko replied coldly.

Amanda did her best to hide her fear, turning to give Elizabeth a reassuring smile, but she could see that Elizabeth was uneasy. Neither of them liked having this large, foreign man drive them to the airport, even if he had shown them his credentials verifying his identity. He had told Amanda that Chad's life, and their lives, were in danger; they had to go to D.C. immediately to meet up with her husband. He had alluded to Chad's upcoming testimony, but was silent on the specifics.

"Why is dad in Washington, D.C., mom?"

"He's got some work to do for the government, honey. It'll be like a vacation! We can see the monuments and visit the White House." She forced herself to sound happy, though it wasn't easy.

"What about school, mom?"

"It's okay, Elizabeth. This is just a little sneaky vacation." She glanced at Danko who sat expressionless in the driver's seat. Twenty minutes later, Danko pulled into a private, "executive" airport as he described it, and escorted them to the small private jet that awaited them on the tarmac.

The captain was at the jet door, standing at the top of the steps, "Come on up ladies, welcome aboard."

Upon boarding the jet, Amanda was amazed at the plush seats, electronics, and amenities. *Is this standard FBI equipment?* she wondered. Elizabeth went straight for a lazy-boy-like chair that reclined in front of a television. Amanda sat next to her in an adjacent chair while Danko sat up front, facing them in what looked to be the most uncomfortable seat on the plane.

"If you want to eat let me know," Danko said.

Amanda wanted to sleep. She wanted to fall asleep, wake up and be back home with her daughter without any of this happening. She turned toward Elizabeth to make sure she was comfortable with this unordinary experience, but with characteristic childhood resilience, Elizabeth had already eased into the setting, distracted by the extravagance as well.

"Elizabeth, why don't you pick a movie and I'll see if I can get us some snacks, ok?"

Amanda stood to release some of her nervous energy, "Is there anything I can get for us to drink—sodas maybe?"

Danko looked at her gloomily, "Ok, sit down and I will get it for you." His sharp tone surprised her and she immediately sat back down.

"Ladies and gentlemen this is your captain. We are now taxiing for take-off. Please be seated and buckle up until further notice. We will be flying directly to Washington, D.C. If you have any requests please ask the flight attendant and we will do our best to accomodate you. Enjoy your flight."

Amanda leaned back in her seat and looked out the window. *Chad, what the hell have you done? You better not have screwed up too big…for your daughter's sake.*

Chapter 32: Washington, D.C.

Dulles International Airport

Eight hours and two connections after boarding his first flight out of Seattle, Chad Davis now walked down the arrivals corridor toward baggage claim at Reagan National Airport in D.C. He was completely drained. His hair was a mess, his slacks and shirt were heavily wrinkled. Even though he hadn't had anything to eat for the past 10 hours, he was past the point of hunger. He noticed friends and relatives waiting for their loved ones as well as the limo escorts in suits and their "I'm-a-limo-driver" hats holding signs with names of their customers. Flipping open his cell phone he saw he had only one message from an apparent missed call.

"Dr. Davis, this is Grace Wilkinson. I got your message and called as soon as I could. Please call me back as soon as you get this message."

He contemplated calling Grace back, but quickly checked his watch, which showed it was after 8 P.M. Seattle time, making it past 11 P.M. here. *Chances are she's probably asleep, getting rest for tomorrow, but maybe I should call anyway.* His thoughts were interrupted when among the limo drivers he noticed two men holding a sign with his name, "Dr. Chad Davis." With a sense of relief he walked toward them. *Hans, you came through!*

He approached the men and pointed to their sign, "Excuse me gentlemen, I'm Chad Davis."

One of the men replied, "Mr. Davis, we were sent to escort you to your destination. We have a car waiting outside. May I take your bag?"

"Thank you."

Davis handed his carry-on to one of the men, but kept his briefcase in his hand as he followed them out of the main terminal, heading east toward the valet section.

"How was your flight, Mr. Davis?" asked the escort with the bag.

"The flight was fine. I'm just very tired."

"Of course," The man nodded knowingly while his companion continued to remain silent.

The two men escorted Davis to a black stretched limousine. *Pretty nice for the FBI, I owe you one Hans!* As they neared the car, a driver emerged from the front seat. The driver placed his carry-on in the trunk and then reached for his briefcase. Davis handed it to the driver without thinking but soon realized he was about to place it in the trunk.

"I'm sorry can I please have my briefcase with me?"

"Yes, sir," replied the driver, "I'll bring it up for you."

Davis settled into the plush limo, followed by his escorts. The driver came around, handed him his briefcase, and then closed the door. A moment later, he felt the limo start to move forward. Inside it was dark, but small runner lights illuminated the limo cabin with soft neon hues. His eyes and ears caught the array of drinks at the bar, as the bottles softly chinked together with the limo's movement. His eyes were like that of a man trying to find water in a dessert.

"Please help yourself to anything you like, Mr. Davis," said his more vocal escort, noticing Davis eyeing the bar.

"Thank you," replied Davis, "Can I fix you a drink as well?"

"No, thank you. I can't drink on the job."

Of course. Davis leaned over and reached for the crystal containers full of dark and clear liquids. He surveyed the bottles and found what he was looking for. *Whiskey.* He dropped a couple of ice cubes in a glass and poured the whiskey in. The swishing sound it made brought him comfort.

"Well I don't mean to tease you with the drink, but cheers!"

"No problem, Mr. Davis. I'm used to it."

Davis took a gulp. *Ahhhhhh*. He leaned back and sunk into the seat as deep as possible. The limo was now exiting the airport and heading toward downtown. Out of the right side window he could see the Washington monument illuminated, climbing high into the D.C. skyline. He reached for his cell phone, remembering he had to call Grace.

One of the men interrupted, "I'm sorry Mr. Davis, I'd ask that you not use your cell phone until we arrive at our destination."

"Umm…ok. Sorry," replied Davis at once, quickly pocketing his cell phone. *That's strange.*

After another sip of his drink, Davis asked, "Have you worked long for the FBI?"

The men looked at Davis realizing what he must have thought, and then briefly at each other. The one that had spoken up to this point hesitated for a moment before answering.

"I don't work for the FBI." The silent man cracked a slight grin.

Davis paused. His stomach dropped. He turned to his glass and took another gulp.

He wasn't sure if he should even look at his escorts. *Do I attempt to escape? Can I survive a 70 mph lunge from the back of a limo onto a busy highway?*

"Our employer has asked us to take you to your hotel. But first you have an arranged meeting with Mr. Payne."

Davis now took another swig of his whiskey. *Ok, no problem. He just wants to see me and possibly try and sway tomorrow's testimony.*

"So do you work for Mr. Payne then?" asked Davis.

Neither man answered. For the next couple of minutes the car was absolutely silent, except for the occasional swallow of whiskey he took to keep his mouth from drying up.

The limo pulled into the hotel's drop-off area, coming to a stop. The driver quickly came around the back and opened the passenger door.

"Sir, right this way."

Davis was guided out of the limo and handed his carry-on bag.

"Thank you," he replied trying to reach for a tip.

The driver quickly stopped him, "That won't be necessary, sir. I insist."

Davis looked up from his fumbling hands and said, "Oh, ok. Well thank you."

The other two men escorted him in, "Mr. Davis, please go ahead and check in, we'll then take you to Mr. Payne's suite."

"Okay. Give me a minute please."

"We *will* be right behind you, Mr. Davis."

What a surprise. Davis walked up to the front counter and let his carry-on drop to the floor.

"Good evening! Checking in, sir?"

"Yes," replied Davis as he pulled out his driver's license and placed it on the counter.

"Ok, Mr. Davis, one moment please. I have you staying with us for two nights, is that correct?"

"Yes."

"Check-out time is 11 A.M., but if you have any problems please call us and we'll make the necessary arrangements. Here is your key card for room 1006, king-sized bed, nonsmoking. Is there anything else?"

How can this woman be so peppy all day?

"No, thank you."

Davis grabbed his license and room key. He turned and headed toward his escorts for the evening.

"Mr. Davis, please give your bags to the bellhop. We'll be heading straight to Mr. Payne's suite."

"He's staying in this hotel as well? How convenient."

Davis did as instructed but he kept his briefcase that contaned his papers and laptop with him. *That thing is not leaving my sight.*

The elevator ride up to the penthouse suite was quiet. Davis's last year of work on Advice flashed through his mind. *It's not like I'm meeting a mafia boss or something.* During his many visits to this hotel, he'd never been up to the penthouse suite floor before. A hotel host greeted them as they exited the elevator.

"Gentlemen, welcome. Please follow me."

His heart began to beat faster. They approached the penthouse doors slowly, giving him time to take in the luxurious paintings and crafts that adorned the hallway.

As the doors opened a butler greeted them, "Welcome gentlemen. May I take your coats?"

The men refused. Davis followed their lead. Without another word, the butler escorted them to the study. Once inside, he turned to Davis.

"May I get you something to drink, Dr. Davis?" he asked.

"Whiskey, please, on the rocks." The butler departed while a door on the opposite side of the room opened.

Chris Payne entered the study in a dark Armani suit, with an air that radiated confidence and success. Davis was speechless. They had met only a few times before in very formal settings during the evaluation of Advice's software, though he had always admired the man and respected his achievements. Somehow, Chad sensed that this meeting would be quite different.

Payne stood across from him and extended his hand, "Dr. Davis, I'm glad you could make it tonight. We have some things to discuss."

Chapter 33:   Washington, D.C.

Chris Payne's Hotel Suite

To the right of the study, Davis's escorts opened a double set of doors that revealed what appeared to be a meeting room. He followed Payne into the large room with a long, dark oak table in the center. The room was dim and the walls were covered with dark-striped wallpaper, bordered on the top and bottom by ornate molding. Chris Payne walked to the far end of the table where twelve chairs were arranged; five on each side and one on either end.

"Please, have a seat. I trust you had a good flight?" Payne didn't wait for Davis's response, instead motioning to a chair at the opposite end of the table from himself. As he sat he heard the doors creak closed behind him. The room was cold; he had noticed that immediately. He had expected to be in his own hotel room now, under the careful watch of the FBI, but something had gone wrong. *Where are Hans's guys?* His mind again began to race with thoughts of Baff's CD, the testimony, and the bugs in his house. He was having trouble fully contemplating his current situation.

"You may be wondering why I've asked you here this evening," Payne said.

Asked? Did I have a choice? Davis thought to himself.

"I assume it's about tomorrow's testimony?" Davis responded.

"Partly. I'd like to begin by thanking you for the review you gave our product a few months ago for *Infoweek*. You've helped us get where we are today with public acceptance of electronic voting."

"The tests I ran came out pretty well. I just called it like I saw it at the time."

"In any case, thank you. It's inevitable you know. Computers have permeated every aspect of commercial and government transactions. Did you know that 41 percent of Americans filed their taxes electronically last year? Forty-one percent! Amazing, really. Our government is controlled by computers. I'm proud to be a part of bringing voting into the 21st century. It's only a matter of time before paper votes become obsolete altogether."

"It must have been a difficult sell to Congress, though. You are creating a single point of failure for the election of the most powerful person in the world. Surely you've come up against some formidable resistance."

"The timing was right; people are still reeling from the 2000 election fiasco. E-voting promises to reduce some of those risks. Look at the traction that physical electronic voting machines are getting at the state and local levels. The people are ready. For the time being we're just a small piece of the puzzle—we only process the absentee ballots. In close elections though, definitive results can be held up for weeks with the archaic process they have now—waiting for the mail, sorting ballots. Look at what the last election did to the economy. When we didn't know who was President for a few weeks the stock market went to hell. I'm no economist but I think that was the catalyst for the whole dot-com bust. The people suffered, hell, on paper *I* lost more than the GDP of the Bahamas!"

Davis remembered the effect of the last election on the market all too well. He had just graduated from day-trading stocks to options. He knew the mathematics, he had studied the Black-Scholes equation—the mathematical basis for calculating option and futures prices. In a particularly bold move, two days before the 2000 election he bought $10,000 worth of call options on Intel's stock; he was positioned to triple his money if the stock went up just 8 percent. Options, though, were a risky proposition. They allow someone to control an enormous amount of shares at a relatively low price but the downside is that options expire: if they aren't exercised in time, they're worthless. By the time a winner was declared several weeks later, the stock market had dropped 18 percent, taking Intel and Davis's $10,000 along with it.

"What about the potential for someone to tamper with results? In the old days, it would take a massive conspiracy, dozens of officials would have to be involved to make a real impact. Now, a single individual might be able to manipulate results on a large scale. You're asking people to put a lot of faith in software, Mr. Payne."

Payne's countenance changed slightly, he seemed unsettled by the implication.

"So, what do you think of this place?" Payne asked as he outstretched his hands, quickly changing the subject. "I've taken out a two-year lease on it. It lets me keep an eye on things here in D.C."

"It's nice. A bit extravagant for me, though. I didn't know that this hotel leased out its suites."

"Let's just say that the manager is a reasonable man; when it comes down to it, it's all about money." Payne paused; he took a sip from a glass of wine that had just been delivered by the butler. "Excuse my manners," Payne paused and waited for the butler to deliver Davis his drink. Once the butler served him, Chris held his wine glass up and spoke, "A toast. To a successful testimony and a brighter future for our country, our children, our children's children."

Chad didn't care much for the toast but drank more out of need, "Mr. Payne, thank you for the drink."

"Call me Chris, please."

"Chris, I've had a really long flight and…"

Payne interrupted, "Do you know who that is?" Payne asked as he pointed to a framed portrait on the wall. The painting was large, roughly three feet by two feet by Chad's estimates. It had a unique frame, dark wood with gold highlights. It looked *rich*, like a Presidential portrait that would hang in the White House, and it appeared to be the central focus of the room. The man in the portrait was young, perhaps no more than 30. He was seated and wearing a blue suit with a red tie. Chad noticed a striking resemblance between the man in the painting and Chris but still wasn't sure who it was.

"No, I don't believe I do."

"That, Dr. Davis, is a picture of David Payne, my little brother. He was a real prodigy. By 30, he had his own brokerage in New York. Fortune called him 'the man who would conquer Wall Street'."

"You must be proud."

"Oh I am, we were very close. I'll tell you Dr. Davis, there's nothing more precious than family."

Davis's thoughts turned to Amanda and Elizabeth. He thought about the birthdays he'd missed, the special moments in Elizabeth's life; and his wishes for a second chance. This business with Baff, the CD, and the bugs was overwhelming. He needed the compassion of a loved one to escape from this mess, even if it were only for a moment of relief.

"I would have to agree."

Payne's countenance again changed, something indistinguishable rippled below the surface. His voiced dropped a level and he leaned forward in his chair. "Let me ask you a question, Dr. Davis. What if everything you loved, everything you treasured, were wrenched from you; stolen, never to be returned. What if your whole life was broken by one cold, desperate, cowardly, unthinkable act. What would you do to the people who took everything from you?"

Davis sat silently. Neither man spoke for a few seconds.

Payne continued, "I have had to face that pain, Dr. Davis. My brother, my life, was stolen from me. His office was on the 52nd story of the World

Trade Center. I spoke to him the night before; he sounded so content, so alive." Payne paused, "He was engaged, he had an excellent life ahead of him personally and professionally, but it was taken."

Payne's voice started to tremble. "Those bastards took everything. They must pay; they will pay! Their homes, their cities, their families should be made to suffer; suffer like I've suffered and the thousands like me have
suffered!"

He was taken aback by Payne's sudden mood change. He could see that Chris had suffered a devastating loss. He felt his rage, his intensity, but also saw another glimpse of an emotion he wasn't able to pinpoint at first, and realized Payne was on the verge of madness. "Chris, I'm sorry. I can't imagine what that must be like..." Davis trailed off, wondering what to say and where this conversation was headed.

"My life ended that day, too. I wake up with nightmares constantly. My heart is so full of rage, it has driven me for the last few years. Make no mistake, though, there are others that have suffered too, Dr. Davis; so many others. Some have come to accept it, move on with the rest of their lives. But there are those of us that cannot. A debt exists that can only be repaid in blood."

"Hatred is a very destructive emotion. It can stop you from enjoying the life you have left."

"Destructive?" Payne replied. "If I had my way, we would start bombing every home city of every terrorist we know about. That would make them pay, make their families pay! That would make the cowards come out!"

Davis stared across the table in shock. He was no longer looking at Chris Payne, ambitious billionaire, strong-willed entrepreneur and savvy software mogul. His hatred had turned him into something else. A man obsessed, a man precariously teetering on the edge of insanity.

"Think about what you're saying. You're talking about mass murder!"

Payne slammed his fists onto the table. It startled Davis, who now regretted speaking those words to a man who was obviously beyond any hope of reason.

"Murder?" Payne shouted angrily. "You son of a bitch, it's *justice*." Chris Payne's voice echoed through the room. He was now standing.

Chad did not speak. He was terrified. He had heard such sentiments before, in interviews of family members of those who lost their lives in the September 11th tragedy. Chad could not condemn them for their thoughts. *What if it was Elizabeth that died that day?* he used to ask himself; it was only human to lash out. This conversation with Payne, though, was disturbing because Payne *had* the resources to act on his rage in a catastrophic way. This was the man whose software was about to be used to select the next leader of the free world. Davis was now convinced: *This man will do anything to avenge his brother, including manipulating the U.S. Presidential election.*

"Pardon me, Dr. Davis. I get very emotional when I talk about my brother. I apologize. I'd like to talk to you candidly about tomorrow's testimony." Payne's demeanor suddenly calmed, his rage quickly disappearing. He sat back in his chair and continued, "As you probably know, a lot is riding on your final report to the Congressional Election Committee. This is an important event for Advice and for me, personally. I know you may have some, how shall I put it, reservations, as of recently about our product. Let me assure you that the ramblings of a hacker are meaningless; this system will be a bold step for the American people and ultimately for our way of life."

Ramblings of a hacker. God! Baff, but how did he know?

Payne continued, "Mr. Lexicon's death was unfortunate. He tried to stand in the way of progress and sometimes the needs of the many force us to make difficult decisions."

Davis's entire body went numb. He couldn't wrap his mind around the situation. He spoke without thinking. "You? You had Baff killed?"

"Come now, Chad, we have more important matters to discuss. Tomorrow we have a real opportunity; an opportunity to change the world." Payne stood up and began to walk around the table.

"There are others you know. People who share my vision. We have a strong society of committed men and women who want things to change; who understand that the wicked must be punished."

Chad swallowed hard. His fear was starting to turn to anger. *These people have been manipulating me for months. I'm a pawn in this sick bastard's chess game.*

"I know about Mezonic," he said in a defiant tone.

"Ah yes, Mezonic. A real stroke of genius I think. Did you know that over 90 percent of new video cards ship with a Mezonic chip? When we first came up with the idea of subliminal suggestion through computer monitors it was purely a marketing plan. We hired a psychologist and spent a fair amount of time refining the suggestive techniques. We were going to use it to push some of our software products to consumers. It's better than an ad during the Super Bowl. It ended up being a back-burner project."

Payne pulled out a chair and sat next to Davis.

"When the planes struck the World Trade Center, I was devastated. It was the lowest moment of my life. A few months later I met a man who shared my pain and vision. He had been running a manufacturing company for years when his wife and daughter were killed in an embassy bombing overseas. I knew he would be motivated. A few months later we founded The Mezonic Corporation. It was the best way we could think of to reach the people, to help them make the choices that they should make, that they had to make."

"What about Senator Shift? How does he fit into all of this?"

"William Shift is a good man, a good American; the man is a visionary. He understands what this country is and what we need to do to preserve it. He has felt pain, too; he shares our vision."

"Why are you telling me this?"

"So that you can understand!" Payne's voice resonated through the large room, in an angry, desperate tone.

"You're psychotic! The committee is going to know everything. I *will* testify tomorrow, don't worry about that." Chad was incensed. He stood and quickly felt a hand on his left shoulder. He turned to see two large men in dark suits standing behind him; the first he recognized from the limo ride, the second was much larger and looked significantly more menacing. He sank back into his seat.

"I had hoped that you were a patriot, Dr. Davis; a man who would be reasonable and understand our cause."

"Your cause is lunacy! You want to go on a killing spree!"

"Lunacy!? Is that what you call patriotism!?" Payne spoke with genuine hurt. He motioned to one of the men behind Davis. The man disappeared through a small corridor on the opposite side of the large room. "I had really hoped that it wouldn't come down to this. Sometimes one is blinded and cannot make reasonable choices, but I want to make this choice easy for you Dr. Davis. Tomorrow, you *will* testify before the committee, you *will* endorse our software, and we *will* succeed in getting Senator Shift into office."

"And why in the hell would I *choose* to do that?" Rage had now blocked all sense of fear and self preservation in Davis.

"I thought I might have to make this choice a bit more personal for you. We are in a state of war Dr. Davis and in every war there are casualties; innocent people who have to suffer for the obstinacy of some." Chris motioned his hand towards the corridor.

A large man walked in, with a short military hair cut and a black full-length trench coat. Davis recognized him immediately.

Danko, my god!

Davis's mind spun with the implications. He sat with his mouth open slightly. Payne could see that he had rattled the man.

Danko approached slowly and began to speak, "We meet again, Dr. Davis."

"Is this a threat, Payne? Testify or you'll send one of your flunkies after me?"

Danko was not amused. His face hardened.

"Oh no, Dr. Davis. I wouldn't dream of it, but, I thought that I needed to put things a bit more in perspective for you," Payne said.

Danko pulled a miniature video camera out of his left coat pocket. He swiveled the LCD display so that it was visible and sat it on the table in front of Davis. He pressed the play button and the video began.

At first, Davis could not make out what was happening. The picture was jumping, like someone was walking while filming. On the screen he saw a door getting larger and heard footsteps as the filmmaker approached. The door creaked open and it took a second for the room to come into focus. He saw two people sitting on the floor, huddled in a corner, holding each other. As the camera approached he could make out their faces: *Amanda and Elizabeth!* Davis's heart seemed to stop for a moment. In that instant he knew what death must feel like; only, it was worse than death. It was like a sharp dagger tearing at his soul. As the camera approach he heard the voice of Danko on the tape. The shot panned to Elizabeth.

"We are making a movie for your dad. Is there anything you want to say to him?"

Elizabeth's small head stayed down, turned away from the camera. The camera then turned to Amanda. Her eyes were red. There were large dark circles under them. He could just make out dried streaks across her cheeks, from where her tears had run.

"Chad, please..." Amanda said before the tape then faded to black-and-white snow.

Chad's voice was barely audible. He had no breath to form words, "What, what did you..."

Danko interrupted, "You have a nice family, Dr. Davis. Your daughter is very pretty, and your ex-wife, her skin is so," he paused briefly to make sure Chad understood, "soft."

Panic swelled up inside Davis. He felt the terror and rage Payne had showed only moments before. "Where are they? What did you do to them you sick bastard!" Davis lunged towards Danko with his hands outstretched but was quickly and easily subdued by the large man standing behind him. He was now a man possessed. He wanted to kill Danko with his bare hands. He wanted to *feel* him die.

"Now you understand how it feels to have those that you love suffer at the hands of others. But unlike mine, your family is fine. Nothing *will* happen to them as long as things go smoothly tomorrow," replied Chris.

"I'll do anything you want, just don't hurt them! Don't you even touch them!"

"Relax Chad, no harm will come to them, you have my word." Payne spoke with such calmness it grated on Davis.

"You'll never get away with this you know. This is bigger than me."

Payne stood up and walked over to a miniature bar beneath the picture of his brother. "No doubt you are referring to Special Agent Hans Sheridan," Payne said matter-of-factly. "It seems as though Agent Sheridan had a rather unfortunate…accident…after leaving your house."

Danko grinned widely. Davis was awash in emotion. He sat silently with no words or energy left in him.

"Dr. Davis, I'd like to introduce you to someone." Payne pointed to another man that had just entered the room. The man looked to be in his mid-thirties. He was completely bald and wore a white button-down shirt with black khakis. He was of average height but had a muscular build. "This is Luis Sanchez. You will not find a more dedicated or patriotic man." Payne took a sip from his freshly poured scotch. "Luis will be there tomorrow with your wife and daughter. He is a God-fearing man, but make no mistake, he is as committed as I am to making this happen; he will be armed. After the testimony your wife and daughter will be returned to you, *if* you provide the *correct* information for your testimony. You have my word." Payne walked up next to Davis's chair, "Now Chad, why don't you go and get some rest. Tomorrow is a big day, for all of us."

Davis was an eloquent speaker. He had given talks at over 50 conferences and had spoken with some of the smartest people on the planet. In this moment, though, words escaped him. He stood slowly and backed his chair away from the table.

"What's to stop you from killing me and my family after the testimony?" Davis said as the power of speech returned to him.

"You must think I'm some sort of monster who would kill without reason. I need you. Your death would raise questions that I would rather not have asked nor would I want to answer. You're no threat to me alive, who would believe you? Think about it. You have no evidence against me. I can't be linked to Mezonic's activities directly. The so-called proof you think is so important was created by a known hacker. And, as for your wife and daughter, I've already made arrangements to make this look like a kidnapping for ransom if it were to come out. *The Society* is strong Dr. Davis. You have no idea how far it reaches." Davis glared hard at Payne. He turned toward the door and began to walk away.

"Think it through Chad. You are about to commit perjury. If you then turn around and admit you lied and come up with this ridiculous story you'll either be committed or jailed." Payne's voice grew louder as Davis continued to walk through the room door and toward the suite exit. "Either way it's in your best interest to give us a glowing review tomorrow, if not for America, for the continued well-being of your family. We can and will find you no matter where you go."

Davis slammed the door as he left Payne's suite. He headed toward the elevator, briefcase in hand, a defeated man.

Chapter 34:   Washington, D.C.

Chad Davis's Hotel Room

Davis inserted his card key into his hotel room's door. A red light blinked slowly on the lock. He tried again. Same result. *What the?* On the third try the lock released. *Finally!* He turned the handle and pushed open the door. His luggage was sitting inside, near the door, but he didn't notice. He didn't care. The door shut behind him as he stared blankly into the room, and dropped the briefcase to the floor. He was numb. Chris Payne had just taken everything he cared about away from him. His thoughts turned to Amanda; he had spent their entire marriage letting her down, a series of disappointments, of dinners alone, of suffering. And this was her reward? Kidnapped? Held hostage by some deranged psychopath? He thought about Elizabeth. He was ashamed to admit it, but he hardly knew her anymore. She was growing up so fast. She was so young and innocent, and there was a chance she would never reach her teens if he made the wrong decision. He thought about her with Danko. His right hand balled into a fist, and his arm started to tremble uncontrollably with anger. *If he touches her, if he even looks at her, I'll kill him!*

In one fluid motion, Davis cocked back his arm and punched the wall, hard. A small indentation appeared in the middle of the otherwise pristine wall and a droplet of blood eased down the side of his hand between his thumb and index finger, but he didn't notice. He didn't even feel the pain. He picked up his briefcase from the floor, walked toward the desk and sat down in the chair. He felt powerless; Chris Payne held all the cards. There was no other choice, he had to walk into that Congressional committee tomorrow and give the green light to Advice's software, a system to help select the most powerful man in the world; a man who would be Payne's puppet. *But how are they doing it?* Davis thought. He'd studied that software for months and found nothing; no back doors; no security problems; no way to tamper. He thought about the people that would have to be involved if the votes themselves were tampered with before they were counted by the server. It would have to be dozens of people, each holding some official role in the election process; there was no way Payne could get to all of them. *How the hell is he going to manipulate the vote?*

Davis tried to reason out their plan. Mezonic was a good idea to garner support for Senator Shift but there wasn't enough time before tomorrow's primary, and there were only so many people that could be influenced by Mezonic's chip. *There must be some back door in the e-vote software. Why else would Payne be so obsessed with getting it approved?* So many had been hurt or killed to make this happen. His thoughts turned to Hans, and Amanda and Elizabeth; all victims of Payne's madness. He thought of Baff and after a brief moment of silence stood up suddenly, like he had an explosion go off in his head.

Somebody did know about the flaw! Baff! Davis opened his briefcase and pulled out his laptop. The machine came to life and the CD drive began to whirl.

"Come on Baff, talk to me." Davis watched as the machine booted. He looked over the files that now sat on his hard drive from Baff's CD. There was one mystery still left to uncover: what was in the last encrypted file, encrypted2.dat? He had already gone through trying to use Baff's original decryptor.exe on it with no success. It was obvious that this was something different.

He opened it up in a hex editor.

encrypted2.dat in a Hex Editor

```
WinHex - [encrypted2.dat]
File  Edit  Search  Position  View  Tools  Specialist  Options  File Manager  Window  Help

encrypted2.dat

Offset      0  1  2  3   4  5  6  7    8  9  10 11  12 13 14 15
00000000   F2 BE C2 3F  42 7B 70 6F   23 79 68 75  76 6C 72 71   ⊡¾Â?B{po#yhuvlrq
00000016   40 25 34 31  33 25 23 68   71 66 72 67  6C 71 6A 40   @%413%#hqfrglqj@
00000032   25 78 77 69  30 3B 25 42   41 10 0D 3F  79 72 77 68   %xwi0;%BA..?yrwh
00000048   41 10 0D 23  23 3F 76 77   64 77 68 41  5A 64 76 6B   A..##?vwdwhAZdvk
00000064   6C 71 6A 77  72 71 3F 32   76 77 64 77  68 41 10 0D   lqjwrq?2vwdwhA..
00000080   23 23 3F 73  64 75 77 7C   41 44 70 68  75 6C 66 64   ##?sduw|ADphulfd
00000096   71 3F 32 73  64 75 77 7C   41 10 0D 23  23 3F 66 72   q?2sduw|A..##?fr
00000112   78 71 77 7C  41 3F 32 66   72 78 71 77  7C 41 10 0D   xqw|A?2frxqw|A..
00000128   23 23 3F 73  75 68 66 6C   71 66 77 41  3F 32 73 75   ##?suhflqfwA?2su
00000144   68 66 6C 71  66 77 41 10   0D 23 23 3F  66 64 71 67   hflqfwA..##?fdqg
00000160   6C 67 64 77  68 41 5D 28   23 55 68 38  37 6F 82 82   lgdwhA](#Uh87o⊡⊡
00000176   3B 78 7C 7A  43 26 3A 3C   6D 6B 23 6F  72 74 7A 81   ;x|zC&:<mk#ortz⊡
00000192   43 26 67 3F  32 66 64 71   67 6C 67 64  77 68 41 10   C&g?2fdqglgdwhA.
00000208   0D 3F 32 79  72 77 68 41                              .?2yrwhA
```
Page 1 of 1   Offset: 0   = 242   Block: n/a Size: n/a

He noticed that the encrypted characters were very different from those in the last file. There were more patterns here and there was a much smaller set of characters. The repetitiveness led Davis to infer that the encryption scheme was pretty basic. *It looks like a simple substitution cipher.*

Substitution ciphers were among the easiest forms of encryption to crack. Each occurrence of a character in the plaintext (unencrypted document) is replaced with exactly one and only one other character. This meant that the word 'beer,' for instance, would look like 'cvvt' or 'fjja' or some other pattern, but the two characters in the middle would always be the same.

The easiest way to crack a substitution cipher was through frequency analysis: compare the frequency of occurrences of a particular character in the encrypted document with the average frequency with which that letter occurred in the English language. The method was simple and effective but it also made the assumption that the encrypted file was text. This was almost certainly not the case. Based on the results of the last encrypted file, Davis figured that it was either some type of executable, or possibly, a formatted file of some sort. Frequency analysis would probably be a waste of time.

Baff must have left me something, some clue.

Davis again opened the second text file that Baff had left for him:

```
Mr. Davis, there is a flaw in the software that your country is about to
use in its Presidential election of MMIV. This flaw, I believe, was
created on purpose.


I believe that there are people who know what I have discovered. If this
is true, you must bring these things to light.


I warn you, these are powerful people who have been giving me visions,
manipulating my very mind and yours. Do not give these files to anyone, I
fear what may happen if some of my associates gain access to them.


I cannot say more here, the risk is still too great. Do not try and
contact me. I will lay underground for some time. It is the safest thing
for me and you until this matter is resolved.


B.L.
```

Davis stared intently at the screen. *There's got to be something I'm missing here.* When he and Hans had first read the letter it seemed like the ramblings of someone in a mental institution. "Visions" and mind manipulation just seemed too far-fetched to be credible. Chad now knew differently. God knows how long Mezonic had been playing with peoples' minds. He continued to browse through the letter. There was something he noticed that had also struck him as odd during their first reading, the line "Presidential election of MMIV." When he had first seen it he didn't give it much thought, but now it seemed particularly odd. *MMIV is the Roman numeral for 2004, why the hell didn't the guy just write 2004? Could it have some other meaning?*

Davis sat with his hands holding his head. This was a puzzle that had to be solved. He had nothing else, no other place to focus his attention.

Roman numerals?

Roman numerals?

"Roman numerals!" he exclaimed out loud. Suddenly it hit him; Baff's final message had been revealed. Davis thought back to his cryptography classes and one of the first known implementations of cryptography. The Roman emperor Julius Caesar would encrypt secret communications using a very simple substitution cipher now known as the Caesar Cipher. It was possibly the simplest and most well-known encryption algorithm in history. Davis couldn't believe he didn't make the connection earlier!

The premise of the Caesar Cipher was incredibly simple: replace each letter with the letter three characters ahead in the alphabet. So, A was replaced by D, B was replaced by E, and so on. If Davis was right and the file was encrypted with a Caesar Cipher, all he would have to do is subtract three from the ASCII value of each character in the file. Doing it by hand would take too long. He quickly opened a new text file and began to write a program in C to do it for him:

```c
//This program decrypts a file that has been encrypted
//using the Caesar cipher.

#include <stdio.h>
#include "sys\stat.h"

int main()
{
        int data, output;
        long long int count=0;
        struct stat statbuf;
        char enc_file[260], dec_file[260];
        FILE * sourcefile;
        FILE * destfile;

        printf("\nEncrypted file path: ");
        scanf("%s", enc_file);
```

```c
printf("\nOutput file path: ");
scanf("%s", dec_file);

/* get the size of the source file */
if ((sourcefile = fopen(enc_file, "rb"))== NULL)
{
    printf("\nCan't open encrypted file %s.\n", enc_file);
    return(4);
}


fflush(sourcefile);
fstat(fileno(sourcefile), &statbuf);
fclose(sourcefile);


/* open all the necessary files. */
if ((sourcefile = fopen(enc_file, "rb"))== NULL)
{
    printf("\nCan't open encrypted file %s.\n", enc_file);
    return(4);
}


if ((destfile=fopen(dec_file,"wb"))== NULL)
{
    printf("\nCan't open destination file %s.\n", dec_file);
    return(4);
}



/* Subtract 3 from every character and write the new characters*/
while (count < (statbuf.st_size))
{
    data=fgetc(sourcefile);
    output=(data-3);
    fputc(output,destfile);
    count++;
```

```
        }

        /* Close the files */
        fclose(sourcefile);
        fclose(destfile);

        return 0;

}
```

Davis compiled the program and ran it on the new encrypted file.

Program Run on the New Encrypted File

Seconds later he had the decrypted file. His first impulse was to open it in a hex editor.

File, Reopened in a Hex Editor

```
WinHex - [decrypted2.dat]
HEX File  Edit  Search  Position  View  Tools  Specialist  Options  File Manager  Window  Help

decrypted2.dat

Offset      0  1  2  3  4  5  6  7   8  9 10 11 12 13 14 15

00000000   EF BB BF 3C 3F 78 6D 6C  20 76 65 72 73 69 6F 6E   ï»¿<?xml version
00000016   3D 22 31 2E 30 22 20 65  6E 63 6F 64 69 6E 67 3D   ="1.0" encoding=
00000032   22 75 74 66 2D 38 22 3F  3E 0D 0A 3C 76 6F 74 65   "utf-8"?>..<vote
00000048   3E 0D 0A 20 20 3C 73 74  61 74 65 3E 57 61 73 68   >.. <state>Wash
00000064   69 6E 67 74 6F 6E 3C 2F  73 74 61 74 65 3E 0D 0A   ington</state>..
00000080   20 20 3C 70 61 72 74 79  3E 41 6D 65 72 69 63 61     <party>America
00000096   6E 3C 2F 70 61 72 74 79  3E 0D 0A 20 20 3C 63 6F   n</party>..  <co
00000112   75 6E 74 79 3E 3C 2F 63  6F 75 6E 74 79 3E 0D 0A   unty></county>..
00000128   20 20 3C 70 72 65 63 69  6E 63 74 3E 3C 2F 70 72     <precinct></pr
00000144   65 63 69 6E 63 74 3E 0D  0A 20 20 3C 63 61 6E 64   ecinct>..  <cand
00000160   69 64 61 74 65 3E 5A 25  20 52 65 35 34 6C 7F 7F   idate>Z% Re54l■■
00000176   38 75 79 77 40 23 37 39  6A 68 20 6C 6F 71 77 7E   8uyw@#79jh loqw~
00000192   40 23 64 3C 2F 63 61 6E  64 69 64 61 74 65 3E 0D   @#d</candidate>.
00000208   0A 3C 2F 76 6F 74 65 3E                            .</vote>

Page 1 of 1          Offset:        0      = 239  Block:              n/a  Size:          n/a
```

He looked at it and immediately recognized the format. "It's an e-vote!" he said out loud. Davis had worked with Advice's electronic vote format for months, he knew it by heart.

The format itself was quite simple, it was text based and stored as an XML file that was then interpreted and displayed in Advice's program. When the file was stored, it contained no personally identifiable information about the voter. The voter would make their candidate selection from within the voting program and the application would then encrypt the name of the candidate selected. The vote would then be uploaded to the submissions server through a secure web site.

The precautions were taken so that if someone were to intercept the stored vote they could not trace it back to the voter nor could the candidate voted for be deciphered. Davis loaded the vote file in Internet Explorer to better inspect its contents.

Vote File in Internet Explorer

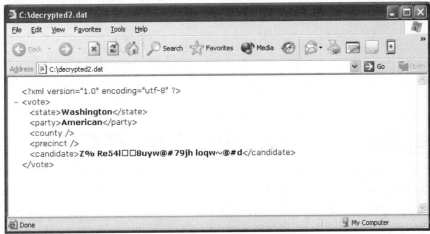

Nothing out of the ordinary. Davis was perplexed. The vote looked like hundreds he had seen before. *There must be something here. Baff had to have a reason to send this to me.*

Davis closed the browser and ran the counting server component. He selected the "acquire vote" menu item. A screen popped up asking him to fill in various options related to how the vote would be counted. He filled in the appropriate options, requesting the software to process the single vote file he had just looked at.

Davis fell back into the chair as he read the results.

Baff's vote had apparently done something that he and countless other experts had reported as impossible. He couldn't fathom the implications.

Baff had voted for himself; an outcome that was certainly possible given that the voter could enter a write-in candidate name. What was shocking, though, was the *number* of votes recorded.

The single file that represented one vote had caused the system to register 12.3 million votes for Bartholomew Lexicon. Baff had figured out that *they* had the power to swing the vote by 1 or 12 million, whatever they needed. *Considering all of the subconscious promotions for Shift, I doubt they would need to swing that many.*

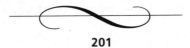

Chapter 35:   Washington, D.C.

Chad Davis's Hotel Room

Chad Davis lay in bed staring at the red luminescent numbers of the alarm clock sitting on the hotel room nightstand. 6:59 A.M. He had been watching the clock since 4:30 that morning when he had finally laid down. There was no hope of sleep. His testimony was slated for 9:30 A.M., and he still had no idea what he was going to do. Amanda and Elizabeth never left his mind. Where were they? Were they really safe? Would he ever see them again?

The clock flickered as the numbers changed to 7:00 A.M. The alarm began to sound but he was oblivious to it. His mind was somewhere else, far away, safe at his home with his wife and daughter. *How could I let this happen?*

Davis became aware of the blaring clock and immediately reached to silence it. He moved slowly to a seated position on the bed. He had spent hours working on Baff's file, trying to understand why it did what it did. He couldn't believe that he had missed it in his own analysis. Baff had found a buffer overflow in the counting server, one so subtle and insidious that Payne's company would have easily passed it off as a coding error; one that thousands of programmers make. It would be impossible to prove that Payne had knowledge of the flaw if it was discovered; complete deniability. The flaw, however, gave him ultimate power over the election. He could control the outcome of the absentee ballots, and with a close election, ultimately control who would get a party's nomination.

If the system went national as planned he would control who the next president was. After Davis's testimony, it would be a near guarantee.

He stood and walked slowly toward the bathroom, and reached for the hanger with his suit that he had tossed into his bag several hours earlier. He looked in the mirror and barely recognized his reflection; his face was drawn and pale, his eyes evidence to the previous night's insomnia. He sunk to the floor and sat up against the bathroom cabinets with his elbows balanced on his knees and his head in his hands.

He was about to make the most important decision of his life.

Chapter 36: Washington, D.C.

Chris Payne's Suite

The older you get, the better prepared you are for it: the death of a loved one. It's a rite of passage for any man or woman. For any human. Chris Payne started preparing in his early twenties. Every night, as he lay in bed praying for peaceful dreams and a good night's rest, he would think of that moment. He thought of what he would say. What he would do. What he would feel. And as he lay there, he would ask himself those questions in a soft whisper so that he wouldn't wake his wife.

He thought about where he would be when that moment arrived. When someone would call and tell him his father, who had been ailing in the past few years, had died. Maybe he would be at home, the phone would ring and he would notice that the house was eerily still—nothing moving—everything was extraordinarily quiet. He would pick up the phone and feel the sadness before any voice delivered the news.

Or maybe he would be at work. And as the phone rang all the commotion and conversations around him would phase out as he reached to answer in his usual business manner. And he would say nothing, just listening to the voice on the other end filling his heart with pain.

Maybe he would be there in person. He could barely imagine that. He feared this scenario the most. *There is nothing more horrible. How could you hold your dying father in your arms without dying inside?*

Chris was wrong, though. The phone call he received was regrettably different. It felt just like he thought it would, all those nights preparing for it. As he reached for the phone at work that day, he didn't even remember saying anything. Somehow he knew it was the call he had dreaded his entire life.

Only it was his father's voice on the other end, "Your brother is dead."

He was prepared for his father's death. He assumed that he would outlive him, but there was no accepting the death of his younger brother; not even from a terminal sickness like cancer or a heart attack. To hear that he died so horribly, so meaninglessly from a terrorist attack made it infinitely more painful, and even more, so unacceptable.

Those bastards are going to pay!

It was during the 2001 holiday season when Chris Payne met Steve Watts at a New York City fundraiser for the families that had lost loved ones at the World Trade Center disaster. They hit it off after only a couple of minutes of conversation, and it was during this first meeting that both decided to make a change in their lives for the good of the American people.

Although details were not discussed, both men understood each other. Their passion and dedication said it all. Steve was excited and just as committed as Chris was about righting the wrong.

"We can never forget why we are here, the monsters who brought this suffering into our lives," Steve said.

"We won't," replied Chris lowering his voice, "believe me, we won't."

A month later Chris Payne and Steve Watts met for the second time, now with a new purpose and under a new name. They had founded *Patriotic Americans for Change*, a nonprofit organization whose sole purpose was to help direct victims of the World Trade Center attacks by creating a children's college fund and further education and job placement resources for surviving mothers or fathers who now had to work double time to put food on the table. *Patriotic Americans for Change* was a 501(c) organization under Internal Revenue Service (IRS) guidelines. Although more politically motivated organizations such as *Moveon* were classified as chapter 527s by the IRS, Chris Payne decided to classify *Patriotic Americans for Change* as a 501(c) organization for good reasons.

Although both chapter 527 and 501(c) organizations can raise money for political activities, Payne knew that 501(c)s had some key advantages. Organizations such as *Moveon* state upfront that their purpose is to run ad campaigns to help influence the election of one candidate or another. Additionally, chapter 527 organizations must disclose their spending quarterly. Chapter 501(c) organizations do not have to reveal how much money they spend until well after an election, and they do not have to reveal who their donors are. Although 501(c)s do run political ads, they operate under the caveat that these ads address specific issues relevant to their cause and are not meant to influence the election for any individual; a subject of much controversy and interpretation.

A chapter 501(c) organization like the National Rifle Association (NRA) could run an ad campaign on gun control, for example, but could not endorse a specific candidate that supported their interests. Although it is obvious what the NRA's agenda and interests are, Chris Payne's *Patriotic Americans for Change* motives were less transparent. They had a much broader and more hostile agenda, and that agenda was about to be fully realized.

It was a cool morning in the District of Columbia, and even though five floors below him Davis was lying awake, Chris Payne was just getting out of bed in his penthouse suite. Breakfast was ready, brought up minutes earlier by room service and now delivered by his butler. After rinsing off his face and giving his reflection a triumphant smile, he walked out of the bathroom and sat down to eat.

We finally made it.

Chris thought back to the first few days of *Patriotic Americans for Change*. He thought of his brother. He thought back to that horrible day and about how close they now were to getting justice. *David would be proud.*

As he slowly ate his breakfast, thoughts of a brighter future filled his mind. With Senator Shift in power Chris Payne was ready to build his nation's empire and then exact his revenge. He knew gaining national control would take time. Slowly, but surely, Advice's voting systems would spread to other states after the Washington Primary proved it successful. Before the next Presidential election he would have in power select politicians in all the right places with very little resistance—after all, the *people* voted them in. They would then push for adoption of Advice's e-vote system not just for use in absentee ballots but also for use in the general election. Advice's software then would be able to sway the votes as needed and still not raise any red flags when voter audits were performed. *The beauty of no paper trail.*

With the national elections under Advice's—or more accurately Chris's—control he then would initiate his plan to avenge the attacks that took his brother and so many other innocent lives. The Middle East would pay. He would fight fire with fire. He would rally the nation to expand its war in the Middle East. The potential was unimaginable.

Chris sipped on his now lukewarm coffee as he stared out of one of his suite's expansive windows. The view of Washington, D.C. was exquisite. Morning traffic was beginning to thicken. In the distance, the Arlington National Cemetery seemed almost surreal. He picked up the newspaper that his butler had brought in. The front headlines were typical—the Iraq war, European news, Presidential news, and among others, a story on today's primary and the congressional meeting on electronic voting. The story went on to promote the e-vote that both Chris Payne and Chad Davis would cast outside of Congress after the testimony *if* it gained approval. He noted the article quoting him saying that he was "confident the analysis and research would show just how reliable and secure their electronic voting system truly is."

He rose and headed for his bedroom, deciding to make a quick phone call before his shower.

"Good morning Mr. Danko."

Danko was awake but not known to be a morning person. He replied, "Yes. Good morning."

"I'm sure you took care of Dr. Davis last night, making sure he went directly to his room and stayed there without making any unwanted phone calls."

"Of course Mr. Payne, I would not have done otherwise."

"I'd like for you to keep an eye on him until we make it to Congress."

"Fine, Mr. Payne. What should I do with his wife and daughter? I cannot bring them together."

"I understand," replied Chris, "have Luis escort them. I need you on Davis."

"Ok, I will watch Davis. Do not worry, if he even thinks of making a wrong move, his wife and daughter will suffer."

Chapter 37: Washington, D.C.

U.S. Congress: Waiting Room

Chad Davis sat alone. The waiting room had a few chairs and a couple of tables, but was otherwise bare. A small buffet table hosted two coffee pots, glass mugs, silverware, and the usual coffee and tea condiments. There was no food in sight and Davis thought it for the best. His stomach was in no condition to hold anything. Maybe a glass of whiskey, or a bottle of it, would help soothe his nerves. *I'm sure someone's got some.*

Last night was still a blur. It was too surreal for him to even begin to question if it really happened or not. The one thing he was certain of was that in a few minutes he would testify. In those few minutes he would have to determine how his testimony, his decision, his reality, would affect not only the U.S. Presidential election, but more important to him, his ex-wife Amanda and their daughter Elizabeth.

He could easily walk in and keep his game face on. Smile when need be. Be serious when required. He could tell the committee what they needed to hear, answer their questions with just enough insight to pacify their concerns, and walk out of the room without anyone knowing the difference. *But would they let Amanda and Elizabeth go? No bad guy ever plans to release the hostages…they always kill them, no matter what happens.* His paranoia overtook him. *Does it really matter what I say? Will Chris let them go? He's already had Hans killed.*

He picked up his palms from the table and noticed their sweaty outline on the imitation wood top. He got up and grabbed a napkin from the coffee bar, wiping his hands and forehead.

"Okay," he spoke to himself quietly, "If I tell the truth will they believe me? Who the hell is Baff to them? That doesn't matter, I have the file. I could very easily have written that file, show it as an example during my testimony and claim Advice's system is corrupt. They could easily claim I made it up because I wanted money or I didn't like them or something."

He paced back and forth in the small room, turning continuously. With one hand in his pocket and the other rubbing his head he continued to think aloud. *What if I just tell them I think that the whole idea of electronic voting is dangerous? They'll just ask me for my evaluation of Advice's system. They'd say: 'This isn't a general overview. It's a detailed evaluation.'*

He sat back down, leaned back uncomfortably in the chair, and rubbed his face with his hands hoping to refresh himself. He then dropped both elbows on the table and began to rub his neck, *What if I let the testimony go as planned? All is well. The software is okay except, of course, for a few minor glitches. Nothing that can't be fixed in time. Nothing that can't be certified. And then what if…?*

He was silent. His eyes gazed off in the distance as he contemplated his actions. *What if?* Davis was in such serious thought that he would have been oblivious to anyone entering the room. In that silence he formulated his plan. How he would execute it was still a little unclear to him. Whether or not it would work was also a chance he would have to take. *It's my best bet.*

A knock brought him back to cold reality. A woman opened the door and peaked inside, "Dr. Davis?"

"Yes?" he replied.

"We're ready to begin."

"Okay, thanks. I'll be right there."

Davis rose from his seat and collected his papers, placing them back in his carry-on. He looked down and gathered his thoughts one last time before stepping out from the waiting room's peacefulness.

As he neared the door his heart began to beat faster, his stomach fluttered. There was nothing but nauseating discomfort running throughout his body. The hallway was busy; reporters, men and women in business attire, and the rare casually dressed spectator.

As he stepped out into the hallway he thought, *for Elizabeth*.

Chapter 38: Washington, D.C.

U.S. Congress

"When do we get to see dad?"

Elizabeth was anxious. She had woken up later than usual for a Monday morning. Her typical routine meant waking up at 5:30, showering, and preparing for school, but today had been completely different. Today, she and her mother had awakened in a strange room, escorted by strange men that wouldn't let her see her father.

"Elizabeth, we'll see him after his speech. We'll just have to wait till he's done."

"Okay, mom. So are we sight-seeing afterward? I think I'd rather just go home."

Amanda smiled sadly, "Let's just wait for your father and we'll see how much time we'll have here. I want to go home too, honey."

"Please follow me," said Luis, their escort. He walked close to Amanda and Elizabeth as they entered the building that would hold the Congressional hearing, and sat them just outside the hearing room where the testimony would take place.

Chris Payne approached. He was dressed in a dark, tailored suit, polished shoes, a clean shave, and perfect hair, not a strand out of place. He neared their bench and sat next to them, acknowledging Luis. He smiled, "Good morning ladies. How are we this morning?"

Amanda replied coolly, "How do you think we are?"

"You're in good hands with Luis," continued Chris, pointing to the hearing room just across the hallway. "I'll be inside, seated near your husband. Trust me, if Chad is as smart as we believe him to be, this will all be over soon. I know both he and I look forward to seeing you at the vote after the testimony."

Amanda did not speak. She held Elizabeth's hand and clenched the bench with the other. Chris stood and walked through the open doors toward his table. They could see him greet a small group of distinguished-looking men Amanda took to be Senators. She looked back at Elizabeth and noticed her anxiousness, "It's gonna start pretty soon sweetheart."

As she spoke, a door down the hallway opened. Davis walked out with a look of concerned nervousness accompanying his disheveled appearance. It seemed like a lifetime before he walked up to them. He spotted them immediately and stopped to lean down and kiss Elizabeth. He looked over at Amanda who peered at him silently, before he reached to hug her for the first time in over a year.

"Don't worry. We'll be ok. I'll make this up to you, I swear."

With her head against his shoulder Amanda nodded. She pulled away and calmly said, "Good luck with your testimony. We'll be waiting."

She turned to Elizabeth who was smiling at her father, and squeezed her hand.

Davis stood straight and fixed his eyes on the door. The sign read, "Room SH–216." He stepped into the room, the doors closing behind him, and walked toward the table facing the committee. He immediately turned his attention to the lone man sitting at a table next to his, Chris Payne. *That son of a bitch.* He slowly made his way to his table, quietly greeting members of the press and representatives he knew.

A voice from behind interrupted him before he was about to take his seat, "Dr. Davis, is everything alright? I got your message last night and tried to call." He turned to see Grace Wilkinson standing in front of him with a look of concern. He wanted to tell her everything, but he knew she couldn't help him now; nobody could.

"Sorry about that, Grace, I was just calling to confirm which room the proceedings were going to be held in today. I can be so absent-minded sometimes. I hope I didn't disturb you?"

"Why…no, not at all. I see you've found your way."

"I have, thank you."

"Well, I wish you the best of luck today, Dr. Davis. We've made it this far!"

"Thank you, Grace." She smiled again, though eyed him carefully before making her way to her seat.

He set his briefcase down and turned to look at Payne.

"Dr. Davis," Payne said with a smile, "long time, no see."

"Mr. Payne," he replied coolly, ignoring the hand Payne had extended.

"How was your flight?"

"A bit bumpy but I made it."

Although the attendee court was small, the room was filling up quickly. Around them Senators, members of Congress, reporters, photographers, and others had created a buzz. Davis and Payne spoke almost like they were in a protective bubble, impervious to the sounds and people surrounding them.

Payne calmly said, "This is a monumental day in your career, Dr. Davis."

Davis remained silent. Rage had again overcome him.

Payne continued diplomatically, "Your report is excellent, Dr. Davis. I read through it last night. I think we can address your concerns and have a certified system by November."

"Of course, Mr. Payne. We wouldn't want it any other way," Davis replied through gritted teeth.

"I'm looking forward to today's testimony and Q&A. I think it's imperative that we educate our government on our ever-improving technology. We are creating history today, Dr. Davis. I am glad to see that your family came out to be part of this."

Can I just hit this bastard? What if I just called a guard over, told them every-thing? Would Amanda and Elizabeth be safe? Would there be repercussions? Chad had never hit anyone. He had never even thrown a punch at a bag. He peered into Payne's eyes, knowing exactly how his family ended up with him.

"I'm delighted to have them here, Mr. Payne. And I look forward to spending time with them afterward," Davis replied loudly so that those around him could hear.

"Let's get through the testimony first."

Davis nodded. He reached for his briefcase, pulled out his laptop and grabbed some papers he had been scribbling on.

A loud voice exclaimed, "Ladies and Gentlemen…"

It's time thought Davis.

Chapter 39: Washington, D.C.

U.S. Congress

The Chairman, Honorable Joshua Fielding, opened the testimony, "This hearing of the Congressional Elections Committee is called to order. Present with us today are Representatives Adam Milkien, John Brown, Beatrice Harris, and Alan Kingsworth. Also in attendance are: Ms. Grace Wilkinson, Voting Systems Director of the Federal Election Commission and Mr. Sam Eliot Mann, Chairman of the Center for Elections. Testifying before us today are Dr. Chad Davis, Professor of Computer Science at the University of Washington, and Mr. Chris Payne, President and CEO of Advice Software, Inc."

The Chairman paused for a second and looked around him. Chris Payne and Chad Davis were listening intently while the committee members fumbled through their papers, preparing for their opening statements. This was their daily routine; sitting in meetings, making nation-sweeping decisions as a matter of practice. For Davis this was not only a new experience, but one that held his family's life and the fate of the nation in the balance.

The room was smaller than Davis had expected. It held two small tables where he and Payne sat, each with a free-standing microphone. Facing the tables was a much longer table raised on a platform in front of a row of seats where the committee sat, each with a microphone in front of them. Just like in courtrooms, a stenographer was seated off to the side and had begun to type the Chairman's call to order.

The Chairman continued with his opening statement, "Today, the Congressional Elections Committee will receive testimony on the evaluation of Advice Software's electronic voting system by Dr. Chad Davis, Professor of Computer Science at the University of Washington and world-renowned software security expert. The 2000 U.S. Presidential election brought to light the vulnerabilities and limitations of our current voting systems. It also raised more general election system issues that transcend the voting systems themselves, such as the training of election precinct staff and the role of election system manufacturers and their adherence to the Federal Election Commission's standards, as well as state voting system standards. Before we begin with today's testimony and before I call upon Ms. Wilkinson for her opening statement, I want to provide some background on how we have arrived at today's proceedings. As you are all aware, the state of Florida ultimately decided—or more appropriately, ultimately became the deciding state—for who the 43rd President of the United States of America would be. Among all the hanging chads, overvotes, undervotes, no votes, and the controversial list of felons that would not be permitted to vote, we did our best to resolve the matter as quickly and accurately as possible and announce to the American people and to the world our new President.

"The limitations of the punch card voting system, which I will let Ms. Wilkinson describe in more detail, led our government at the local, state, and federal levels to initiate a search for a better way to hold elections. This initiative began in April of 2001, when this committee and representatives from the Federal Election Commission and the Center for Elections met to discuss our approach to researching, selecting, evaluating, and implementing an improved voting system. Specifically, today we are meeting on the absentee voting process and its move to a more efficient computerized system. After careful research by a number of software, security, and election experts we narrowed our selection from a total of four manufacturers and six voting systems to the voting system and supplier we have with us today, Advice Software.

"I think it is imperative that we all understand the importance of why we are here today. There has been much talk and discussion—from sensationalistic media to respected scientific and legal analysts—on the 2000 U.S. Presidential election and the right of every eligible American citizen to have their vote counted anonymously and accurately. Needless to say we cannot address every open issue or question today about voting systems or voting in general. Our purpose here today is specifically the evaluation of Advice Software's e-Vote system.

"And with that I want to let our speakers, Dr. Davis and Mr. Payne, know that we will be as critical as possible during this testimony. Your expert analysis, experience, and dedicated work is why you are here today gentlemen. I would now like to call upon Congressman Alan Kingsworth, and hear his opening statement."

Alan looked at the Chairman, acknowledging his invitation to the microphone. He then looked across to Chad Davis and Chris Payne facing himself and the committee. Chris offered an abbreviated, almost covert smirk. Alan's lips rolled inward as he ever so slightly nodded at Chris. He looked down at the papers in front of him and began his opening remarks.

"Thank you Mr. Chairman. First and foremost, it is my honor to be a part of this committee and I appreciate all the hard work my fellow members, Ms. Wilkinson, and Mr. Mann have devoted to our cause. Without a doubt the secure, accurate, and anonymous tabulation of votes for local, state, and national elections is of the utmost importance when considering any voting system, not just that of Advice Software. I think that fact alone speaks volumes for Mr. Payne, his company, and his highly skilled staff. They have worked extremely hard to develop this e-voting system and have worked diligently with us—the committee—to help us better understand how such systems work. Additionally they have worked closely with Dr. Davis, Independent Testing Authorities, the Federal Election Commission, and the Center for Elections. I think Advice Software has demonstrated their commitment to this project as well as their openness to continuous product improvement based on outside evaluations and recommendations.

"Like you mentioned, Chairman Fielding, this committee is here today to address this specific e-vote system and its nationwide implementation for the 2004 U.S. Presidential election. I just want to remind everyone that we as citizens of the greatest country in the world have a duty not only to our government but to the great people of this country. I don't believe the United States is considered a great nation because of wealth or big cars, or big homes, or of all the conveniences some say we have spoiled ourselves with. We are a great nation because this republic has given its citizens the power to elect their government and they also have the ability to remove from power those elected officials that the people have deemed unable to perform. It is this privilege that we have, to vote democratically, that defines us, and I for one look forward to improving the process to better meet the needs of the people. And with that I would like to call upon Ms. Grace Wilkinson for her opening statement."

Grace was listening to Alan as he finished his statement. Alan had been behind the move to electronic voting from the beginning. He passionately spoke at several of the closed door meetings about Advice's software and Grace could sense his tone of satisfaction as they pushed through this final hurdle toward its implementation. She was ready to begin her speech, feeling much more confident after her conversation with Davis in the hall.

"Thank you Mr. Kingsworth, and thank you for your inspiring remarks. As Voting Systems Director at the Federal Election Commission my job for the past three years has been very clear: evaluate an electronic voting system for implementation in 2004. We have all worked hard over these past three years. I understand the manufacturers—not just the one we have here today—but all companies and their products we have diligently poured over have dedicated an enormous amount of time to developing these systems.

"I want to begin by reviewing what criteria we look for in any voting system and then I will turn the floor over to Dr. Chad Davis. A voting system should allow a voter to anonymously select his or her candidates of choice from an easily comprehensible ballot. After the voter has completed his or her selections, the ballot is submitted to the precinct for tabulation and storage. Vote tabulation can be performed at the precinct or at a central location where the voting system shall count the votes accurately and again anonymously. The votes are then stored either physically or electronically for future reference or recounting. Before I go any further with today's topic I also would like to talk a little bit about what happened in Florida in 2000. The punch card systems as we've come to find out are flawed. The real shame here is that those problems have been around for almost four decades. The ballot itself cannot be accurately interpreted by human eyes when a manual recount is called for. What I mean is that a voter may have attempted to vote for a candidate, but because of some mechanical malfunction or human error, the voter's intent was not clearly captured on the punch card ballot. This is what we have come to know as the infamous hanging, dimpled, and pregnant chads. We must make sure that voter intent is as close to 100 percent clear as possible, not only when votes are machine-counted but also when they are hand-counted. When we began our evaluations of a number of different systems from a number of different manufacturers these upper-level criteria such as voter privacy, easy of use, and ballot count and recount accuracy were our roadmap for selecting a system. Our task was to determine which voting system or systems best filled these roles.

"This is where outside analysis was solicited. We had experts in numerous fields evaluate each system and make their recommendations. Today we ultimately are discussing the issue of Advice Software's e-Vote system and its security and operation. Having worked with Dr. Davis now for the past year it has been a pleasure to be able to get a glimpse into what he does, how he does it, and how great Dr. Davis is at explaining such complicated technical jargon to individuals like myself. I think I speak for most of us here today when I say we are laymen or women when it comes to the degree of technical detail that Dr. Davis has evaluated the voting systems. Dr. Davis, I ask you to please not restrict yourself when explaining such matters and allow us to interrupt you when necessary for more simplified explanations. With that, Dr. Davis, the floor is yours."

A silence fell upon the room. Davis nodded and stared down, first at his papers and then over at his laptop that was now powered up. Chris Payne watched him cautiously. This next speech would make or break his cause, his country's cause. Davis coughed to clear his throat, took a sip from the glass of water and began, "Thank you Ms. Wilkinson, Mr. Chairman, members of this committee, for allowing me to be a part of such an important assessment. I believe we are here today to decide how voting will be implemented in the United States, not only for our upcoming election, but for years to come. When I was asked to join this effort I was honored, and have since then devoted the majority of my time to evaluations, meetings, and the like regarding this matter. When I looked at the various electronic voting system candidates and their software, I considered the following four points:

"Number one, who is making the software and system? Are they a reputable company? Are they established in the field? Can they support the implementation for years to come?

"Number two, how easy is the software to use? How will I, as a voter, navigate through the voting screens and make my choices? Are the features easily discoverable? Is there ambiguity in their procedures?

"Number three, under what operating environment will the software run? This includes operating system and supporting software and hardware.

"Finally, number four, which is arguably the most pressing of all the criteria and where the majority of my work was focused: Can I find vulnerabilities, exploits, operating errors, software bugs, anything that may cause this software and system to operate outside of its intended parameters?

How will these—and I will use the word bugs generally here—how will these bugs affect a voter, the tallied votes, and ultimately the election at hand? What could an attacker do to this system in terms of exposing user information or tainting the election results?

"I have submitted my official analysis report on Advice Software's e-voting system and would ask that it be published in full for the record."

The Chairman interrupted, "Yes, Dr. Davis, we have received your report and we all have copies with us here today. Your report will be published in full barring any confidential information we feel should not be made public."

"Thank you Mr. Chairman," Davis continued, "I would like to take a couple of minutes just to summarize my findings and then we can move onto a Q&A session. Overall the research and analysis that my colleagues and I have performed show that the Advice Software e-Vote system is our best choice for implementing an electronic voting system today. Its ease of use, operation, and robustness clearly surpass any other system we have evaluated." He reached again for his glass of water, turning his head slightly in a fluid motion. He glimpsed Payne, whose face had maintained a perceptible smirk. *You arrogant son of a bitch,* Chad thought to himself. He continued to address the committee, "With that said, my report does point out a number of bugs, including a couple of critical run-time errors when a voter selects a specific set of choices. These are described in detail in my report and I would be happy to answer any questions about them during our Q&A.

"I would ask this Committee to carefully review and consider my report as well as the recommendations included regarding additions to the Federal Election Commission's electronic voting standards. It is important to note that each state is required to adopt these standards. The FEC has done a great job to foresee this technology and has created a set of standards that I believe are a reasonable start for electronic voting. In addition, State Election Departments have taken steps to produce their own voting system standards. My recommendations, I feel, will help steer those standards in the right direction. Again, thank you Mr. Chairman, and the committee for allowing me to be a part of this important process."

As Davis finished speaking, Payne nodded quietly in his seat, and looked over at him, realizing that his dreams, the society's cause was monumentally closer to fruition. There was a brief moment of silence as the members shuffled through their papers and laid out their lists of questions. The Chairman's microphone came to life with the sound of his papers rustling, "Thank you, Dr. Davis. We sincerely appreciate all your hard work regarding this matter. I will unanimously move this meeting into Q&A unless any other member has any additional comments."

He scanned the room and found none, "Thank you all. Dr. Davis, Mr. Payne, as you can imagine our expertise is not in software or electronic systems. We are here to oversee a due process by which we can select the best system for our country's needs. Mr. Payne, can you explain to us in some detail how your system works? How does one go from a computer program to an entire system that can record votes, store them, tabulate them, and determine a winner during an election?"

"I'd be happy to, Mr. Chairman. Let me begin, however, by thanking you, the committee, and Dr. Davis for your hard work and dedication on this issue. It has been my company's, and my personal, distinct pleasure to work with Ms. Wilkinson, Dr. Davis, and the others involved in narrowing the field. Our company has worked hard to create a system that we believe is ideally suited to serve the American people.

"To address your specific questions Mr. Chairman, I will first go through the voter registration procedure and then move on to how the election process itself works. Our pilot implementation was restricted to those persons eligible to vote in Washington state who would, for a variety of reasons, require the use of absentee ballots. Washington was chosen because it historically has one of the highest proportions of absentee voters in the nation and, of course, Advice Software's headquarters are located in Redmond. To participate in the absentee electronic voting program, an eligible voter must first register. For those many soldiers serving abroad in the military, this can be done completely electronically with the appropriate Military ID containing an integrated smart chip. For others, suitable citizenship and identification documents must be presented face-to-face to a trusted agent such as a military officer, embassy, or local election official. At the time of registration, the voter is provided with a 16-character passkey that they must then use when their vote is uploaded during their Internet voting session. Voters are then required to have a PC running the Microsoft Windows operating system, with either the Netscape Navigator or Internet Explorer web browser.

"The voting system itself is composed of three primary software entities. The first is a ballot application that registered voters are instructed to download from the official state elections web site; in the case of our pilot implementation, this application was available from the Washington State Election Board web site. The second is an Internet application, which the user interacts with to upload their votes to a central server. This second application is implemented as a separate web-based service and actually was developed and maintained by a third party under contract from the federal government. Once votes have been collected, the third software component, Advice's E-Count Server, collates and counts the votes. I would like to explain how each of these components work by walking this committee through the voting process of a typical user and then tracing that vote through acquisition, counting, and reporting. Before I continue, however, I would like to remind the committee that the web acquisition system was not produced by Advice and so I speak on it solely based on the design documents I was given. I understand that its use has been ratified by this committee?"

Grace Wilkinson jumped in, "Correct. Our focus today is Advice's components, but I would ask you to please outline the Internet vote acquisition system as well, especially as it relates to your software."

This was still a sore spot for Payne. Originally, Advice had proposed to build and implement the entire system, end-to-end. They would have complete control over how votes were created, delivered, and counted.

The committee, however, decided to separate the roles, fearing that too much would be under the control of a single company. This forced Payne to make some important changes to his plan. He *needed* control.

"Thank you for the clarification, Ms. Wilkinson. I'd like to continue then by considering the vote and voting experience of a typical but fictional voter. For discussion purposes, I will call this voter 'Joe.' Joe is a resident of Washington state and will be in Florida during the presidential primary election. He has submitted the appropriate identification and information to a local election official in Washington before leaving for Florida. Joe then received a card with a unique passcode and a web site to navigate to. In order to vote, Joe's first step is to download Advice's e-Vote application. Joe would then launch the application and be prompted with an absentee ballot very similar to the paper versions in use today. I would like to direct the committee's attention to Figure 3A of the Advice software proposal, which I believe you all have."

The committee shuffled through their papers and one by one found the figure Payne was referring to.

Figure 3A from Advice Proposal: Advice's e-Ballot Application

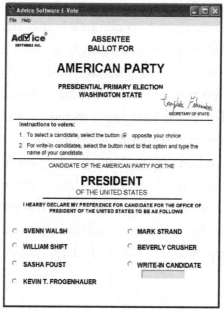

"Joe would then select the appropriate circle next to his candidate of choice. Alternatively, he can select the button associated with the write-in candidate option and then type the name of the desired candidate. Once Joe is finished he saves the file, which is stored as XML in the Advice VTE format. Again, I would like to refer you to the proposal, Figure 4B.

Figure 4B from Advice Proposal: Vote Saved in the Advice VTE Format

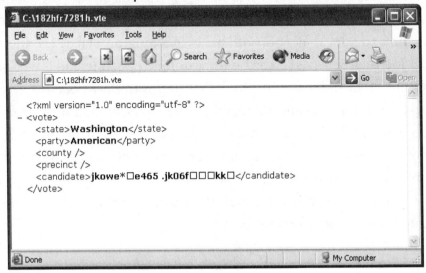

"Notice that the county and precinct elements are blank. This data is appended to the file when Joe submits his vote through the Vote Procurement Server, or VPS, web site. Also notice the candidate field contains what appears to be nonsensical data. This is actually an encrypted version of the candidate name that Joe selected on the ballot. The encryption is to ensure that even if someone were to intercept the vote and could infer that it belonged to Joe (because they found it on his hard drive, for example) they would still be unable to determine *who* he voted for. Once Joe saves his vote, he then logs on to the submission web site and enters the number he was issued that uniquely identifies him, along with his social security number and birth date. I'd like to refer the committee to Section 3 of the Advice Software Proposal titled Integration, where you will find Figures 19B and 19C."

Figure 19.B from Advice Proposal: Vote Procurement Server Web Site

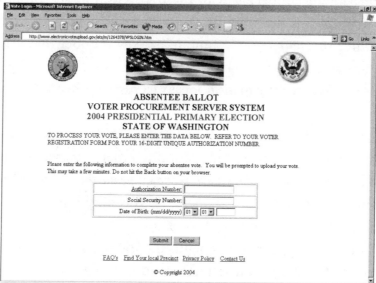

Figure 19.C from Advice Proposal: Continuation of Vote Procurement Server Web Site

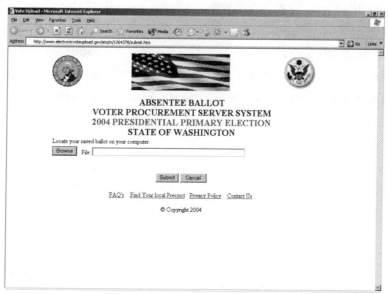

Payne continued, "The information being sent back and forth between Joe's computer and the submission server is encrypted using SSL, Secure Socket Layers; thus reducing the risk of anyone intercepting and deciphering or tampering with the transaction in any meaningful way. Joe then uploads the vote file through the VPS web site and submits his vote. Once this happens, the unique passkey number that was issued to Joe is now invalid and he cannot change his vote, nor can he or anyone else with that information log in to cast another vote. Joe's job is now done."

Payne reached forward to grab his glass of water to take a sip. He surveyed his audience. Several of the committee members seemed completely uninterested. *These guys have probably heard this 20 times already.* Payne didn't care, this was his moment; he was only hours away from the next critical step to realizing his dreams.

"The VPS web application appends the district and precinct information stored for Joe and no other information. Finally, the vote file is passed off to a central repository for counting through an encrypted connection.

"When the cutoff time for votes is reached, all of the vote files are retrieved by three computers at different locations manned by two individuals each. Each group then runs the Advice e-Count Server application on the locally stored vote files and the software produces a report. The server application is shown in Figure 7 of the proposal."

The committee again hurriedly turned pages to get to the figure Payne was referring to.

Figure 7 from Advice Proposal: Advice E-Count Server Interface

Payne continued, "The three reports are then printed and carried by hand to the Secretary of State who certifies that the totals match and records the official absentee electronic vote tallies. The redundancy exists so that a single person or group at one counting location cannot manipulate the software or the count. Figure 9B illustrates the process at a high level."

Figure 9B from Advice Proposal: Absentee Electronic Voting Process

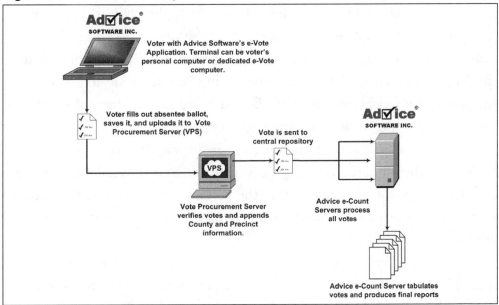

Payne paused as the committee members shuffled papers and glared at the figure. After a few moments, member Brown leaned forward to his microphone and began to speak, "Mr. Payne, does the system require identifying information from the voter in order to limit an individual to a single vote? If so, how do you preserve the voter's anonymity?"

After dealing with government officials for the past few years Payne was used to repeating himself. No matter how thoroughly he went through something there would always be someone who would ask him to repeat the very point he had just made.

"The Vote Procurement Server deals with limiting a single individual to a single vote by asking the voter for his or her unique passkey along with a series of other information before they are permitted to upload their vote. After the process is completed, the passkey is no longer valid; one and only one vote can be cast per passkey. Additionally, the system prevents against attackers randomly trying to guess the passkey of another voter—and thus vote on behalf of that individual—by monitoring the number of connections made to the server. Again, I cannot speak with authority on the VPS as it was designed by a third party. What I can speak to, however, is that once the vote is sent to the central repository for counting it has no personally identifiable information about the voter, only the voter's county, precinct, and selection. I have been assured that the VPS renames the files to a random string and keeps no log of which file was submitted by which voter. Also, files are deleted from the VPS once they are sent to the repository for counting."

The Chairman asked, "How different is the voting process compared to, let's say, the absentee voting process in place today? What I'm getting at is what does the elections staff at the precincts need in terms of information and education to operate and oversee these systems when they are implemented?"

"Well, Mr. Chairman, conceptually, this system is similar to the manual one in place now. Presently, citizens register to cast an absentee vote with proper ID and are given an absentee ballot. They complete the ballot and a form with their personal information—it's an affidavit saying that they are who they claim to be and they voted under their own will. The ballot is placed in an unmarked envelope and that envelope is placed in a larger envelope with their personal information form. This larger envelope is mailed into their precinct where an elections official opens it. The official first verifies the personal information form to ensure the voter indeed is registered in that precinct and is registered as an absentee voter. Finally, the official places the voter's absentee ballot, sealed in the envelope, in a ballot box where all absentee ballots are held until they are to be counted. The differences exist only in how these tasks are carried out. Filling in a vote is done by a click instead of with a pencil. Votes are submitted through the Internet instead of through the postal system. Counts are done by redundant machines instead of redundant humans. All the pieces are there. As for education, the system is highly automated. The Vote Procurement Server is manned around the clock during the voting window by both a trained system administrator and an election official. As for the operators of Advice's e-Count Server, a comprehensive user's manual was prepared and personnel must pass a hands-on exam on its use. Additionally, support personnel are on-site from Advice in the unlikely event that any issues arise. Our biggest challenge has been voter education. Voting using a computer significantly changes the user's voting experience. A great deal of effort has been put into awareness programs and educational pamphlets and software for voters. We have also set up a technical support hotline that users can call if they have any questions while submitting their vote online."

"Dr. Davis," asked member Kingsworth, "Can you go over in some detail the bugs that you discovered in the Advice Software e-Vote system? Also, what issues or bugs do you feel are most critical to overcome to achieve implementation?"

"Yes sir. My colleagues and I spent the first month of the evaluation process creating testing criteria on which to both examine and compare the various candidate voting systems. We spent the next several months executing these tests. Of the systems tested, Advice's product was judged as the most secure and robust. Like all software, though, it has bugs. The bugs that I and the other evaluators have unearthed in the system, however, are common to many applications. The client e-Vote application is relatively simple and we have found no significant issues. I was not personally involved in the testing of the Vote Procurement Server, but after reading the reports, I believe that all the open issues have been addressed. As for the Advice e-Count Server, my colleagues and I have found several reliability issues under resource deprivation fault-injection testing. The results were detailed in my report."

Davis again went for a sip of water. He turned his head toward Payne, who had a stern and severe look on his face as he discussed the bugs in Advice's software. He wanted Payne to suffer. *If it wasn't for Amanda and Elizabeth I'd spill the whole thing right now. Hans, Baff, Mezonic, Danko, all of it!* He took a sip from his glass and continued, "None of these flaws, however, should cast doubts on the results from the pilot implementation in Washington. We also outlined a plan of how we thought these could be remedied."

"Mr. Payne, I assume you are aware of these bugs? You have been working closely with Dr. Davis?"

Payne hesitated, apparently caught off guard, "Yes, of course," he replied.

"Mr. Payne, how will you go about making any recommended changes? Additionally for the issues without recommended solutions, how will you approach and improve your system to take into account Dr. Davis's observations?"

"We have worked diligently to make the recommended changes. Thanks to the input of Dr. Davis and others we believe the system is now ready and robust enough to handle an election of any scale. I welcome and encourage Dr. Davis and the other evaluators to reexamine the system."

"Mr. Payne, as you know a recount was required in Florida after the 2000 U.S. Presidential election. This recount required quite a bit of manpower and was extremely time-consuming. How long would it take for this system to tabulate the absentee votes and recount them if necessary?"

"Our latest benchmarks show that counting 100,000 votes and verifying their integrity takes just under 90 minutes. The procedure easily could be repeated any number of times with the same result."

The Chairman asked, "As we all know, this system is going to be used after this testimony for both you and Dr. Davis to cast your votes in the Washington primaries if we approve. We have connections set up outside where the media also wants to take a peek at the process. Additionally, it will be used by absentee voters who opted to vote electronically in the Washington primary. How ready are you, Mr. Payne—and by you I mean Advice Software, Inc.—to deploy this system nationwide if we decide to implement it? Is your company ready to scale up and support this system both physically and from a technical point of view?"

"Mr. Chairman, we have conducted significant testing and evaluation of the system under double the volume of votes it would likely handle during a national election. I can say with complete confidence that we are ready to implement this system on a wide scale. Our company employs over 11,000 people and we have a dedicated team of 500-plus that have already been trained and tested to both help implement and support the system for every state in the nation in November should this committee and our government see fit to use it."

"Look gentlemen," interrupted member Brown, "I'm gonna cut to the chase here. I mean, this software has been tested and it's been evaluated and I'm sure you all have gotten to the finer details during your evaluations. What I need is a simple, straightforward answer from you, Dr. Davis; can we confidently deploy this system? Will the American people be served better by it? And more importantly, when my grandchildren, and all our grandchildren for that matter, do a term paper on electronic voting 20 years from now and they look in the history books will they say we made the right call?"

Davis's left hand began to tremble and he quickly hid it under the desk. This was the very bluntness he was trying to avoid. He glanced over at Payne, whose forehead was now lightly beaded with sweat. *This is it.* He took a deep breath and began to speak, "Well Mr. Brown, nothing is ever a guarantee." He paused, noting Representative Kingsworth eerily focused on Chris Payne. Davis continued, "I would have to say, though, that this system is the best the marketplace has to offer, and I have no doubt that 20 years from now your grandchildren will look at you with nothing but pride." With that, Davis could feel a piece of himself melt away; lost and never to be returned.

The room degraded into silence. The chairman put his hand over his microphone and spoke quietly to Representative Brown who was seated to his left. He removed his hand and began to speak. "Are there any more questions for either Dr. Davis or Mr. Payne?" His head swiveled from left to right as he surveyed the panel. "Since there are no further questions, I would like to thank both Dr. Davis and Mr. Payne for their insights on this matter. I would ask that the two of you please excuse yourselves for the remainder of these proceedings."

The two men stood up. Davis felt instantly nauseous. He walked closely behind Payne toward the door. Payne opened the door, allowing him to pass through first, grabbed his shoulder and spoke softly, "I am a man of my word, Dr. Davis; your family is waiting for you down the hall. You've done a great thing for America today, Chad." Davis gritted his teeth and remained silent. In his mind he had already punched the man. His thoughts turned to Baff. He loosened his jaw and a calm swept over him.

I have a feeling that the election may not go your way after all, Chris.

Chapter 40:   Washington, D.C.

U.S. Congress

Davis walked quickly down the hall toward the seating area with Payne following closely behind. As he rounded the corner at the end of the hall he saw Amanda and Elizabeth sitting on a bench with Luis standing opposite them. As Davis approached, Luis moved closer to Amanda. With a quick gesture, Payne waved him off, and Luis retreated back to the wall. Chad could see her eyes were red. As he approached, she turned her head toward him and then quickly stood. He embraced her and pulled her close to him. "Everything's going to be fine. It's over," he whispered in her ear. She said nothing but tightened her grip around his waist. Her tears came freely and flowed onto his shoulder.

"Is everything going to be okay?" Elizabeth asked as she stood next to them. Chad extended his arm and pulled her in close to them. "Everything's fine, baby," Amanda said, raising her head.

Chris Payne and Luis walked quietly toward the exit. Davis watched them walk into a small gathering of reporters and photographers stationed outside. Amanda sat back down on the bench and Elizabeth gave her a squeeze. *Does Elizabeth know what's going on?* He thought to himself. She let go and stood in front of her mother, who quickly embraced her. Davis had no words. He felt a consuming guilt over what he had put them through. He saw an envelope on the bench that hadn't been there moments before. Opening it up, he found three airline tickets.

"He made reservations for the three of us to go back to Seattle together. Our flight leaves in three hours." Davis said.

Amanda looked up at him, still in the embrace of Elizabeth, and said nothing; she was too emotional to speak.

"There's just one last think I have to do. You and Elizabeth wait here. I'll be back in a few minutes."

Elizabeth immediately let go of her mother turned and put her arms around Davis's waist, desperately clinging to him, "Dad, don't leave!"

"Elizabeth, honey, I just need to do one thing, I'll be gone for about 20 minutes and then we can go home."

He looked at her face. It was puffed, tears swelled in her eyes. His heart sank, "Honey, I'm so sorry I haven't spent much time with you these last few months. That will never happen again, I swear! You mean everything to me!"

She threw her arms around her father's neck, "I love you, dad."

"I love you too, Elizabeth!" Chad stood, "I'm gonna be right back, okay?" Elizabeth nodded her head. He glanced over to Amanda who looked at him with understanding.

"Go on, you need to finish this," she said, waving him toward the exit. "We'll be here when you get back."

"This will be the last time, I promise." He then turned and walked toward the exit.

As Davis made it through the grand entranceway there were two clusters of press. The first was around Payne and the second had surrounded Grace Wilkinson, who had apparently just exited through a separate door. Grace was only a few yards away, when she began to speak.

"Ladies and gentlemen, the committee has decided to endorse the Advice e-Vote system for national implementation for the November election."

A din of questions came from the reporters. Grace pointed to one of them and the man began to speak, "Ms. Wilkinson, does this mean that the option to cast an absentee vote electronically will be made available to every resident in the 50 states in November?"

Grace quickly began her reply, "Each state must make that decision, but with this recommendation and given the system's success in today's pilot primary election in Washington we expect that most states will choose to adopt it. It has the potential to save thousands of man-hours of error-prone vote counting."

Chad felt a hand grab his shoulder. "Ready to cast your vote, Dr. Davis?" It was Payne accompanied by at least six reporters. Davis looked over at him coldly. "Very ready," he replied.

The two men were escorted by an aide back inside the building to a small room that had been set up with an Internet connection. "Gentlemen, the room is yours. I assume you would like to use your own laptops?"

"Yes," Payne responded quickly. As they stood at the door, Payne turned to face the reporters.

"This is truly a great day for America," Payne said, "We are finally bringing democracy into the 21ˢᵗ century. As we cast our vote today for the Washington primary, I hope that officials in other states take note; this is the new standard for voting." Payne turned toward Davis and outstretched his hand in a sweeping motion toward the door to the voting room, "Dr. Davis, after you."

Davis turned to face the reporters, "On such a monumental occasion I believe it is only fitting that you go first, Mr. Payne. I absolutely insist."

Payne walked into the room with laptop bag in hand. He closed the door behind him. The reporters now shifted their attention to Davis. "Dr. Davis, do you honestly believe that Advice has the capacity to deploy this system nationwide before November?"

"From what I've seen, I believe they do, but I believe that is a question best suited for Mr. Payne."

"Dr. Davis, what will be your ongoing role in the evaluations?"

Davis began to sweat. He felt uncomfortable answering the questions from the press. He leaned over to the aide, "Where can I get a glass of water?"

"We have a fountain just down the hall," the aide pointed to his right. "Ladies and gentlemen, if you will excuse me just for a moment."

Davis walked toward the fountain. His mind swirled with the day's events. He leaned down to take a sip, resting his laptop bag next to the fountain. As he drank, his thoughts again turned to Amanda and Elizabeth. The last couple of days had filled him with regret over what he had let slip away. *Over what, work?* He was sick at the thought that he could have ever put his family second.

He turned to walk back toward the voting room.

Just outside the room he now saw Payne awash in reporters and handheld microphones. As Payne saw Davis approach, he motioned for him. "Ah, Dr. Davis, are you ready to make history?"

With a forced smile he thought, *Payne you smug son of a bitch!*

He walked into the room and closed the door behind him. As soon as he heard the click, he sprang into action. He quickly unpacked his laptop, plugged in the Ethernet cable seated on the small table, and powered his laptop on. He had to work quickly; there were plenty of modifications he had to make to his vote before submitting it.

Ten minutes later, Davis emerged from the voting room. "Ah, Dr. Davis, we were beginning to think you fell asleep in there," Payne said wryly, still with a smaller number of reporters outside.

"Just savoring the moment!" Davis responded. He couldn't help but smile. He *was* savoring it. The events he had just put in motion in the voting room were his own form of justice. Baff's last secret had given him what he needed to bring Payne down, anonymously. *Something tells me that you are going to have one hell of a bad day tomorrow.*

Epilogue

Flight 304, Washington D.C. to Seattle, WA

Chad loosened his seatbelt and reclined his aisle seat. It had been only 45 minutes since their flight had taken off, but already Elizabeth was asleep in the middle seat next to him. They'd all had a traumatic day. Amanda, seated at the window, had not spoken to Chad since they got on the plane. She was quiet, drained from what she and Elizabeth had gone through the past couple of days.

"Amanda?" Chad said quietly trying not to awake Elizabeth, "Things are going to be different now. I want to spend more time with Elizabeth…and you." Amanda did not respond. She sat staring blankly at the small television monitor in the seat back in front of her. "Amanda, it's okay, it's over," he said reassuringly.

After a long pause she began to speak, "I know it is. But I just can't get over what that man said to me—'Your husband is doing a great thing for America.' I can't believe that psychopath is going to get away with this!"

Chad hesitated, not knowing exactly how to respond. He turned his body toward her and said in a soft voice, "Trust me when I say it's amazing how things tend to work themselves out." She smiled hesitantly, but did not respond. Instead, she put on her headphones, hoping to lose herself in distraction.

A minute later she reached across Elizabeth and tapped Chad on the leg, "They're about to announce the results from the absentee votes."

Chad grabbed his headphones, plugged them into the jack in his arm rest and turned the channel to CNN.

"Thank you for joining us live for our election 2004 coverage. The race for the primaries is heating up! Senator William Shift and his closest competitor, self-made millionaire Mark Strand, are neck and neck going into the Washington state primary. Exit polls show that Senator Shift has a one-percent edge on Mr. Strand. A big factor in this primary, however, could be the absentee ballots. One interesting note, Washington state has the largest number of absentee voters of any state. For this primary election, a whopping 62 percent of those voters have registered to use the electronic voting system implemented by Advice Software. Because of the new electronic voting system in Washington, we expect to have some preliminary results momentarily.

"Okay, we are receiving word that the absentee votes have been tallied."

The anchorman paused and pressed his finger up against his earpiece waiting for the results. A look of shock and concern came over his face. He looked to his right where his support staff stood watching. He mumbled toward them, "Is this right?"

They stared back and shrugged, assuming it was.

"Ladies and gentlemen it appears that 99 percent of the electronic votes cast were for Senator Shift. We are waiting for verification of this data, but it has come straight from our elections correspondent in Washington." The anchorman put his hand over the microphone attached to his tie and turned to his news director who was staring agape at him from behind one of the side cameras. The anchorman's words, though faint, could still be heard through the broadcast, "Twelve million absentee votes for Shift? There aren't even that many people in Washington state are there?"

The anchorman dropped his hands to his desk and grabbed the blank papers in front of him, "We'll be right back."

He took off his earpiece, "Can somebody verify this? What in the hell is going on? I'm on live, people!"

The feed quickly cut to a commercial.

Amanda's back was perfectly straight and she was positioned at the edge of her seat. She turned her head quickly to Chad, smiling. He sat grinning, beaming back at her, "I love democracy."

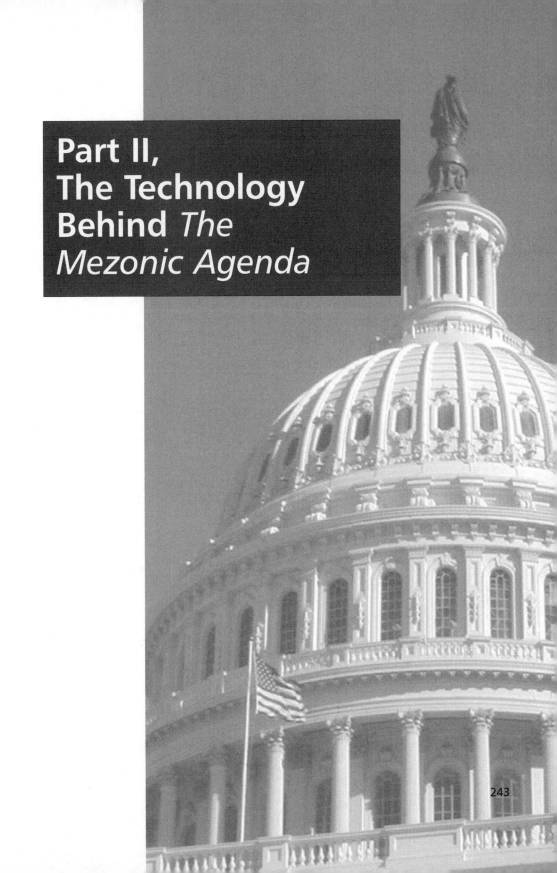

Part II, The Technology Behind *The Mezonic Agenda*

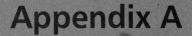

Appendix A

A Brief History of Voting: Origins to Modern Implementations

Topics in this Appendix:

- **Voting Systems and Their History**
- **Voting System Manufacturers and Voting Controversy**
- **Electronic Voting**
- **Internet Voting**

Introduction

The right to elect the leaders of one's country is at the very heart of a free and democratic nation. Although the principle of democracy is simple to grasp, it can be difficult to implement. One particularly thorny issue has been the voting process itself: how does one record and quantify the will of the people fairly and accurately? This appendix takes a look at how voting systems have evolved and discusses the benefits and challenges of modern electronic voting systems. The purpose of this appendix is to briefly review voting systems that have been and are presently used in the United States; we will go over some inherent flaws in these systems, and review the leading players in the electronic voting movement as well as the controversies surrounding this fast-growing field.

Before we start, first let's review the use of the Electoral College, which is fundamental to the Presidential elections of the United States.

A Brief Review of the Electoral College

When the United States was founded, its founding fathers had a dilemma. At the time, the nation had no political parties, nor were any desired. And, as the Constitution was drafted to limit the power of the central government, the real challenge was to set up a system to elect the President for 13 states spread across thousands of miles with limited transportation and communication among the states. Initially it was thought that Congress would elect the president, but the possibility of corruption, "vote selling," and even international influence quickly put an end to those plans. Another idea was to allow State legislature to elect the president. This concept was thought to "undermine the whole idea of a federation." A direct election via a popular vote also was considered, but rejected because most states would elect a candidate close to them (their hometown hero) and probably no one candidate would receive an overall majority of the vote. Also, a candidate from a smaller state (i.e., smaller population) would almost certainly be beaten by a candidate from a larger state that had votes to cast. The founders' education led them to select a system that can be traced back to the Centurian Assembly of the Roman Empire. In this system the adult male citizens of Rome were divided into groups of 100, or Centuries, based on their wealth. Each Century was allowed to cast one vote for or against items brought to them by the Roman Senate.

Although political parties were looked down upon in early America, they were inevitable. By the fourth presidential election, parties began to take form and the election ended in a tie between Thomas Jefferson and Aaron Burr. After 36 attempts and some "bargaining" in the House of Representatives, the tie was broken with the election given to Jefferson. The Electoral College has gone through a number of revisions and amendments before evolving into the system we have in place today.

Currently, each state is assigned a number of Electors to the Electoral College equal to the number of its U.S. Senators (two per state) and the number of the state's U.S. representatives (which depends on the population of each state). Figure A.1 shows the number of Electoral Votes each state is assigned based on the 1990 census population tallies. Note the number of Electoral College votes *per capita* for each state. The six most populous states actually receive the least number of electoral votes per capita, whereas the least populous states received the most. So, for example, if you wanted your individual vote to count "more," just move to Wyoming! This apparent discrepancy is an inevitable consequence of a system designed to represent the concerns of less populous states.[1,2,3]

Figure A.1 Number of Electoral Votes for Each U.S. State in 1990

State	No. of Electors	No. of Electors [%]	Population	Population [%]	Electoral Vote per Capita*
California	54	10.04%	29,785,857	11.97%	1.00
New York	33	6.13%	17,990,778	7.23%	1.01
Texas	32	5.95%	16,986,335	6.83%	1.04
Illinois	22	4.09%	11,430,602	4.59%	1.06
Florida	25	4.65%	12,938,071	5.20%	1.07
Pennsylvania	23	4.28%	11,882,842	4.78%	1.07
Ohio	21	3.90%	10,847,115	4.36%	1.07
New Jersey	15	2.79%	7,747,750	3.11%	1.07
Michigan	18	3.35%	9,295,287	3.74%	1.07
Massachusetts	12	2.23%	6,016,425	2.42%	1.10
Georgia	13	2.42%	6,478,149	2.60%	1.11
Maryland	10	1.86%	4,780,753	1.92%	1.15
Virginia	13	2.42%	6,189,197	2.49%	1.16
North Carolina	14	2.60%	6,632,448	2.67%	1.16
Louisiana	9	1.67%	4,221,826	1.70%	1.18
Missouri	11	2.04%	5,116,901	2.06%	1.19
Indiana	12	2.23%	5,544,156	2.23%	1.19
Kentucky	8	1.49%	3,686,892	1.48%	1.20
Arizona	8	1.49%	3,665,339	1.47%	1.20
Alabama	9	1.67%	4,040,389	1.62%	1.23
Wisconsin	11	2.04%	4,891,769	1.97%	1.24
Tennessee	11	2.04%	4,877,203	1.96%	1.24
Washington	11	2.04%	4,866,669	1.96%	1.25
Minnesota	10	1.86%	4,375,665	1.76%	1.26
South Carolina	8	1.49%	3,486,310	1.40%	1.27
Kansas	6	1.12%	2,477,588	1.00%	1.34
Colorado	8	1.49%	3,294,473	1.32%	1.34
Connecticut	8	1.49%	3,287,116	1.32%	1.34
Oregon	7	1.30%	2,842,337	1.14%	1.36
Iowa	7	1.30%	2,776,831	1.12%	1.39
Oklahoma	8	1.49%	3,145,576	1.26%	1.40
Arkansas	6	1.12%	2,350,624	0.94%	1.41
Mississippi	7	1.30%	2,575,475	1.04%	1.50
West Virginia	5	0.93%	1,793,477	0.72%	1.54
Utah	5	0.93%	1,722,850	0.69%	1.60
Nebraska	5	0.93%	1,578,417	0.63%	1.75
Maine	4	0.74%	1,227,928	0.49%	1.80
New Mexico	5	0.93%	1,515,069	0.61%	1.82
Nevada	4	0.74%	1,201,675	0.48%	1.84
New Hampshire	4	0.74%	1,109,252	0.45%	1.99
Hawaii	4	0.74%	1,108,229	0.45%	1.99
Montana	3	0.56%	799,065	0.32%	2.07
Idaho	4	0.74%	1,006,734	0.40%	2.19
Rhode Island	4	0.74%	1,003,464	0.40%	2.20
South Dakota	3	0.56%	696,004	0.28%	2.38
Delaware	3	0.56%	666,168	0.27%	2.48
North Dakota	3	0.56%	638,800	0.26%	2.59
District of Columbia	3	0.56%	606,900	0.24%	2.73
Vermont	3	0.56%	562,758	0.23%	2.94
Alaska	3	0.56%	550,043	0.22%	3.01
Wyoming	3	0.56%	453,589	0.18%	3.65
Totals	538	100.00%	248,765,170	100.00%	

* Normalized based on California's data

One of the more controversial consequences of adopting the Electoral College system was the results of the 2000 U.S. Presidential election. The election took a scandalous turn when the results from Florida's voters were too close to determine accurately which of the two frontrunner candidates—Al Gore and George W. Bush—would receive Florida's 25 electoral votes. What followed over the next few days and months were revelations of voter disenfranchisement, machine miscounts, and political shuffling, all to try and sway the results one way or another. The entire voting procedure, the systems used, and the Electoral College system were under fire as officials on both sides debated the outcome. Many of the manual voting systems, such as the use of punch cards, were particularly criticized by the media and election officials. The 2000 election forever changed the way voters would cast their ballots and incited a movement toward more reliable ways to capture and quantify voter intent. The election of officials and religious figures has been going on for centuries, if not millennia, and the U.S. general election of 2000 was certainly not the first shrouded in controversy.

Voting Systems and Their History

One of the earliest forms of voting dates back to 508 B.C. and was introduced by Cleisthenes. Every year the voters would select a government official they would want to see exiled for 10 years. The official would have to receive 6,000 votes in order to be banished, and if no official received more than 6,000 votes then they would all stay. A 13th century Venetian system, or approval voting system, worked by having voters cast one vote for the candidate(s) they found acceptable and no vote for any candidates the voters did not approve of. One form of voting that was utilized in ancient Athens was the use of distinct clay balls for each candidate, which were dropped into appropriate pots assigned to candidates. Another early voting practice involved placing a small ball into an urn for the candidate under consideration—a white ball for an affirmative vote or a black ball for a negative vote. This practice led to the phrase "black-balled" to mean "rejected" or "prohibited from participating." This practice also gave us the word "ballot," derived from the Italian word *ballotta*, meaning small ball.[4,5,6]

Moving further ahead in time, there's an interesting painting by George Caleb Bingham titled *The County Election*, which gives some insight into voting practices of the mid 1800s. In the painting, Bingham portrays a Saline County, Missouri 1846 election poll showing that voter verification was a mere oath sworn by the voter indicating that he was eligible to vote and had not done so yet. The candidates were campaigning right at the polling place and the voters did not have to write down their vote, they could just voice it and the clerk would record it. The clerk really held the power of elections because it was his vote tallying that decided the outcome. There was no paper trail, no punch card or record of votes.[4] This is a sharp contrast to the procedures and practices in place today. In this section we look at how such systems have evolved and discuss the different types of voting systems, their advantages and drawbacks, as well as any controversial role they played in elections. The systems we'll be covering include:

- Paper Ballot
- Mechanical Lever Machines
- Punch Cards
- Optical Scan Ballots (Marksense)
- Direct Recording Electronic (DRE) Ballots
- Absentee Ballots (and Internet Voting)

Each system has served and continues to serve its purpose both in the United States and abroad. Figure A.2 shows a brief history of the voting systems mentioned in this list.

Figure A.2 A Brief History of the Voting Systems

Voting System	Paper Ballot	Mechanical Lever Machines	Punchcards	Marksense (Optical Scan)	Direct Recording Electronic (DRE)
Description	Voter marks his or her choice on paper and drop their selection in a sealed ballot box.	Levers used for each candidate. As voter pulls on lever of choice, a mechanical system turns the appropriate counting wheel a set amount. At the end of the election the wheel's position determines the number of votes per candidate.	Voter punches his or her choice on a card and places the card in a ballot card. The card is read by a tabulating device at the voting precinct	Voters us a card and fill in an empty circle, triangle, square or oval next to their choice. Their card is placed in a sealed ballot box and read by a device using "dark mark logic."	Electronic version of Mechanical Lever Machine. Voter choices are shown on a touch screen. Voters selects candidate by touching the appropriate area on the screen orpush-buttons. A keyboard is available for write-in votes. Data storage such as a memory cartridge, disk, or smart-card is used to store all votes for tabulation.
Use	1.7% of registered voters as of 1996	20.7% of registered voters as of 1996	37.3% of registered voters as of 1996	24.6% of registered voters as of 1996	7.7% of registered users as of 1996
Application	Mostly in small communities, rural areas, absentee ballots	Over half the U.S.'s votes were cast by this method by the 1960's.	Applicable in many jurisdictions. Georgia was first state to implement in 1964 primary election	Their use is on the rise	Implemented in many precincts for 2004 elections
Of interest	First adopted in Victoria, Australia in 1856. It became known as the "Australian Ballot." The first state in the United States to adopt the paper ballot was New York in 1889.	First official use in Lockport, NY in 1892. Also known as the "Myers Automatic Booth." These machines are no longer made.	Infamous for the 2000 Florida voting hanging chads, overvotes, and undervotes. The "Votomatic" type card uses numbers to indicate the candidate choice. The "Datavote" type card has the candidate names written on the card	"Dark mark logic" tabulators select the darkest mark within a predetermined set as the correct choice. Other "optical scan" techniques exist beyond the Marksense system. Marksense has been used for decades in standardized testing (remember high school tests?) and state lotteries.	Diebold was recently in trouble of using uncertified software in the voting systems to be used in the 2004 U.S. Presidential Election. Analysis by top security experts concluded that such systems are still vulnerable to various types of attacks that may compromise an election.

Ref. www.fec.gov/pages/elections.html

251

Paper Ballots

Although the Australian state of Victoria lays claim to the first paper ballot system used in 1856, Rome used paper ballots to hold an election circa 139 B.C. The first use of a paper ballot in the United States was to elect a pastor for the Salem Church in 1629. There were, however, several fundamental differences between the Australian ballot and those that preceded it. Before the Australian ballot system, most paper ballots were torn newspaper campaign ads that voters would take to the polls. Alternatively, voters would be given a Straight Party Ticket that had all candidates for President, Senate, and so on, of one party already printed for them. All the voter would have to do is go to the voting polls and drop his ballot off.

Even in such simpler times parties did their best to gain an edge over their competitors. A voter could take a party ticket and scratch off candidates they did not wish to vote for and write in candidates from another party. The parties quickly caught on and began to print tickets that made it difficult for voters to remove their party's candidates and write in others. The Australian ballot solved this problem by printing all party candidates on one ballot and allowing voters to select candidates of their choice. Having all parties on one ballot also meant that the printing costs would be covered by the government instead of each political party, who had previously printed their own "influential" ballots.

Another way to manipulate votes was to stuff ballot boxes. This easily could be accomplished by one voter who would hide many ballots within one folded ballot that he dropped into a ballot box, or the clerk himself would "stuff" a ballot box or vote count. This led to many ballot boxes being clear so that election officials could look and see that voters were dropping in only one vote.

Although Australian ballots did offer an improved level of accuracy and voter integrity, the elections could still be influenced by those counting and even by laws specifying how a voter would mark his or her choice. For example, Michigan law not only specifies that a voter uses an

X or a checkmark to select candidates but it also specifies the position and shape—that's right, shape—of that X or checkmark in order for the voter's ballot to count. In other words, if an X or checkmark does not adhere to strict requirements, a voter's ballot legally could be thrown out as invalid.[4,5]

Mechanical Lever Machines

The first official lever machine was developed by Jacob H. Meyers, and became known as the Myers Automatic Booth. It debuted in Lockport, New York in the 1892 elections. At that time, lever machines were at the edge of technology. They quickly dominated the election market and by the 1930s were used in almost every major city in the United States, because they made voting simpler and more private for the voter. A lever machine is a device much like an odometer in a car, only it has many odometers—one for each candidate. The machine tallies votes for each candidate only when a voter pulls on a lever to select that candidate as his or her choice. Lever machines also helped reduce the number of "over votes." Over votes are instances where a voter selects more than one candidate for the same office. A lever machine is able to prevent users from voting for two different candidates for one particular office by forcing them to pull only a single lever.

Two companies eventually emerged in the forefront of production for mechanical lever machines. One was Shoup, founded by Ransom F. Shoup, and the other was Automatic Voting Machines (AVM), founded by a direct descendant of Jacob H. Meyers. Both companies built fairly similar machines with some differences in ballot layout and booth style. These machines became so popular that most people "…born in mid-century grew up assuming that all voting machines were and would always be lever machines."[4,6]

Although the lever machines did ease the fears of ballot tampering and ballot interpretation, they, too, had weaknesses. The biggest concern was that lever machines kept no record of the votes placed in each machine. The counters were the only mechanism that stored the votes placed for each candidate. The machines also were complicated and had a large number of moving parts. It has been noted that a large number of vote totals from lever machines ended in 99. This has been attributed to the counters jamming at 99, probably because it takes more force for the counter to turn over to 100. Lever machines are no longer manufactured but parts are still available for maintenance for those still being used.[4,7]

Punch Cards

The punch card originally was developed by Herman Hollerith and was used by the Baltimore Board of Health in the 1890 census. University of California at Berkley Professor Joseph P. Harris improved on the initial card design by patenting an "easier to use" punch card voting machine (see the following note) and founded Harris Votomatic, Inc. In 1964, in Georgia counties Fulton and De Kalb, Harris' Votomatic punch card system was the first to be used in a primary election. In 1965, IBM bought Harris Votomatic, Inc., after it had been implemented successfully in several counties nationwide.

> **NOTE**
>
> Although Harris's patent improved on earlier technology, patents from the 1960s and 1970s on punch card systems spoke of design flaws that would cause clogged machines, incomplete punches, and other such machine errors. Following is a quote directly from an October 27, 1970 U.S. Patent No. 3,536,257 that builds on earlier designs and references Harris's U.S. patent no. 3,240,409:
>
> *"…It is necessary to insure that the chips or card portions punched out of the selected, prescored areas on the ballot are positively separated from the ballot and retained in the vote recorder so that errors will not be made when processing ballots because of a chip being only partially removed and remaining attached to the ballot during counting.*
>
> *In prior vote recording devices, such as the type shown in U.S. Pat. No. 3,240,409 to J.P. Harris, a plurality of elongated strips…Because a number of strips are needed for each vote recorder and because the*

Today there are essentially two types of punch card systems used: the Votomatic and the Datavote.

Votomatic

The votomatic punch card design is a card with numbers designating voter choices. No candidate names or affiliations are printed on the ballot, making this card economical and applicable to many different elections and precincts. The card and the apparatus in the voting booth allow the voter to place the card in its designated slot without the chance of the card being placed upside–down or backward. The voter would then attach the booklet with the names of the candidates over the punch card and begin his or her selections. As the voter turns the pages of the booklet different rows (or columns) appear for the voter to punch. Roughly 33 percent of the punch card systems used today are Votomatic.

Datavote

In the Datavote system, the name of the candidate is printed next to the hole to be punched for that candidate. Because of the extra room required for this, these cards do not hold as many holes as the Votomatic type and are therefore more expensive to implement, count, and store. It is estimated that the Datavote punch card system is used in only 4 percent of the polling stations in the Unites States.[7]

Figure A.3 shows how a punch card system works and Figure A.4 gives an example of a Votomatic punch card used in the 2000 U.S. Presidential election in West Palm Beach, Florida. In Figure A.4, note the use of the infamous "butterfly ballot" where candidate choices are alternating between the right and left side. Also note how one row of holes is exposed from the punch card. If one were to turn the right page over, a new row of holes would be exposed for the next set of candidates.

The term "chad" has almost become a pop icon after the 2000 elections. Dr. Douglas W. Jones of the University of Iowa has a great site on the history of punch cards and chads that is worth a glance. His site can be found at www.cs.uiowa.edu/~jones/.

Figure A.3 How a Punch Card System Works

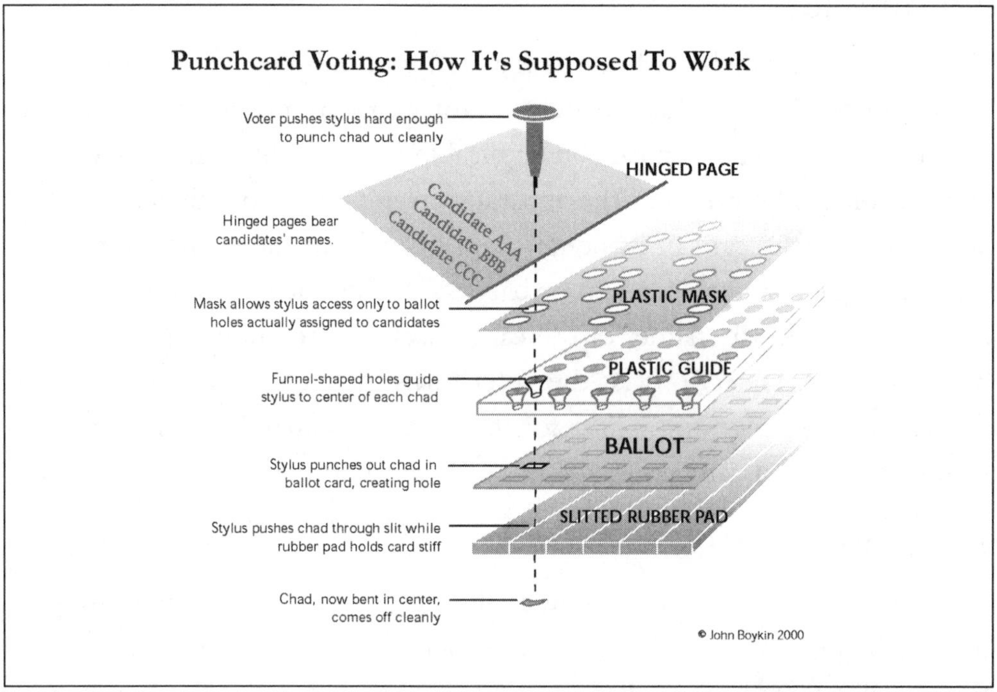

Punchcard Voting: How It's Supposed To Work

Voter pushes stylus hard enough to punch chad out cleanly

HINGED PAGE

Hinged pages bear candidates' names.

Candidate AAA
Candidate BBB
Candidate CCC

Mask allows stylus access only to ballot holes actually assigned to candidates

PLASTIC MASK

Funnel-shaped holes guide stylus to center of each chad

PLASTIC GUIDE

Stylus punches out chad in ballot card, creating hole

BALLOT

Stylus pushes chad through slit while rubber pad holds card stiff

SLITTED RUBBER PAD

Chad, now bent in center, comes off cleanly

© John Boykin 2000

(Image courtesy of Mr. John Boykin, 2000)

Figure A.4 Butterfly Ballot from West Palm Beach Used in 2000 Election

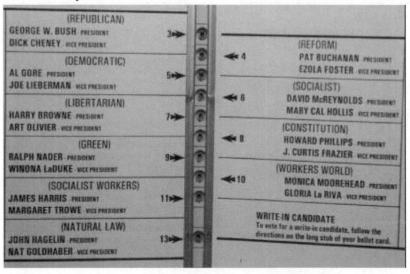

Depending on how complete the punched hole is on a card, the chad is defined as hanging, dimpled, or pregnant. Chads could also have filled holes on otherwise properly punched cards when all the cards were stacked together for counting. Figure A.5 shows various malfunctions of a punch card system. Problems with punch card systems are well known and have existed since the 1960s. Largely because of this, IBM dropped its Votomatic business in 1969. Votomatic later became Computer Election Services, Inc. (CESI), which was eventually purchased by Election Systems and Software (ES&S).

The 2000 election brought to light just how nonstandard the punch cards are when it comes down to a manual recount. A paper ballot with a check next to a candidate or a write-in vote leaves very little to interpretation; but the varying chads on a punch card open up a number of interpretations regarding what the voter's intentions were. This ambiguity is arguably as bad as no voter record at all since the voter's intent at times is open to interpretation from the holes made in the card. It was this ambiguity that mired the Florida Presidential election recount of 2000.

Figure A.5 Punch Card Malfunctions

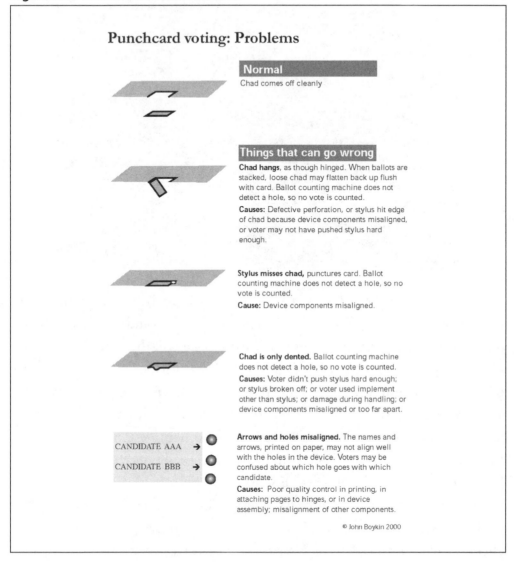

(Image courtesy of Mr. John Boykin, 2000)

Optical Scan Ballots (Marksense)

Optical Scan Ballots have been in use for many years, primarily in the academic world. You probably have used optical scan forms when taking exams such as the Scholastic Aptitude Test (SAT). In most uses, a paper with numbered choices is given to you and you are required fill in an oval next to your choice for each question, typically with a No. 2 pencil. The sheets are then counted based on the electrical conductivity of graphite from the pencil lead.

Although these types of forms have been used extensively in academia and standardized testing since the mid-20th century, they still have a number of drawbacks. Based on their calibration, at times the systems may be too sensitive and they record erased marks. At other times they may not be sensitive enough and do not record marks that are dark enough. Marksense—a name that has become synonymous with optical scan systems—readers are also known to reject cards that fail to read, for unknown reasons.[7]

Marksense systems have been developed by IBM, Westinghouse, Data Mark Systems, and American Information Systems. American Information Systems (AIS) later became known as ES&S after it merged with Business Records Corporation. Diebold also makes optical system counters. Figure A.6 shows two different types of optical scan ballots.

Though many have hailed optical scan systems as the best bet for accuracy and ease of use, Bev Harris's digging (www.blackboxvoting.com/) uncovered a slew of optical voting system errors from around the country and in varying elections. The most severe cases were found in the 2000 Presidential election, where in Volusia County, FL, a total of 412 people voted. Diebold's optical system reported a total of −16,022 (that's right, *negative* 16,022) votes for Al Gore and 2,812 votes for George Bush.[11, 12]

Another interesting incident occurred in 2003. "I know I voted for myself," said Rafael Rivera during a Lake County, Illinois election in April 2003. The systems used ES&S's optical scan voting machines and apparently recorded zero votes for Mr. Rivera. He figured he'd get at least one, the one he cast for himself. The county clerk attributed the problem to their optical-scan machines.[12]

Obviously these errors were caught and corrected, but what about errors that aren't as obvious? What about errors that do not change the total number of votes or report minus votes, but simply skew the proportion of votes for a particular candidate?

Figure A.6 Marksense Ballot. The Voter selects his or her choices by (a) filling in ovals, squares or circles next to the candidates's name or (b) by completing a broken arrow.

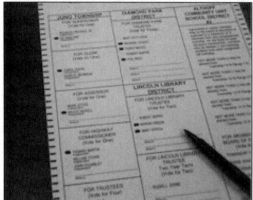

Direct Recording Electronic Systems

It's quite surprising to note that Direct Recording Electronic (DRE) systems have been around since the 1970s. One can draw a parallel between the lever machines of old and the modern DREs. Both are relatively easier to use than preceding technologies and help protect against over votes and under votes. DREs typically do not offer a voter record or a paper trail; instead the votes are recorded into memory, a card, or disk, and are the sole record of the votes at the polling precincts.

Although DRE systems are being implemented in more and more precincts (30+% precincts for 2004), the public and the scientific community—more specifically, the computer science, software, and security communities—are asking for a much closer look into the technology and how to properly implement it. There are a number of studies and technology reviews on the DRE systems that bring up security concerns. If one wanted to quell any precinct's desire to purchase such a system, all that would have to be uttered is, "Diebold."

A large proportion of the news and flaws reported focused on Diebold's election systems; however, for a more complete listing of voting machine errors refer to Bev Harris's book, *BlackBox Voting* (www.black-boxvoting.com). *Wired* also has a collection of articles on voting and electronic voting titled "Machine Politics," which can be found at www.wired.com/news/evote. This collection contains all the *Wired* articles referenced in this appendix as well as others of interest. We urge all readers to look up the references listed here as well as other articles that you may find on other sites. This is a topic of heated debate and we welcome questions, comments, corrections, and any new happenings that can be brought to our attention. Please visit www.mezonicagenda.com for contact information.

How Do DREs Work?

A DRE voting system is similar to an ATM, and in some cases, a voter must insert a smartcard to vote in much the same way that an ATM client inserts a bankcard. Indeed, the leading DRE manufacturer, Diebold, is one of the largest manufacturers of ATMs as well. For DREs, voters register with a poll worker and obtain a smartcard or some activation card. The voter then inserts this card into the DRE machine and begins the voting process. Once the voter has made his or her choices, the DRE device will ask the voter to verify his or her votes. The voter then confirms his or her choices and casts a vote. Votes are tallied in the "backend," the part of the system that stores and counts the votes in the DRE machine. At the end of the polls, workers compile each machine's tallies and one or more reports are produced. System design, aesthetics, and software design, of course, varies from manufacturer to manufacturer, but the systems do have Voting Systems Standards (VSS) that they are required to adhere to from both the Federal Election Commission and each state. Figures A.7, A.8, and A.9 show Sequoia DRE machines and a Hart InterCivic DRE.

Figure A.7 Sequoia *Edge* DRE

(Photo courtesy of Sequoia Voting Systems)

Figure A.8 Sequoia AVC Advantage DRE

(Photo courtesy of Sequoia Voting Systems)

Figure A.9 Hart InterCivic *eSlate* DRE

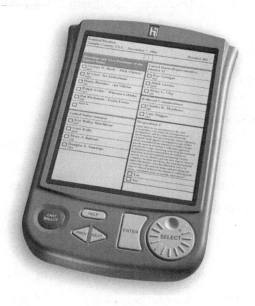

(Photo courtesy of Hart InterCivic)

Diebold (www.diebold.com)

Diebold Election Systems makes DRE systems as well as the optical scan Marksense counters. Diebold offers two DRE voter interface models, the AccuVote-TSX and the AccuVote-TS. Diebold's DRE systems operate on Windows CE platform, using their Global Election Management Software (GEMS). You've probably heard of Diebold when their CEO, Walton O'Dell, was quoted from a letter he wrote that said,

> "I am committed to helping Ohio deliver its electoral votes to the president next year."

O'Dell later admitted the remark was a mistake and he would keep a "lower political profile." This isn't the only newsworthy appearance Diebold has made. In January 2003, Bev Harris, a book publicist turned voting activist/investigative reporter, uncovered an FTP site on Diebold's systems in which she found roughly 40,000 files including source code for their DRE machines, GEMS software, a Texas voter's registration list, firmware upgrades, and "...live vote data from 57 precincts in a 2002 California primary election."[12]

In the *Wired* article titled "How E-Voting Threatens Democracy," Bev Harris said that that the time stamp for the vote data was 3:31 P.M. on election day even though polling precincts are not allowed to release votes until polls close (usually 8 P.M. of election day). This led Harris to suspect that Diebold was able to obtain vote data in "real-time" during an election.[11,12]

In March 2003, an unidentified hacker gained access to one of Diebold's private servers and made off with approximately 1.8 GB of files. The files were provided to *Wired*, which released an article on August 7, 2003. *Wired* reported the contents of these files to be internal discussion-list archives, a software bug database, and other software.[9]

In July 23, 2003, four researchers released a report that appeared as a Johns Hopkins University Information Security Institute Technical Report (TR-2003-19). This report—deemed the Hopkins Report—was later published in May 2004, *IEEE Symposium on Security and Privacy 2004*. The report was critical of Diebold's AccuVote-TS system, as it showed how voters could cast numerous votes, change other's votes, and access administrator status on Diebold's system. It is important to note that Dr. Avi Rubin, one of the four authors, was forthcoming with information that he was a board member of a competing voting systems company, VoteHere, Inc at the time of the article's publication. In August 2003, Dr. Rubin resigned from the board and returned his stock options of VoteHere, Inc., due to apparent conflicts of interest between his report and his involvement with a competing company. On January 20, 2004, a report published by RABA Technology's Innovative Solutions Cell under the request of the State of Maryland reviewed this Hopkins Report as well as a number of other related reports that followed.[10, 19, 29]

Rob Behler, a former worker at Diebold's warehouse in Georgia claimed that the company patched voting machines after they were certified for use in Georgia's 2002 gubernatorial election. Behler claimed that the machines would act erroneously when they were tested just before being shipped to the counties. He said, "It's hard to track down a problem when you go out to your car and the first time it starts, the next time the headlights don't work, the next time you start it the brakes are out, and the next time you start the door falls off. That's really the way they were."[12, 18]

In November 2003, Doug Stone, spokesman for the secretary of state of California, found out that Diebold may have used uncertified software in their voting machines used in California's gubernatorial recall election. California then suspended the certification of Diebold's AccuVote-TSx system, which was slated for use in the state's primary elections in March of 2004. Audits of the voting machines revealed that Diebold had installed uncertified software, skirting both federal- and state-level certifications in some cases, in all the counties in which their systems were used. Diebold Election System's (DES) president, Bob Urosevich, sat before California's Voting Systems Panel to answer questions regarding this matter. Diebold faced decertification and banning from the state of California as well as possible criminal and civil charges against DES.[13, 14, 15, 16]

Election Systems & Software (www.essvote.com)

Election Systems & Software promotes their iVotronic DRE system as well as the Automark system geared toward disabled voters. ES&S originally was founded by Todd and Bob Urosevich under the name American Information Systems. What's interesting here is that Bob Urosevich, who was founder of ES&S, became Diebold Election Systems's CEO. Thus the two largest voting systems companies are headed by brothers. And as it so happens, ES&S isn't impervious to machine count errors either.

In Broward County, Florida ES&S's iVotronic touch screen systems were reported to perform without a hitch in their November 2002 election. The day after the polls had closed the County Elections office found out that 103,222 votes had not been counted.

Back when ES&S was still known as American Information Systems (the name changed in 1997), Richard Hagel was their CEO from November 1993 to June 1994 and Chairman from July 1992 to March 1995. On January 29, 2003, *The Hill* reported on Senator Richard Hagel's interests in ES&S as well as the McCarthy Group, which is ES&S' parent company. Apparently ES&S's voting machines—and only ES&S machines—were used to count votes when Mr. Hagel ran for Senate election in 1996 and 2000 in Nebraska. His 1996 win was considered a big upset by the Washington Post.[12]

Dominance of Diebold and ES&S

So here we have Diebold Election Systems, headed by Bob Urosevich, while his brother Todd was steering the ship at ES&S (Aldo Tesi has been ES&S's President and CEO since 1999). From a cached web page dated June 8, 2004, we were able to find that Todd Urosevich's title is "Vice President, Customer Support" although another search on his name brings him up as "Vice President, Aftermarket Sales." On February 12, 2004, Election Data Services (EDS) released a report that surveyed 3,114 counties to determine the type of election system that will be used in the 2004 U.S. Presidential election. The report breaks down the voting system types as paper, lever, punch card (Datavote or other), optical-scan, electronic (DREs, touch screen), or mixed (mixed being two or more systems). Table A.1 shows the breakdown of the models and the percentage of registered voters for optical-scan and electronic systems based on EDS's report. Roughly 45 percent of the votes in the November 2004 elections will be cast using optical voting systems and 21percent will be cast via electronic systems. Notice that 27.2 percent of the nonmanufacturer declared optical-scan machines are under the generic label "optical scan," and roughly 5.4percent of the electronic voters are under "Electronic Voting" and "Direct Recording Electronic." We contacted Mr. Robert Grundstad at EDS and asked about these entries. He replied that jurisdictions have been asked to provide the *type* of voting system used and not any specific model or manufacturer information. He also said they are implementing a plan to include more specific vendor and model information in the next six to eight months. Using the proportions of machines where manufacturers were reported and applying these proportions to the generic categories we calculate that of the 45 percent of the optical votes, 13.4 percent will use Diebold's systems and 25.7 percent will use ES&S's. Of the 21 percent of electronic votes, 6.67 percent will use Diebold's systems and 1.04 percent will use ES&S's. Doing some quick addition brings Diebold's total votes to be read in November 2004 to approximately 20 percent and that of ES&S's to approximately 26 percent. The Ulrich brothers thus lead the companies whose machines record approximately 46 percent of votes for the 2004 presidential election.[22]

Table A.1 Breakdown of Models and Percentage of Voters Based on EDS's Report

Optical Scan Systems		Percent Registered Voters	Electronic Systems		Percent Registered Voters
Accuvote	Diebold	4.82	Shouptronics	Shoup Voting Solutions Inc.	0.16
Optical Scan		27.2	Electronic Voting		1.09
Air Mac Tech		0.06	Sequoia Pacific A.V.C. Advantage	Sequoia	2.09
Mark-A-Vote	DFM Associates	0.22	Microvote	Microvote General Corp	2.18
American Information Systems	ES&S	3.56	Votronic	ES&S	0.96
C.E.S. – Optech	ES&S	0.03	Direct Recording Electronic		4.27
Optech II	ES&S	0.19	Accuvote TS	Diebold	6.17
Optech III - PE Mark Sense	ES&S	4.69	eSlate	Hart InterCivic	0.03
Optech 3P Eagle	Sequoia	2.28	Patriot	Unilect	0.06
Mark Sense	ES&S	0.96	Shouptronics 1242 DRE	Shoup Voting Solutions Inc.	4.46
Global ES-2000	Diebold	0.22	**Total Electronic Systems**		**21.47**
Scanner M100	ES&S	0.48			
Optech III	ES&S	0.03			
Diebold Election Systems	Diebold	0.26			
Optech IV	ES&S	0.06			
Scanner M150	ES&S	0.32			

Continued

Table A.1 Breakdown of Models and Percentage of Voters Based on EDS's Report

Optical Scan Systems		Percent Registered Voters	Electronic Systems	Percent Registered Voters
Global/GEMS	Diebold	0.06		
Global Opt. Scan	Diebold	0.03		
ES&S M100's 3.0.0.1	ES&S	0.03		
Total Optical Systems		**45.5**		

Sequoia

Sequoia manufactures the AVC Edge and Advantage DRE systems. The AVC Edge is a desktop model and the AVC Advantage is a floor model capable of serving voters with disabilities. Sequoia's southern regional sales manager was allegedly involved in a kick-back scandal with Jerry Fowler, Louisiana state elections chief. Although Sequoia's CEO felt the allegations were "without merit," Jerry Fowler pleaded guilty.

Sequoia is also famous for hiring state elections officials and regulators. For example, executive director of the Denver Election Commission, Michael Frontera, became a Sequoia Regional Manager after they were awarded $6.6 million in contracts from Mr. Frontera's Election Commission.

On October 29, 2003, *Wired* reported a source code leak from Sequoia. This time an FTP server with public access owned by Jaguar Computer Systems was the culprit. Sequoia lashed out at Jaguar for their lax security. The information leaked was binary code of parts of their software as opposed to the Diebold leak discussed earlier, which was source code. Refer to the Reverse Engineering chapter regarding binary code and how much information could potentially be drawn from it.[12, 20]

Hart InterCivic (www.eslate.com)

Hart InterCivic produces the eSlate brand of DRE voting systems. The eSlate is PDA-like in its design and function. A voter uses a turn wheel to select his or her choice and pushes a vote button to make a selection. Hart InterCivic spun off from Hart Graphics, developed by David Hart. Although the finances of Hart Graphic remained under the eyes of the Hart family, Hart InterCivic was funded through venture capital from Triton Ventures, RES Partners, and an investor from Hicks, Muse, Tate & Furst. Both Sequoia and Hart InterCivic will count less than 5 percent of the electronic and optical votes cast in November 2004 in the United States.[7, 12]

SERVE and Internet Voting

Internet-based voting has made some attempts to get off the ground but so far has not been as successful as DREs. If implemented, Internet-based voting likely would be used initially for overseas or absentee ballots. The voter would register and then be able to access a secure online ballot and cast his or her vote(s). This encrypted vote then likely would be held by a central server such as that described in the Secure Electronic Registration and Voting Experiment (SERVE) program. The local election officials from each county would download their appropriate absentee votes from this server and decrypt them. Figure A.10 shows how such a system may work. Note that the figure and the process is quite similar to the one portrayed in the fiction section of this book.

Figure A.10 Example of Internet-based Voting System

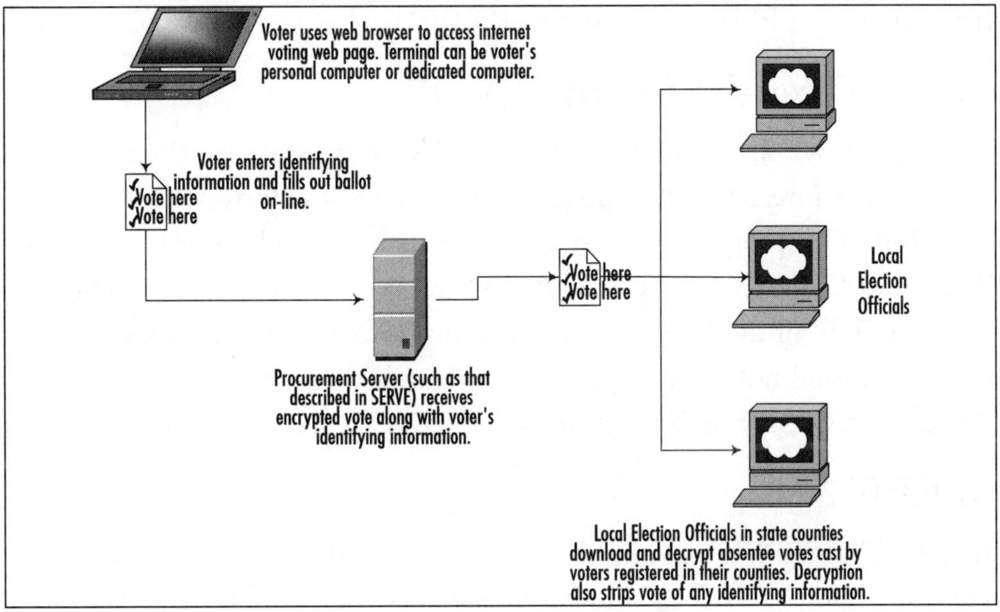

Voter uses web browser to access internet voting web page. Terminal can be voter's personal computer or dedicated computer.

Voter enters identifying information and fills out ballot on-line.

Vote here
Vote here

Procurement Server (such as that described in SERVE) receives encrypted vote along with voter's identifying information.

Vote here
Vote here

Local Election Officials

Local Election Officials in state counties download and decrypt absentee votes cast by voters registered in their counties. Decryption also strips vote of any identifying information.

California's Internet Voting Report

In January of 2000, the California Internet Voting Task Force reported their findings on the status and feasibility of Internet voting. One point of interest in this report is the classification of the different types of Internet voting methods that could be applied. The report defines an Internet voting system as:

> ...an election system that uses electronic ballots that would allow voters to transmit their voted ballot to election officials over the internet.[25]

The report differentiates between Polling Place Internet Voting (PPIV) and Remote Internet Voting (RIV). In PPIV a voter would use an Internet voting system at traditional polling locations supervised by elections officials that authenticate the ballots before the votes are cast. In RIV a voter would cast his or her ballot using any computer and no official would be able to authenticate the vote before it was cast and sent to the procurement server. The report outlines how Internet voting could be implemented slowly via evolutionary multiphase, multistage steps beginning with PPIV and arriving at RIV.[25]

Voting Over the Internet (VOI)

The VOI program was one of the Federal Voting Assistance Program's (FVAP) first Internet voting programs contracted to Booze-Allen & Hamilton. This program was used by four states (Florida, South Carolina, Texas, and Utah) to record a total of 84 *real* votes in the 2000 general election. Fifty of the 84 votes were cast in Florida. Although 84 votes typically would not be enough to swing an election, the close race for the U.S. Presidency in 2000 is proof enough that *every vote counts*.

SERVE

In 2001, The SERVE was implemented as part of the Department of Defense's (DoD) FVAP. U.S. military personnel, their families, and American citizens living abroad typically have to go through a lengthy process in order to place an absentee ballot vote. This program's goal was to make voting for overseas citizens easier and more convenient. A report issued on January 21, 2004[19] described the analysis and findings of a Security Peer Review Group (SPRG) and the FVAP on the SERVE program. The report strongly recommended that the SERVE program and any program like it be halted due to numerous Internet-based vulnerabilities that possibly could compromise an election. In the days following the report's issue, the Pentagon, along with the Information Technology Association of America (ITAA), maintained support for the system. The ITAA's members include DRE manufacturers that were criticized in the report. In February of 2004 the Pentagon finally shut the SERVE program down.

When the DoD sent out a request for proposals for this $40 million effort, they received seven proposals. The SERVE contract was awarded to Accenture (previously election.com \www.election.com) with VoteHere's proposal coming in as FVAP's second choice.[23-28]

VoteHere (www.votehere.net)

VoteHere was founded by Jim Alder, who received funding from Compaq Computer, Cisco Systems, and Northwest Venture Associates totaling approximately $15 million by November 2000.[12] VoteHere's proposal included a way that the company claimed voters would be able to verify that their votes were cast as they intended. The concept is similar to how one can track a UPS or Post Office shipment by a tracking number that does not reveal any personal information. Only the voter would be able to interpret the tracking info and verify his or her vote. Information on this proposal may be found at www.votehere.net/vhti/documentation/verifiable_e-voting.pdf.

VoteHere also did something unheard of in the DRE/e-vote community: they made the system's source code available for download on their web site, Election.com (www.accenture.com/xd/xd.asp?it=enweb&xd =industries\government\gove_democ.xml). Election.com, as evidenced by this link, is no longer in business. Newsday's Mark Harrington published an article in February of 2003, linking a Saudi/Yemen investment group named Osan Ltd. to election.com. It was reported that Osan Ltd. purchased 20 million preferred shares for $1.2 million controlling about 51.6 percent of the voting power in the company. Election.com announced it had sold its assets to Accenture on July 2, 2003.[12]

The Attacks

In the SERVE analysis report, various attacks were considered that could possibly interrupt or change vote results. Implementing these attacks, as the system is represented in Figure A.10, we arrive at Figure A.11.

Figure A.11 Possible Internet Voting Attacks

Figure A.11 Possible Internet Voting Attacks

Voter uses web browser to access internet voting web page. Terminal can be voter's personal computer or dedicated computer.

Trojans, Worms, Scripts, Viruses. Could be written by voter or outsider unbeknownst to voter or user.

Ballot could be infected with virus, script, etc. Could be accomplished by voter/user or by outside source.

Voter enters identifying information and fills out ballot on-line.

Procurement Server (such as that described in SERVE) receives encrypted vote along with voter's identifying information.

Man in the Middle attack, Denial of Service attack, Web Page spoofs. Can disenfranchise voter or collect and change votes.

Local Election Officials

Local Election Officials in state counties download and decrypt absentee votes cast by voters registered in their counties. Decryption also strips vote of any identifying information.

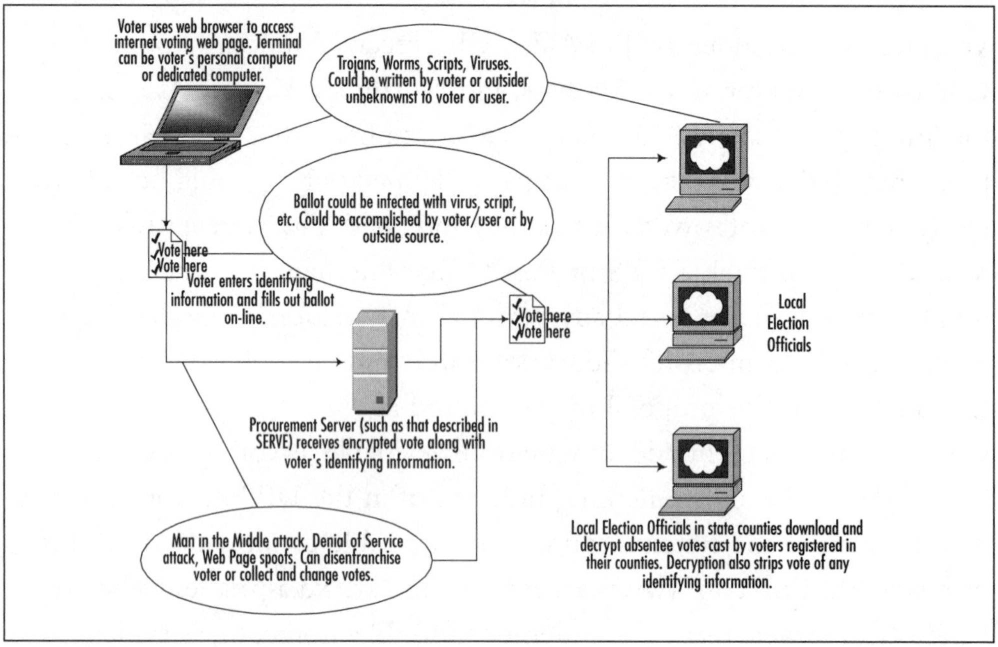

*Trojans, Worms, Viruses, Scripts (a **very** brief overview)*

At one time or another we have probably experienced the inconvenience or complete horror of some worm or virus infecting our computer. These entities can disenfranchise the voter by preventing him or her from casting a ballot on his or her machine. In the worst case, they could be a part of some other software running on the voter's or election official's computer and could possibly collect or modify voter data, ultimately changing votes.

*Man in the Middle, Denial of Service, Web Page Spoofs (a **very** brief overview)*

Man in the Middle attacks can intercept the transfer of data to and from the voter, procurement server, and the local election officials. Even though it is understood that the votes are encrypted, it may still be possible to alter them before they arrive or selectively withhold votes from the procurement server or local election officials. Denial of Service (DoS) attacks could disenfranchise voters by rendering a web site or service inoperable for some time. This DoS attack could even be selective, where it would attack select voter's machines. Web page spoofs could emulate the voting web site and collect voter information (possibly including encryption keys). The voter would place their vote just like they would on the actual web site and assume that their vote was cast safely. The web site spoof would gather the voter information and send its desired votes to the procurement server or possibly emulate the procurement server and spoof the local election officials.

But I've Bought Stuff Online Using my Credit Card... and That's Secure, Right?

E-commerce also has to deal with the same vulnerabilities and attacks in the aforementioned partial list. What's the difference between voting online and buying something on eBay? The SERVE security report detailed the differences in three categories:

1. Different level of security for voting vs. e-commerce.
2. Security structure and legalities differ.
3. Voting is anonymous. E-commerce offers traceability. Additionally your credit card companies usually offer protection against fraud.

The Security Difference

One may ask, "How much security is enough to assure safe online voting?" Good question, and one that is possibly beyond answer presently because the online risk transcends computer software and hardware. Social aspects also would have to be considered in the voting system in order to gauge a system's overall security.

As far as structure is concerned, the SERVE report points out that in e-Commerce one, for example, may allow his wife to make a purchase online using the husband's credit card and personal information. Additionally, a person may appoint another individual to oversee finances.

In the case of voting, a person's vote is nontransferable and it cannot be appointed.

Anonymity

For all of us that have purchased goods, banked, or paid bills online, we have seen the receipts and traceability implemented in these transactions. As mentioned earlier, most credit card companies also offer fraud insurance that covers unauthorized online transactions. In such transactions, the user can verify the money transferred between accounts and the goods received. Any discrepancies can be sorted out with the bank, vendor, or ultimately disputed with the credit card company in case of suspected fraud.

The privacy and anonymity that is required in voting basically removes the element of traceability present in e-commerce. This alone adds immense complexity to the software design and encryption methods necessary to assure a secure and anonymous vote.

Certifying Software

One of the most difficult tasks for any designer or product developer is to come up with a test plan that will take a product or software package through every possible operating condition imaginable including failure modes and states of malicious intent. Products usually undergo Design Failure Modes and Effects Analysis (DFMEAs), Fault Tree Analysis, Red-Teams and other techniques to attempt to measure software quality, reliability, and security.

When it comes to software—more specifically voting software—government requires that the software and voting system be tested by a licensed independent testing authority (ITA). The voting systems are then passed on to the state where a Logic and Accuracy (L&A) test is performed before the systems are used. The L&A tests are considered black-box testing because source code is not examined. The tester will pass sample ballots through the machine and make sure the machine records and counts them correctly.

As noted earlier, Diebold was in the news for using uncertified software in their voting systems. Wyle Laboratories, one of the licensed ITAs (others include Ciber, Inc. and SysTest), does not inspect source code directly; rather, it tests the system's hardware and firmware. After the systems are tested and approved by the ITAs, they cannot be changed without being reevaluated and recertified. When Bev Harris looked over Diebold's source code found on their FTP site, she found lines like:

> Remove SCWinApi module till pass WYLE certification

and

> Merge WYLE branch into the stable branch.12

The point of testing software, in most cases, is to gain some level of confidence that it behaves as intended. However, it would be extremely difficult, time-consuming, and costly to completely evaluate software under every imaginable operating condition. Also, the vulnerability landscape continues to change with new methods of exploiting how a software system works emerging regularly. Herein lies the fundamental paradox of software testing: it can be used to prove the existence of a bug, but for any non-trivial application it cannot prove the absence of bugs. This basic law of software testing casts doubt on the meaning of the certification of a system, no matter how thorough.

Conclusion: What's the Right Answer?

We have evolved from the days of paper ballots, punch cards, lever machines, and optical scan machines to the electronic and Internet-based systems slowly being implemented today. In the past, people figured out how to stuff paper ballots or buy other's votes, and how to compromise lever machines. Punch cards and Marksense systems have also had their own design flaws, and face similar voter fraud vulnerabilities. In short, given enough time, someone, somewhere, will figure out a way to break into, cheat, and manipulate the voting systems in an attempt to affect election outcomes.

We know that 100 percent security and accuracy is unattainable. We can only do our best to create systems that can be trusted with the public's votes and be transparent enough that an audit can reveal and correct errors in a timely manner.

It can be agreed that the issue of security and voter accuracy goes beyond the machine in which the vote is cast. The entire voting process must be carefully considered when implementing any voting machine/system—including election officials training, security, traceability, and most importantly, gaining voter's trust.

We hope this appendix has you asking questions, maybe even angered you a bit. We urge you to do your own research, find out all you can about the voting system(s) your county, city, state, and country are using, the companies that make them, and how they are implemented. Most importantly, we hope you exercise your right to vote. The question of which machine, process, or mechanism is best to record and count that vote is far from being answered.

References

1. *How the Electoral College Works.* www.fec.gov/pages/ecworks.htm.

2. Kimberling, C. William. *The Electoral College.* Federal Election Commission Office of Election Administration.

3. *How the Electoral College Works.* www.howstuffworks.com/electoral-college.htm.

4. Jones, W. Douglas. *A Brief Illustrated History of Voting*, work in progress. University of Iowa, Department of Computer Science, www.cs.uiowa.edu/~jones/voting/pictures/.

5. O'Connor, J.J., and Robertson, E. F. *The History of Voting.* JOC/EFR, August 2002, www-history.mcs.st-andrews.ac.uk/HistTopics/Voting.html.

6. Bellis, M. *The History of Voting Machines.*
   www.inventors.about.com/library/weekly/aa111300b.htm.

7. Ruttledge, E. Lori. *Voting Systems in the United States: An Examination of Histories, Degree of Use and Performance Characteristics.* Capstone Report presented to the Interdisciplinary Studies Program, University of Oregon, Applied Information Management Program, June 2002.

8. "Electronic Voting Firm Site Hack," *Wired News.* Dec. 29, 2003, www.wired.com/news/privacy/0,1848,61764,00.html.

9. "New Security Woes for E-Vote Firm," *Wired News.* Aug. 7, 2003, www.wired.com/news/privacy/0,1848,59925,00.html.

10. "New E-Voting Machine Furor," *Wired News.* Aug. 20, 2003, www.wired.com/news/politics/0,1283,60116,00.html.

11. "How E-Voting Threatens Democracy," *Wired News.* Mar. 29, 2004, www.wired.com/news/evote/0,2645,62790,00.html.

12. Harris, B., with Allen, D. *Black Box Voting: Ballot Tampering in the 21ˢᵗ Century.* Plan Nine Publishing, 2003.

13. "Suspect Code Used in State Votes," *Wired News.* www.wired.com/news/evote/0,2645,61092,00.html.

14. "E-Voting Undermined by Sloppiness," *Wired News.* www.wired.com/news/evote/0,2645,61637,00.html.

15. "Diebold May Face Criminal Charges," *Wired News.* www.wired.com/news/evote/0,2645,63191,00.html.

16. "E-Vote Firm on the Hot Seat," *Wired News.* www.wired.com/news/evote/0,2645,63172,00.html.

17. "Con Job at Diebold Subsidiary," *Wired News.* www.wired.com/news/evote/0,2645,61640,00.html.

18. "Did E-Vote Firm Patch Election?" *Wired News.* www.wired.com/news/politics/0,1283,60563,00.html.

19. Kohno, Tadayoshi, Stubblefield, Adam, Rubin, D. Aviel, and Wallach, S. Dan. *Analysis of an Electronic Voting System.* IEEE Symposium in Security and Privacy 2004, IEEE Computer Society Press, May 2004.

20. "E-Vote Software Leaked Online," *Wired News.* www.wired.com/news/privacy/0,1848,61014,00.html.

21. Gruley, Bryan and Cummins, Chip. *Election Day Became a Nightmare, as Usual, for Bernalillo County.* Wall Street Journal, Dec. 15, 2000.

22. *New Study Shows 50 Million Voters Will Use Electronic Voting Systems, 32 Million Still with Punch Cards in 2004.* Election Data Services, Contact: Kimball, W. Brace, Feb. 12, 2004.

23. Dr. Jefferson, David, Dr. Rubin, D. Aviel, Dr. Simons, Barbara, Dr. Wagner, David. *A Security Analysis of the Secure Electronic Registration and Voting Experiment (SERVE).* Jan. 21, 2004, www.servesecuri-tyreport.org/.

24. "Military Voting System Excoriated," *Wired News.* www.wired.com/news/evote/0,2645,62012,00.html.

25. *A Report on the Feasibility of Internet Voting.* California Secretary of State Bill Jones, California Internet Voting Task Force, January 2000.

26. "Risky E-Vote System to Expand," *Wired News.* www.wired.com/news/evote/0,2645,62041,00.html.

27. "Pentagon Gives E-Voting the Boot," *Wired News.* www.wired.com/news/evote/0,2645,62180,00.html.

28. Wagner, Jim. *E-Voting Experts SERVE Up Controversy.* Jan. 22, 2004, www.internetnews.com/infra/article.php/3302311.

29. Dr. Wertheimer, A. Michael. *Trusted Agent Report: Diebold AccuVote-TS Voting System.* RABA Innovative Solution Cell, submitted to Maryland General Assembly, Department of Legislative Services, Jan. 20, 2004.

Reverse Engineering

Topics in this Appendix:

- Who's Doing Reverse Engineering and Why?
- Tools of the Trade
- The Reverse-Engineering Process
- Reverse Engineering and the Law
- Reverse Engineering in *The Mezonic Agenda*

Introduction

In the beginning, there was *machine code*: those tiny, self-contained instructions that told a computer what to do in a very specific way. Early computers were programmed using machine code exclusively; there was no other choice! These instructions were precise but amazingly difficult for a human to follow. Any program that performed more than a trivial task was exceedingly difficult to read, and understanding it required a significant amount of effort. This made maintainability of applications a nightmare and also meant that only a very few skilled people could write software and translate the endless strings of characters such as "6A006889321100 ..." into commands humans could understand.

Enter *assembly language*. Assembly assigns short mnemonics to machine instructions, which allow a programmer to write and read code in a more human-friendly way. Tools called *assemblers* are used to transform assembly instructions into their machine code equivalents. Using assembly language, however, meant that programmers were still "close to the metal," and having the machine instructions was essentially equivalent to having the original assembly code. For example, a programmer would write "PUSH 00" instead of "6A00," its arcane machine-language equivalent on the x86 architecture. The programmer could then easily convert back and forth between the two.

Most modern software is written in what are referred to as *high-level languages*. These languages allow programmers to write code that is more English-like and significantly more readable than assembly language. As opposed to assembly, where a single assembly instruction represents a single machine instruction or a small set of machine instructions, a high-level language statement may translate into hundreds of machine instructions. Compilers transform these high-level commands into their machine instruction equivalents. A three-line program in C++, for example, may compile into a program with 200 machine instructions. Although high-level languages make it much easier to write more complicated and rich applications, they remove the programmer from the inner workings of the processor; high-level languages essentially created a disconnect between the programmer and the machine instructions their programs translate to.

Compilers began to be viewed not only as tools to create working applications but as a way to protect the intellectual capital that went into creating the code for that application. Many software vendors zealously guard their product source code. The prevailing assumption is that once a compiler creates a binary from source code, the code is no longer recoverable.

That's where *reverse engineering* comes in. Reverse engineering is the art of unlocking an application's secrets. Reverse engineers are detectives who follow clues, make inferences, and solve giant, mind-numbing hexadecimal puzzles. Software applications, outside the realm of open source, are generally distributed in binary form; these binaries contain within them secrets that range from proprietary algorithms, encryption keys, and user restrictions all the way up to state secrets.

For years, software developers felt safe and secure that once their program was compiled into executable code, it was safe from prying eyes. After all, the compiler was nothing more than a sort of encryption engine. Using human-readable source code as input, the compiler generated the corresponding computer application binary that most of us are familiar with. The transformation into an application or executable program resulted in a file that was unintelligible binary code—effectively, encrypted source code. For this reason, applications are often referred to as *binaries*.

In practical terms, reverse engineering of software is the art and science of figuring out what and how an application works without the benefit of its *source code*. This is an intimidating task for all but the simplest programs. It requires of its practitioner a solid foundation in computer science. This includes an understanding of high-level programming, assembly language, data structures, and computer architecture. Long considered a "black art," reverse engineering was practiced by a few small enclaves of hackers whose interest in software was to bend it to their will. Their efforts were largely focused on bypassing software-protection mechanisms and changing the behavior of binaries. Their esoteric tools were mystifying to most and sported interfaces that are far from user friendly. Using diassemblers, debuggers, and hex editors, they built an underground empire that predated bulletin boards and newsgroups and has now flourished into thousands of Web sites dedicated to the art of understanding and manipulating binaries.

As you might imagine, this gathering of knowledge in a small group resulted in the refinement of the practice—one that has left the software development community lacking. Without access to the skills and techniques of their adversaries, developers are put at an extreme disadvantage in both developing and evaluating the strength of their software protection measures. Other groups share in the need of these techniques as well. For system administrators to corporate computer virus researchers, unknown hostile code running on their machines is a frequent reality. With unfamiliar malicious code comes a need to understand its inner workings, what it has done or is capable of doing to a machine, and how it spreads. Still other groups face the challenges of legacy components that must be adapted and understood to implement newer systems or update behavior. These groups found this need acute in 1999, amid Y2K concerns.

NOTE

The terms *legacy code* and *legacy components* refer to software that was written as part of an older application version that is still used in newer versions. This is a common practice for software development companies because it allows them to reuse components that essentially don't need to be changed to serve their roles in new applications.

However, many security issues have come about through the use of legacy code. Because this code wasn't written with modern security requirements and the ubiquity of the Internet in mind, it is more likely to contain security flaws. One of the biggest nonsecurity legacy code issues in history involved the coming new millennium, in 1999. Many older components used only two digits to represent a year (for example, 99 to represent 1999) because at the time those programs were written, computing resources were scarce, and using two digits instead of four improved the application's performance. At the time, no one ever dreamed that their software would still be in use in the year 2000; the result was a mad rush to fix the so-called "millennium bug."

Who's Doing Reverse Engineering and Why?

Many groups of people are involved in the practice of reverse engineering. The underground reverse-engineering community, for example, is huge and is the source of many new techniques and tools in the public domain. Underground or hobbyist reverse engineers are motivated by several factors, including the challenge of the work, the desire to subvert some software security mechanism, and potential gain through software piracy. Other groups, however, have a legitimate and compelling need for such skills. For example, corporations must engage in the activity to preserve and support legacy code. However, there is always the possibility of espionage at the corporate level, with competitors reverse engineering each other's software. Likewise, there is significant motivation to build reverse-engineering skills within the government to both test and protect national software assets as well as uncover secrets from applications used by individuals or groups who intend to do harm. Finally, the academic community has paved the way for significant advances in reverse engineering through the development of new tools and techniques to better interpret binary code. In the following sections, we take a look at each of the groups involved in more detail.

Underground Reverse Engineers

This group is made up of people who reverse engineer software for the challenge of cracking the most powerful software protections available. They host Web sites dedicated to the art of binary understanding and create elaborate and exacting tutorials to proliferate knowledge among their cracking brethren. Some of these individuals are arguably the most technically advanced of all the groups, especially when we consider software copy protection. The reverse-engineering "scene" has also spawned less technical individuals, commonly referred to as *leaches*, who glean cracks and other tools from these elite reverse engineers to crack software and attack systems. Some of the motives of underground reverse engineers include the challenge of unlocking a binary's secrets, finding flaws in the software that they can use to exploit systems, gaining respect within the reverse-engineering underworld, circumventing copy protection to steal and distribute software, and last but not least, holding the political belief that software should be free, open source, and accessible to all.

Governments

In the United States, a fair amount of reverse-engineering expertise is housed in several of the national labs, some law enforcement agencies, and the Department of Defense. Probably the most recognized source of expertise in the government exists within the National Security Agency (NSA). The NSA uses reverse engineering to extract secrets from both domestic and foreign software and hardware (embedded) systems. As a mechanism for gathering information, reverse engineering is critical and can be applied to solve many puzzles associated with national security. First, it can be applied to expose the inner workings of software and integrated circuits, where access to the schematics and source code is implicitly denied. For these applications, unlocking a binary's secrets is (or at least it is perceived to be) an issue of national security. Unlike the quasi-open nature of knowledge in the underground reverse-engineering world, government expertise is tightly held, and the tools and techniques are among the most protected state secrets of nations participating in this activity.

Corporations

Corporations reverse engineer to further their business interests. For example, companies may purchase a competitor's applications at retail and reverse engineer these applications to understand how they process data internally. In the early days of software, companies needed to use reverse-engineering techniques to modify applications so they would be compatible with corporate hardware. The issue was a lack of standardization among hardware. Corporations are also interested in determining how application interfaces work. Probably the most memorable and legally interesting cases of corporate reverse engineering involved the Accolade Corporation, which reverse engineered the interface to the SEGA Genesis game console to manufacture its own compatible cartridges.[1]

Other companies need reverse-engineering techniques to identify and neutralize the actions of some unidentified malicious application. A system administrator for a critical corporate infrastructure can only rely on antivirus companies for large, well-distributed viruses and worms that have affected enough people to be cost effective to analyze and distribute patches for. For highly focused attacks using custom-built malicious code, system administrators need access to the techniques to enable them to analyze the impact of an intruding application and arrest its actions. Companies also need access to these techniques to evaluate the strength of the protection mechanisms included in their own software.

Academia

Universities and researchers are another source for and consumer of reverse-engineering techniques. Typically, information in this environment is of a much more theoretical nature than the information found in the underground reverse-engineering community. Researchers tend to focus on topics such as generalized classes of vulnerabilities, protection schemes, or complexity measures and signatures. The Working Conference on Reverse Engineering entered its 10th year in 2003. Its program of talks is filled with arcane titles such as "Java Quality Assurance by Detecting Code Smells."[2] Although such works may advance the theoretical underpinnings of reverse engineering, they are of marginal, if any, use to the practitioner. What is interesting is that much of the reverse-engineering subculture has its roots in academia. Massachusetts Institute of Technology's (MIT's) model railroad club in the 1960s was arguably the first group of hackers. Of course, the great facilitator of reverse engineers, the Internet, had its beginning in academia and the military as ARPANET.

Tools of the Trade

The reverse engineer has a few critical weapons in his or her arsenal. These weapons can be loosely separated into two groups: tools that support static analysis and tools that aid in dynamic analysis. Both are usually required to learn information about the application. *Static analysis* is the process of analyzing a binary while that binary is not executing. Tools here are designed to help the reverse engineer analyze executable files on disk. These tools include hex editors, resource editors, disassemblers, and decompilers. In contrast, *dynamic analysis* is the process of scrutinizing a binary during execution. These tools, also known as *runtime inspection tools*, include debuggers, emulators, application monitors, and system monitors.

Typically, a reverse engineer uses a combination of static and dynamic tools to understand how a particular piece of software works and possibly how it can be manipulated and where key vulnerabilities lie. The following sections present a broad overview of the reverse-engineering toolset.

Static Analysis Tools

Looking at an application's instructions in the raw executable form can give us a huge amount of insight into how the software works. Although it is possible to open an executable file in a text editor, the information that we can gather that way is limited. Instead, we need tools that can aid in the interpretation of a file's contents. This is where static analysis tools come into play. The following sections briefly outline the major categories of static analysis tools.

Hex Editors

Hex editors are one of the most useful tools for the reverse engineer. They are used to look at the individual values and machine instructions that compose a binary. The copy protection of many applications has been broken just using a hex editor—for example, to replace a stored expiry date with a later date. Several freeware and shareware hex editors are available; the one used throughout this book is called WinHex (available at www.x-ways.net/winhex/). Most software development environments include their own hex editors, such as the one that ships with Visual Studio .NET.

Disassemblers

Moving up the food chain for application understanding, we have disassemblers. Unlike hex editors, diassemblers actually try to "reason" about what hex values (representing machine instructions and data) actually mean. The goal of a disassembler is to convert the sea of indecipherable hex values in a file to assembly instructions—human-readable mnemonics that allow us to reconstruct the application's code at a very low level. Diassemblers are essential tools for reverse engineers and are probably used more than any other tool type discussed here other than debuggers. Almost every operating system ships with an assembler and a disassembler. Most flavors of Microsoft Windows, for example, ship with the assembler DEBUG, a command-line assembler. Additionally, some disassemblers are fairly widely available as shareware and freeware. Without a doubt, the most popular and powerful commercially available disassembler is the Interactive Disassembler PRO (IDAPro) produced by DataRescue (www.datarescue.com). IDAPro allows users to graph application execution flow, comment disassembly, and other advanced features that make the process of application understanding easier. It is a must-have tool for the serious reverse engineer.

Decompilers

Decompilers attempt go a step beyond disassemblers, to reconstruct the high-level source code. Decompilers are useful if the logic programmed into them is familiar with the compiler used to create the binary. The problem with decompilers is that they often make "best guess" estimates of what a particular group of low-language commands map to in a high-level language, and they are often wrong.

Other Tools

Several other tools can help the reverse engineer unlock the secrets of a binary. Resource editors, for example, can give critical insight into which image, menus, display windows, and other resources that an application uses. There is also a wide array of executable file explorers that organize information about the binary in an easy-to-reference format.

Dynamic Analysis Tools

Dynamic analysis tools are used to inspect and analyze an application during execution. Watching an application as it runs can give users a tremendous amount of insight into how the application processes data that would be difficult to get with static analysis alone. In some cases, for example, applications encrypt some of their instructions to make static analysis very difficult, but by allowing the application to run and decrypt those instructions at runtime, we can still uncover software's secrets. In the next sections we take a look at the major categories of dynamic analysis tools.

Debuggers

Debuggers allow a user to inspect an application, instruction by instruction, while it is executing. Additionally, many debuggers allow the user to change instructions in memory during an application's execution. This technique is commonly used to bypass security checks by "jumping" past those checks while the application is executing. In general, debuggers are amazingly powerful tools for the reverse engineer because—unlike in static analysis—we can watch the flow of data through the application. Many applications that explicitly keep secrets from the user (such as an electronic book reader that reads encrypted books not meant for public distribution) employ the use of antidebugging techniques that are intended either to not allow a user to inspect the application with a debugger or to use techniques to trip up a debugger and render it useless as an analysis tool. A common antidebugging technique, for example, is for an application to continuously scan its instructions in memory, looking for signs of tampering or manipulation by a debugger.

Emulators

Emulators simulate the entire operating environment of an application, including hardware. Emulators can be powerful analysis tools for the reverse engineer because they often allow him or her to inspect the application under observation in exacting detail and in a controlled environment determined by the engineer.

Other Tools

Several other types of tools can be used to analyze the running application. Process inspectors allow a user to carefully observe all the interactions between an application and every software resource that it interacts with on the machine. Arguably the most powerful tool available for this type of analysis is Holodeck (available at www.securityinnovation.com). There are also some freeware tools that can be used to monitor very specific types of interactions; one example is FileMon (www.sysinternals.com), which monitors all interactions between an application and the file system.

The Reverse-Engineering Process

One of the most common tasks of the reverse engineer is algorithm recovery: discovering exactly what an application is doing. Determining this information usually takes a combination of static and dynamic analysis. We will work through a typical reverse-engineering session by considering an application in binary form that performs an unknown computation on a number. Our target application is compute.exe.

A typical first step is to execute the application and see what we can figure out by the results it produces for various inputs. Let's take a look at what happens when we execute compute.exe. Compute prompts us to enter a value. After we press the Enter key, the application produces a result and then immediately exits. Figure B.1 shows some sample calculations performed by the program.

Figure B.1 We Execute the Compute.exe Application and Feed In Sample Data

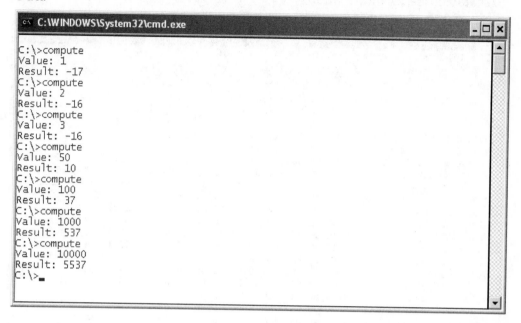

```
C:\>compute
Value: 1
Result: -17
C:\>compute
Value: 2
Result: -16
C:\>compute
Value: 3
Result: -16
C:\>compute
Value: 50
Result: 10
C:\>compute
Value: 100
Result: 37
C:\>compute
Value: 1000
Result: 537
C:\>compute
Value: 10000
Result: 5537
C:\>_
```

Since there appears to be some computation taking place on the value entered, there are a few things we could try, such as coming up with a mathematical model of what we think the application is doing. This can be tricky, though, because we have no idea of the type or combination of types of operations (addition, multiplication, integration, modulus, and so on) the application might be performing. Our next step is to inspect the application's instructions themselves. Opening the application in a hex editor gives us Figure B.2.

Figure B.2 Inspecting the Application in a Hex Editor Provides the Standard Executable Header Information

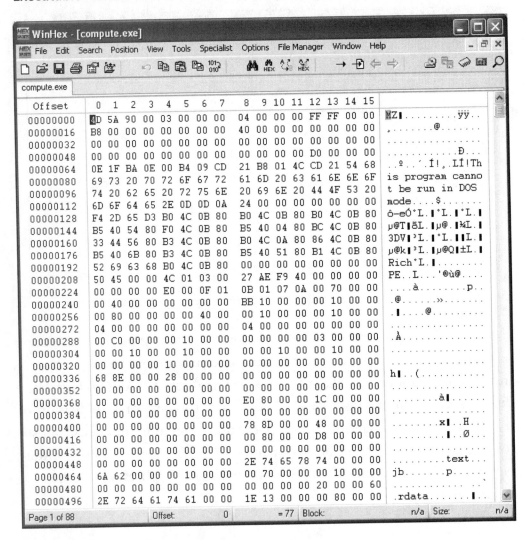

In the hex editor, we see a fairly standard set of data at the beginning of the file, known as the *header*. The letters MZ at the beginning indicate the start of the DOS header for the application. We then see the standard "This program cannot be run in DOS mode" statement that follows shortly afterward. If someone were to attempt to run this application under DOS, that message would be displayed and the application would exit.

NOTE

The statement, "This program cannot be run in DOS mode," might seem misleading, since the program itself launches a DOS Shell. The fact that the program launches this DOS Shell as the interface does not mean the application is running in DOS; in this case, it is running as a Windows console application.

Shortly after this message, we see the letters PE in the hex editor. PE stands for the *Portable Executable* (Windows executable) file format, and those two letters indicate the beginning of the Windows header.

The header contains important information about how that application is to be loaded and where its instructions and data are located in the file. The code section of the file begins at offset 4096 (decimal) of the file (see Figure B.3). We can find this location by either wading through the header information or using one of the many tools that organize the presentation of executable files. (See www.sourceforge.net for several open source applications that do this.)

Figure B.3 A Closer Look at the Hex Representation of the Application Reveals Some of the Machine Instructions

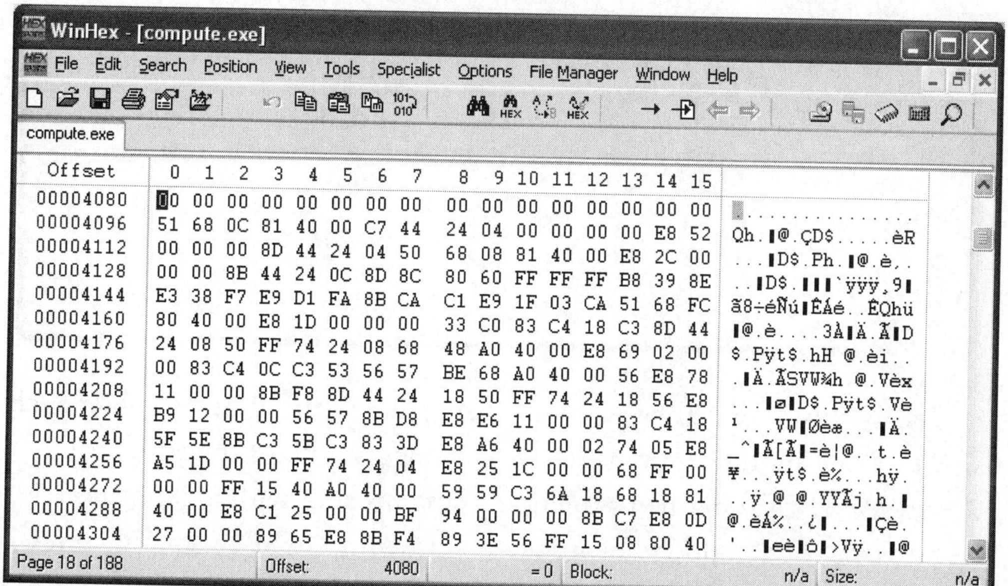

The first part of this hex data initially seems like gibberish:

51680C814000C744240400000000E8520000008D442404506808814000E82C0000008B44240C
8D8C8060FFFFFFB8398EE338F7E9D1FA8BCAC1E91F03CA5168FC804000E81D00000033C083C4
18C3

These values, however, represent executable instructions. We can learn more using a disassembler—a tool designed to convert machine code into assembly language instructions. Using the Microsoft Macro Assembler (MASM, available with a GUI interface as MASM32 from www.movsd.com/), we can see the assembly mnemonics that those instructions represent in Figure B.4.

Figure B.4 A Disassembler Translates the Machine Instructions of an Executable into Assembly Language

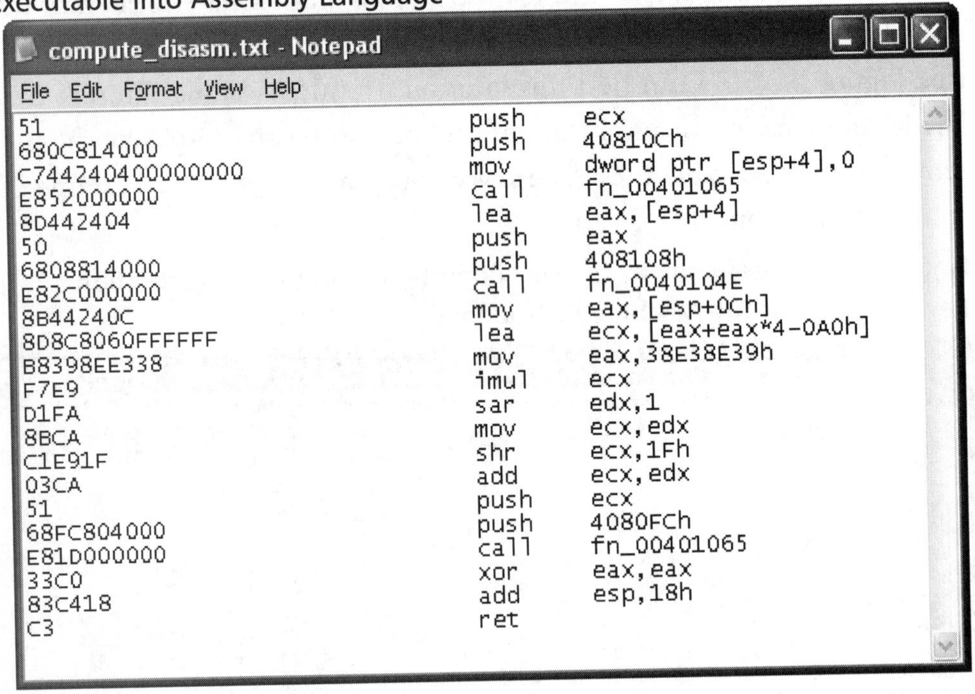

```
compute_disasm.txt - Notepad
File  Edit  Format  View  Help

51                        push    ecx
680C814000                push    40810Ch
C744240400000000          mov     dword ptr [esp+4],0
E852000000                call    fn_00401065
8D442404                  lea     eax,[esp+4]
50                        push    eax
6808814000                push    408108h
E82C000000                call    fn_0040104E
8B44240C                  mov     eax,[esp+0Ch]
8D8C8060FFFFFF            lea     ecx,[eax+eax*4-0A0h]
B8398EE338                mov     eax,38E38E39h
F7E9                      imul    ecx
D1FA                      sar     edx,1
8BCA                      mov     ecx,edx
C1E91F                    shr     ecx,1Fh
03CA                      add     ecx,edx
51                        push    ecx
68FC804000                push    4080FCh
E81D000000                call    fn_00401065
33C0                      xor     eax,eax
83C418                    add     esp,18h
C3                        ret
```

Even more data can be extracted using an advanced disassembler such as IDA Pro.[3] Another route is to use a debugger, one of the principal dynamic analysis tools. Most operating systems ship with a debugger. Most flavors of Windows, for instance, ship with NTSD, a simple command–line debugger that allows you to analyze an executable. Figures B.5 and B.6 show the compute.exe program running under OllyDbg, a freeware debugger for Windows (available for download at http://home.t-online.de/home/Ollydbg/).

Figure B.5 The OllyDbg Debugger Reveals Even More Information About Our Mysterious Program

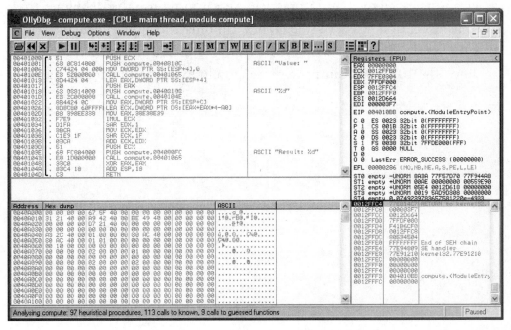

Figure B.6 A Zoomed View of the OllyDbg Output

```
00401000  ┌$ 51              PUSH ECX
00401001  │. 68 0C814000     PUSH compute.0040810C          ASCII "Value: "
00401006  │. C74424 04 000(  MOV DWORD PTR SS:[ESP+4],0
0040100E  │. E8 52000000     CALL compute.00401065
00401013  │. 8D4424 04       LEA EAX,DWORD PTR SS:[ESP+4]
00401017  │. 50              PUSH EAX
00401018  │. 68 08814000     PUSH compute.00408108          ASCII "%d"
0040101D  │. E8 2C000000     CALL compute.0040104E
00401022  │. 8B4424 0C       MOV EAX,DWORD PTR SS:[ESP+C]
00401026  │. 8D8C80 60FFFF(  LEA ECX,DWORD PTR DS:[EAX+EAX*4-A0]
0040102D  │. B8 398EE338     MOV EAX,38E38E39
00401032  │. F7E9            IMUL ECX
00401034  │. D1FA            SAR EDX,1
00401036  │. 8BCA            MOV ECX,EDX
00401038  │. C1E9 1F         SHR ECX,1F
0040103B  │. 03CA            ADD ECX,EDX
0040103D  │. 51              PUSH ECX
0040103E  │. 68 FC804000     PUSH compute.004080FC          ASCII "Result: %d"
00401043  │. E8 1D000000     CALL compute.00401065
00401048  │. 33C0            XOR EAX,EAX
0040104A  │. 83C4 18         ADD ESP,18
0040104D  └. C3              RETN
```

OllyDbg shows the Value: and Result: strings we saw in the program when we executed it earlier (refer back to Figure B.1). The computation on the entered value occurs starting at line 00401022. To see how the application actually works in practice, we can now use the debugger to trace its execution at every step. While running the application, we see that the result entered at the Value: prompt is placed in the EAX register on line 00401022. We can now more closely examine the computations

Figure B.7 A Flowchart Showing the Operations Performed on the Number Entered into Compute.exe

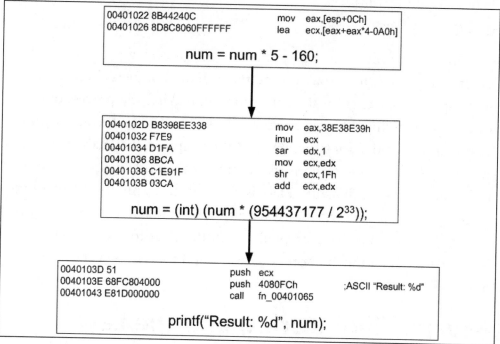

performed on this value. Figure B.7 shows a flowchart of the operations performed on the entered value, which we will refer to as *num*.

Now we begin to see what the application is doing, given that we've translated it into C code by observing the assembly instructions. These calculations appear odd, however. This is one of the challenges of the reverse engineer: to take whatever contrived representation of a calculation or a transformation that was produced by the compiler and not only convert it to its equivalent higher-level language code but draw meaning from those calculations. In Figure B.7, for example, we can simplify the quotient $954437177 / 2^{33}$ as approximately equivalent to 1/9. For integer division and given the size of the operands and the precision involved, these two are exactly equivalent. With this in mind, we can rewrite the calculation as:

Result = (num − 32) * 5/9

This equation looks a bit familiar; it is the conversion formula from Fahrenheit to Celsius!

$$C° = (F° - 32) * 5/9$$

This is an example of the basic reverse-engineering process. In practice, the algorithm to extract can be much more complex. Furthermore, some applications encrypt their instructions, making the process of static reverse engineering difficult because we must first force the application to run and decrypt its instructions and then capture and analyze them. Additionally, some applications are written with antidebugging code to make the process of dynamic analysis more difficult. All known methods of protecting software with software have been broken, because eventually instructions must be decrypted and in the clear to execute. The critical issues are how much effort is required and the value of the information gained.

Reverse Engineering and the Law

Reverse engineering has caused significant debate and actions within the legislative branches of the government in the United States, Europe, Australia, and several other countries around the world. Most of the landmark legal decisions regarding software piracy and reverse engineering were made by courts in the United States early in software's history. Much of the debate has centered on the *illegitimate* copying of software, a practice that is often necessary to perform any type of analysis. In this section, we look at the history of software copyrights and legal decisions that have shaped the reverse-engineering landscape.

A Legal History of Software Copyrights in the United States

Copyright law as applied to computer software has a short but interesting history. The first litmus test of "software" copyright happened long before the advent of the computer as we know it. In the late 1800s, the Apollo

Music Company produced a player piano known as the Apollo. These devices looked like standard pianos but used perforated rolls to produce music automatically, without a human playing the keys. These rolls were essentially "software" that the player piano could read to produce a melody. In 1902, it is estimated that there were between 70,000 and 75,000 of these machines in use in the United States.

The issue of copyright was raised by the White-Smith Music Publishing Company when Apollo produced rolls with two melodies for which White-Smith owned the copyright of the sheet music. Earlier case law had not taken into account that music could be reproduced this way. Instead, copyright law was worded to reflect something tangible, meaning that the author could copyright sheet music or a recording, so the legal issue came down to whether producing the perforated rolls constituted "copying" the sheet music—the item that was lawfully protected. In the wording of Justice Day of the United States Supreme Court, "Only the tangible thing is dealt with by the law, and its multiplication and reproduction is all that is dealt with by the law."[4] The Supreme Court thus ruled that Apollo could continue to manufacture these rolls and that their production did not infringe on the copyright of White-Smith, given the state of copyright law. However, the court did allude to the fact that copyright law needed to change and essentially passed the buck to the legislative branch of government.

To find the first software copyright, we fast forward to 1964. The U.S. Copyright Office threw caution to the wind and granted copyrights to two computer programs, one that was submitted as a printout of source code and the other submitted on magnetic tape. The Copyright Office recognized the fact that software contains an expression of originality and that once it was in a form "intelligible to human beings," it met the standard of copyright.[5]

In the Copyright Act of 1976, Congress expanded its definition of literary works to include "works, other than audiovisual works, expressed in words, numbers, or other verbal or numerical symbols or indicia, regardless of the nature of the material objects, such as books, periodicals, manuscripts, phonorecords, film, tapes, disks, or cards, in which they are embodied."[6] This further paved the way for software companies to copyright their works, and it was clear that the government intended for the copyright of software and other media. What wasn't as clear was how much protection was afforded to the owner of a software copyright. With this in mind, the National Commission on New Technological Uses of Copyrighted Works (CONTU) was appointed to investigate this issue further. The commission delivered its final report in 1978 and recommended a few significant changes to copyright law. One of them was to redefine a computer program as "a set of statements or instructions to be used directly or indirectly in a computer in order to bring about a certain result."[7] The commission also made some interesting recommendations regarding exemptions to copy protection. Specifically, it recommended that "the rightful possessor of a copy" is allowed to make a copy if "a new copy or adaptation is created as an essential step in the utilization of the computer program" or if the "copy or adaptation is for archival purposes only."

The reasoning behind this wording is that the commission realized that any legitimate user of software would necessarily have to copy it to some other medium—to a computer hard disk, for example—to be useful. What is particularly interesting here is the use of the word *adaptation*. At the time the commission delivered its report, the majority of software sold was not the shrink-wrapped "install and go" software of today. Most applications had to be modified, enhanced, adapted, or translated between languages to be useful on the diverse array of corporate computer hardware. When we look at the Digital Millennium Copyright Act (DMCA), you will see how the seeds planted in 1978 have influenced current law.

The changes recommended by CONTU were enacted into law in 1980, with the minor change of the wording "rightful possessor of a copy" to "owner of a copy"—apparently to escape the case of legitimate renters or lessees copying a protected work. This provision to exclude renters of software became unnecessary in 1990 when President George Herbert Walker Bush signed into law the Computer Software Rental Amendments Act, prohibiting the rental, lease, or lending of a computer program for direct or indirect commercial gain unless authorized by the owner of the program's copyright. Aside from some obscure amendments made in 1998 under the DMCA relative to maintenance, backup, and repair of machines, this is where we leave the issue of software copyright.

Reverse Engineering

One of the first legal tests of software reverse engineering came to a head in 1992 with Atari vs. Nintendo, when engineers at Atari essentially reverse engineered raw machine instructions running on the Nintendo Entertainment System to understand how the interface worked so that the company could produce its own games to be compatible with that system. In that case, the Supreme Court ruled that "reverse engineering object code to discern the unprotectable ideas in a computer program is a fair use" under the copyright act.[8]

About a month later, Sega sued Accolade for, among other things, reverse engineering. The Sega Corporation manufactured a game console called Genesis. The Genesis played game cartridges that were also manufactured by Sega and a few other vendors to which they sold licenses. Accolade made game software and entered into negotiations with Sega to become a licensee so that it could get the specifics on how to make cartridges and software compatible with the Genesis. Accolade broke off negotiations when Sega insisted that, as part of the licensing agreement, Accolade make software exclusively for Sega. This left Accolade with a dilemma: The company saw the popularity of Genesis and wanted to benefit from it, but the revenue lost from its other software endeavors by entering into an exclusive contract with Sega was too steep a price to pay. Instead, Accolade engineers bought three Genesis game cartridges and a console and wired in a decompiler that extracted the information needed to painstakingly reverse engineer the specifics of the interface between them. Accolade used this knowledge to manufacture its own cartridges containing its own software and sold them to the public. On October 20, 1992, the U.S. Ninth Circuit Court of Appeals ruled that "where disassembly is the only way to gain access to the ideas and functional elements embodied in a copyrighted computer program and where there is a legitimate reason for seeking such access, disassembly is a fair use of the copyrighted work, as a matter of law."[9] The court also ruled that the intermediate copying of object code that was necessary to perform the analysis was also "fair use" under the law. However, Congress began to realize that current copyright laws didn't accurately define or adequately protect digital works. Efforts to revise these laws resulted in the Digital Millennium Copyright Act (DMCA) of 1998.

DMCA

From the early cases of videogame manufacturers to the growing software for PC users, judges began hearing more and more cases relative to the protection of digital works. In addition, there was a global realization that international copyright law needed to adapt to address rapidly changing technology. In 1996, several countries agreed in principal to the World Intellectual Property Organization Copyright Treaty, the purpose of which was to address intellectual property rights of authors and innovators in a technologically evolving world. To meet these challenges, the United States implemented the DMCA. The road to the DMCA began in 1993, when the Information Infrastructure Task Force (IITF) was formed. This group held public hearings attended by a wide range of interested parties; the result was the 1995 production of the so-called "white paper" that offered recommendations on how to update the copyright laws to keep them current with new technology. Based on the IITF findings, both the House and the Senate introduced legislation to incorporate changes in the Copyright Act. This resulted in a flurry of hearings, meetings, and debates that ultimately stalled any implementation of these amendments for years. Then, in 1998, Chairman Orrin Hatch offered the

Digital Millennium Copyright Act of 1998 at an executive meeting of the Senate Judiciary Committee; the act was adopted and became law that same year.

The original goal of the DMCA was to encourage artists, software developers, and other producers of digital copyrighted works to make their works readily available over the Internet with "reasonable assurance that they will be protected against massive piracy."[10] Among other things, the DMCA strictly prohibits the creation and distribution of tools and techniques whose sole purpose is to circumvent software protections. As you might imagine, the DMCA drew heavy support from the motion picture, recording, publishing, and software industries. The danger, though, was in going too far and limiting the rights of software users and those who had a legitimate need to copy, test, install, and reverse engineer software. The rights of content producers had to be weighed against the chilling impact a too harshly worded amendment could have on security researchers, innovators, and the future development of software security technology. One specific concern was that the spirit of the decision in the Sega vs. Accolade case discussed earlier might be quashed. With concerns like this in mind, exemptions were added to protect certain groups.

Exceptions

Originally, the DMCA had no protection for legitimate reverse engineering, security testing, and research, which critics quickly realized could lead to some pretty ridiculous and stifling consequences. Imagine, for instance, that you are a system administrator who notices a hostile application running on one of your servers, placed there by an intruder. Now imagine that the hostile executable is protected by encryption or some other software protection mechanism. In proposed bills that were precursors to the DMCA, it would be illegal for you to reverse engineer that executable to find out what it was doing to your system! Also, consider a software development company who wants to test the effectiveness of some antipiracy measure it uses. Without exceptions to the DMCA, testers of that product would essentially be performing an illegal act. For these reasons, the DMCA includes exemptions for the following purposes: interoperability, encryption research, protection of personally identifying information, and security testing.

Interoperability

From Title 17, Chapter 12, Section 1201, Subsection f of the U.S. Code: "A person who has lawfully obtained the right to use a copy of a computer program may circumvent a technological measure that effectively controls access to a particular portion of that program for the sole purpose of identifying and analyzing those elements of the program that are necessary to achieve interoperability of an independently created computer program with other programs" (17 USC §1201(f)). Here we see the weight of the Sega vs. Accolade decision. This clause essentially upholds the findings of the court in that case and allows users to engage in reverse engineering to determine the specifics of software's interfaces that would enable new applications to interact with protected, closed-source software. The code goes on to absolve makers of tools that enable reverse engineering for interoperability under the act and permits the dissemination of results strictly for the purpose of interoperability.

Encryption Research

A second major concern of Congress was to avoid stifling the efforts of researchers working on improving the effectiveness of protection measures. For this reason, the DMCA exempts encryption researchers legitimately engaged in reverse-engineering research. The exception in section 1201, paragraph g, states that it is not a breach of the DMCA to circumvent a technological protection measure (given that the act doesn't violate other laws) if (17 USC §1201(g)):

(A) the person lawfully obtained the encrypted copy, phonorecord, performance, or display of the published work;

(B) such act is necessary to conduct such encryption research; [and]

(C) the person made a good faith effort to obtain authorization before the circumvention.

This section goes on to discuss the factors involved in determining exemption, which may involve dissemination, disclosure to the vendor, and if the researcher was engaged in legitimate security research.

The enactment also called for a report to Congress, to be prepared by the Copyright Office and the Commerce Department, to assure them that the enactment of this title did not have any negative impact on encryption research. The report was delivered one year later. Of the responses to the solicitation for comments, "not one identified a current, discernable impact on encryption research and the development of encryption technology."[11] Thus no changes to the DMCA with respect to encryption research were suggested. It is widely thought in the industry that this one-year evaluation period was nowhere near long enough to assess the impact of the DMCA on legitimate security research efforts. These fears were affirmed in threats made by the Recording Industry Association of America (RIAA) to Professor Edward Felton of Princeton University for his research on vulnerabilities in a widely used watermarking scheme for media. We'll look closely at this case in the "First Legal Challenges to the DMCA" section of this appendix.

Protection of Personally Identifying Information

The original wording of the DMCA did not allow provisions for a legitimate user of a product to understand or block an application that was collecting or distributing sensitive information about its user or the system. For this reason, the DMCA includes provisions for individuals who want to investigate or disable the collection and dissemination of personal information by software. According to the DMCA, "it is not a violation [...] for a person to circumvent a technological measure that effectively controls access to a work protected under this title, if the technological measure, or the work it protects, contains the capability of collecting or disseminating personally identifying information reflecting the online activities of a natural person who seeks to gain access to the work protected." The code goes on to state that it is only legal in this case to circumvent software protection mechanisms if the sole purpose of the act is to identify or block portions of the program that reveal sensitive information (17 USC §1201(i)).

Security Testing

The DMCA also contains exemptions for people performing security testing on their products. The wording of this exception is widely considered to be completely off-mark. To begin with, consider the definition of the term *security testing* used in the law, which is "accessing a computer, computer system, or computer network, solely for the purpose of good faith testing, investigating, or correcting, a security flaw or vulnerability, with the authorization of the owner or operator of such computer, computer system, or computer network" (17 USC §1201(j)). This is a very broad, somewhat unhelpful definition for the reverse-engineering practitioner. The wording seems more relevant to network penetration testing than to testing of a binary for its ability to retain its secrets under a reverse-engineering attack. Furthermore, the term *good faith* makes the definition even more nebulous and uninterpretable. The act then goes on to state that security testing is permitted and lists the use and dissemination of the results as the primary factors in determining exemption.

Safe Harbors

Another thorny area in pre-DMCA copyright law was the liability of Internet service providers and others who own and operate critical Internet infrastructure devices and technology. The issue here is criminal facilitation. A Web page, software application, media, and a host of other digital information are copied millions of times a day in the course of normal Internet infrastructure activities. Under the old copyright law, this act of copying data that in some cases is copyrighted (a music file, for example) could be illegal. The DMCA thus made provisions for this situation by creating what are dubbed *safe harbors*—groups that are essentially exempt from the reproduction copyright laws. The four safe harbors named in the DMCA are (17 U.S.C. §512):

- Transitory digital network communications
- System caching
- Information residing on systems or networks at the direction of users
- Information location tools

Congress wanted to ensure that passing such sweeping legislation would not cripple the Internet by making some of its critical operations illegal. By being in a safe harbor, a service provider is absolved from monetary damages that result from its part in copyright infringement. As of this writing, very few relevant cases have been brought to court, and thus, there have been few interpretations of the wording of the law.

First Legal Challenges to the DMCA

The DMCA has faced several legal assaults since it was passed. In the next few sections, we outline some of the early landmark cases challenging the DMCA.

Felton vs. RIAA

On April 9, 2001, Professor Edward Felton of Princeton University, a world-renowned researcher in software security, received a letter from the Recording Industry Association of America (RIAA) threatening "actions under the DMCA and possibly other federal laws"[12] if he were to release his findings of vulnerabilities in the Verance Watermark protection scheme that was in use in some DVDs and other deployed media. Felton and his colleagues, with the aid of the Electronic Frontier Foundation, took the RIAA (and several others, including the U.S. Attorney General) to court to allow them to publish their findings at the 2001 USENIX conference. Felton and his colleagues lost, but the RIAA then agreed to allow Felton and USENIX to publish his results. In return, Felton did not appeal the verdict.

United States v. ElcomSoft and Sklyarov

In July 2001, Dimitry Sklyarov, a programmer for Russia-based ElcomSoft, was in Las Vegas to speak at the infamous DEFCON hacker conference. His talk, titled "eBooks Security—Theory and Practice," discussed how he had cracked the encryption used to protect digital books read through Adobe's eBook reader, to enable his company's product, which operated on ebooks, to work. On July 21, 2001, the day after Sklyarov's DEFCON talk, he was arrested in his hotel room on charges of trafficking in, and offering to the public, a software program that could circumvent technological protections on copyrighted material, under Title 17, Section 1201, Sub-Section b of the U.S. Copyright Act, which was made law by the 1998 DMCA. Sklyarov was also charged with contributory infringement under the DMCA for aiding his company in creating its Advance eBook Processor program. Sklyarov was extradited to California and finally released three weeks later on bail of $50,000 but ordered to remain in California until trial. Sklyarov and ElcomSoft were indicted on August 28, 2001, on five counts of violating the DMCA, four counts of aiding and abetting circumvention, and one count of conspiracy to traffic in a circumvention program. These charges carried a maximum penalty of 25 years in prison for Sklyarov and over $2 million in fines for both him and ElcomSoft. On December 13, 2001, Sklyarov was allowed to leave the United States as part of an agreement that he would testify on behalf of the U.S. government in the case against ElcomSoft. Under the deal, the U.S. government also agreed to drop all criminal charges against Sklyarov personally.

The United States vs. ElcomSoft trial lasted for two weeks, and the decision finally boiled down to whether jurors believed that ElcomSoft knew that its actions were illegal. The DMCA was dealt its first real blow on December 16, 2002, when jurors acquitted the company of all charges. This was the first criminal case under the DMCA since it was made law in 1998, and faced with its first demon, the digital copyright law quivered and fell.

Universal Studios et al vs. Shawn C. Reimerdes et al

Jon Johansen, a Norwegian teenager, just wanted to be able to play his DVDs on his Linux machine. To do that, he had to break the encryption Content Scrambling System (CSS) that encrypts DVDs, for which he produced an appropriately named tool called DeCSS that performs the decryption. A legal and media hurricane made landfall when Eric Corley posted the code to DeCSS as part of an article he wrote for the infamous hacker magazine, *2600*. Corey placed the code to DeCSS on the *2600* Web site, along with links to the program itself. On January 20, 2001, in a nonjury trial, the District Court of New York court entered a permanent injunction barring Corey from posting the code to DeCSS or linking to it from the *2600* site. The appellate courts later upheld this decision.

Sony Computer Entertainment Inc. v. Connectix Corporation

This case is strikingly similar to the Sega vs. Accolade case but takes place in a post-DMCA environment. On January 27, 1999, Sony (the makers of the popular Playstation game console) filed a complaint alleging copyright infringement against Connectix, which produced the Virtual Game Station, an emulator for Playstation games that runs on either a Macintosh or Windows computer. To build its product, Connectix had to reverse engineer the BIOS contained on a ROM chip inside the Playstation. This process involved copying the BIOS multiple times in to be able to understand it, and Sony thus claimed that this violated DMCA provisions protecting the copying of copyrighted software under the DMCA. Sony was granted an injunction against Connectix from selling its emulator or further copying the Playstation BIOS. The court's decision was later reversed on appeal, and the injunction against Connectix was lifted after the appellate court determined that the copying and reverse engineering of the Playstation BIOS was indeed a "fair use" under the DMCA. The court concluded that Connectix's actions were necessary "to gain access to the functional elements of the software itself."[13]

Beyond U.S. Copyright Law

As in the United States, the worldwide legal climate surrounding reverse engineering is in heavy flux. The DMCA, the EU Computer Program Directive with amendments, and many other laws around the world are being implemented to enforce the World Intellectual Property Organization (WIPO) Copyright Treaty (WCT) and the WIPO Performances and Phonographs Treaty (WPPT). Article 11 of this treaty states:

> Contracting Parties shall provide adequate legal protection and effective legal remedies against the circumvention of effective technological measures that are used by authors in connection with the exercise of their rights under this Treaty or the Berne Convention and that restrict acts, in respect of their works, which are not authorized by the authors concerned or permitted by law.[14]

Countries that have agreed to the treaty must therefore enact laws that enforce the articles in the treaty with appropriate punishments. Many countries are making their own revisions to what are considered permissible acts of reverse-engineering software and which actions should be barred.

Legal Implications of Reverse Engineering

As of the writing of this book, software engineers and testers face a nebulous parade of legalese and contradictory rulings to determine whether their software testing is legal. The general spirit of the law seems to indicate that the producers and legal copyright holders of an application have the right to reverse engineer in the context of testing or security research. The copyright holder can also explicitly grant such rights to others. Beyond these narrow circumstances, though, the law is unclear. We are not legal experts, and given the rapidly changing legal climate that surrounds software copyright, we strongly urge you to consult legal counsel before engaging in the reverse engineering of software that you have not produced. That said, it is difficult to imagine that the narrow wording of the DMCA will stand up to legal challenges. The fear of legal reprisal has left software developers and testers wonting for a legitimate source of information on reverse engineering, to create software that is more resistant to the techniques of the attacker community.

Reverse Engineering in *The Mezonic Agenda*

In *The Mezonic Agenda*, Baff Lexicon, noted hacker and software pirate, makes his living from reverse engineering software to defeat its copy protection. Baff is what's known in the software world as a *cracker*, the reverse engineer who "cracks" software protection. Crackers are among the elite of software piracy groups, commonly known as *warez* groups. These groups typically procure, crack, and distribute software on a wide scale. Some groups are in it for profit; others do it as a hobby and simply to trade certain "cracked" applications with other groups. Because of its association with the warez scene, reverse engineering has gotten a bad rap. In actuality, there are several legitimate uses for reverse-engineering skills.

In a later chapter of *The Mezonic Agenda*, Chad Davis uses those same skills to analyze a binary, trying to uncover its secrets. In real life, reverse-engineering skills are used daily by the government, the hacker community, corporations, and the software elite. Some of these uses are legal and legitimate, and others violate copyright law. For legitimate users such as software evaluators, reverse engineering can give remarkable insight into how a compiled application actually works. Sometimes this type of analysis can be more fruitful than just looking at source code. One would hope that the process of evaluating electronic voting software has also gone through such rigorous procedures.

References

1. White-Smith Music Publishing Company v. Apollo Company, Supreme Court of the United States, February 24, 1908, 209 U.S. 1, http://digital-law-online.info/cases/209US1.htm.

2. E. van Emden and L. Moonen, "Java Quality Assurance by Detecting Code Smells," Proceedings of the Ninth Working Conference on Reverse Engineering, 2002.

3. The Interactive Disassembler PRO (IDA Pro) is one of the most advanced disassemblers on the market and is the industry standard. It is sold by Data Rescue (www.datarescue.com), and most reverse engineers use it frequently to analyze an unknown executable.

4. White-Smith Music Publishing Company v. Apollo Company; see note 1.

5. U.S. Copyright Office Circular No. 61, 1964 version.

6. U.S. Copyright Act of 1976, U.S. Code Title 17, www4.law.cornell.edu/uscode/17/101.html.

7. Final Report of the National Commission on the New Technological Uses of Copyrighted Works (CONTU Rep.), ISBN 0-8444-0312-1 (1978) at 12.

8. Atari Games Corporation v. Nintendo of America Inc., U.S. Court of Appeals, Federal Circuit, September 10, 1992, 975 F.2d 832, 24 USPQ2d 1015, www.digital-law-online.com/lpdi1.0/cases/24PQ2D1015.htm.

9. Sega Enterprises Ltd. v. Accolade Inc., U.S. Court of Appeals, Ninth Circuit, October 20, 1992, FN89: 977 F.2d 1510, 24

USPQ2d 1561 (9th Cir. 1992), www.digital-law-online.com/lpdi1.0/cases/24PQ2D1561.htm.

10. Digital Millennium Copyright Act, Pub. L. No. 105–304, 112 Stat. 2860 (October 28, 1998).

11. United States Copyright Office, *Report to Congress: Joint Study of Section 1201(g) of The Digital Millennium Copyright Act,* www.copyright.gov/reports/studies/dmca_report.html (May 2000).

12. Letter from Matthew Oppenheim to Professor Edward Felton, dated April 9, 2001, www.eff.org/Legal/Cases/Felten_v_RIAA/20010409_riaa_sdmi_letter.html.

13. Sony Computer Entertainment Inc. v. Connectix Corporation, U.S. Court of Appeals, Ninth Circuit, February 10, 2000, 203 F.3d 596, 53 USPQ2d 1705.

14. WIPO Copyright Treaty (adopted in Geneva on December 20, 1996), www.wipo.int/clea/docs/en/wo/wo033en.htm#P125_18095.

Appendix C

Cryptography

Topics in this Appendix:

- History of Cryptography
- Symmetric Encryption
- Asymmetric Encryption
- Cryptography and *The Mezonic Agenda*

History of Cryptography

Cryptography—commonly referred to as *crypto*—is the science of keeping messages secret. Cryptanalysis is the science of breaking codes and forcefully decrypting those secret messages. Both cryptography and cryptanalysis are subdisciplines of the larger field of cryptology. The first known use of cryptography dates back roughly 4,000 years, when Egyptians told their buried kings' life stories using hieroglyphics around their tombs. These hieroglyphic texts were publicly accessible but became more and more complex, to the point where most people lost interest in deciphering them and the art died out.

The use of cryptography has evolved and, of course, improved over the past 4,000 years. The ancient Greeks used a skytale cipher, the Romans used a Caesar cipher, and the Arabs made advances in cryptanalysis—the practice of decrypting cipher text without complete knowledge of the cipher. In the United States, the Civil War and World Wars saw widespread use of cryptography for communication and the interception of it from then enemies such as the Nazis and the Japanese.

> **NOTE**
>
> It is interesting to note that some of the most complicated cryptography implemented in early 20th century was created by bootleggers during the Prohibition period in the United States. The U.S. Coast Guard hired Mrs. Elizabeth S. Friedman, wife of William F. Friedman, who was dubbed the father of U.S. cryptanalysis, to help decipher the bootlegger's cryptic codes and messages. Mrs. Friedman reported:
>
> "Some of these are of a complexity never even attempted by any government for its most secret communications ... At no time during the World War, when secret methods of communications reached their highest development, were there used such involved ramifications as are to be found in some of the correspondence of West Coast rum-running vessels."[1]

Figure C.1 shows a very brief cryptography timeline highlighting some uses and key developments in the field.

Figure C.1 A Brief Cryptography Timeline[2]

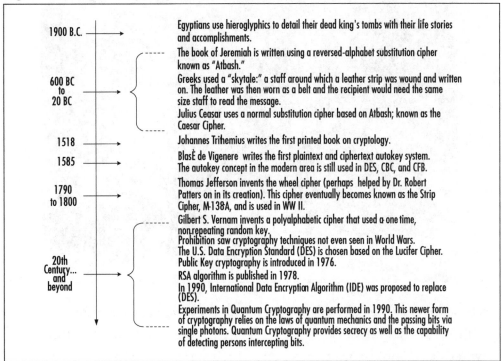

Figure C.2 A Photo of *Kryptos,* a Sculpture by James Sanborn

Photo: www.cia.gov/cia/information/tour/krypt.html and www.elonka.com/kryptos

In the most general sense, cryptography transforms *plaintext* (unencrypted data) into *ciphertext* (the encrypted representation of that data) using a *cipher* (encryption algorithm) with a given *key* (a value that is used with the cipher to create the encrypted data). In the broadest sense, cryptography can be grouped into two categories: symmetric key cryptography and asymmetric key cryptography. Most modern cryptosystems fall into one of these two categories, and most obey a fundamental tenet in cryptography called *Kerckhoffs' Principle.* In symmetric cryptography, the same secret key is used to both encrypt and decrypt a message. In asymmetric key cryptography, a message is encrypted using a different key than the key needed to decrypt. Both schemes have their advantages and weaknesses. The sections that follow discuss these two categories in more detail.

Every widely used crypto system of any value adheres to a fundamental assumption of cryptography known as Kerckhoffs' Principle, named after the 19th-century Flemish cryptographer Auguste Kerckhoffs. Put simply, Kerckhoffs' Principle states that the strength of a crypto system depends on two things: the strength of the key and the strength of the encryption algorithm. The implication here is that encryption strength shouldn't depend on keeping the encryption algorithm itself secret. Most commonly used encryption systems use algorithms that are in the open and widely available for public scrutiny. In the next sections, all the algorithms we discuss are of this type.

Symmetric Encryption

In symmetric key cryptography, a single key is used to both encrypt and decrypt data. To illustrate, let's consider the communications between two people, Adam and Bill. Adam wants to send a message to Bill that is confidential. Adam encrypts the message with a symmetric key algorithm and key k. Bill receives the encrypted message and can decrypt it using the same key that Adam used, k. In this example, Bill must know the key. Obviously, Adam would have to tell Bill what it is ... possibly via steganographic communication!

There are four types of symmetric encryption, which we describe in the following sections. They are:

- Block ciphers
- Barrel ciphers
- Monoalphabetic substitution ciphers
- Polyalphabetic substitution ciphers

Block Ciphers

Block ciphers encrypt data in chunks called *blocks*. In many modern implementations, these blocks are 16 bytes long. Typically, these types of ciphers need to operate on messages that are a multiple of the block size in length. That's where padding comes in. To complete a block at the end of a plaintext message, we need to add some data to increase the message size. Block ciphers are reversible and employ the use of a secret key to both encrypt and decrypt the data.

There are several "modes" in which block ciphers work. Perhaps the simplest is the *electronic code book mode*, or ECB, in which each block of a long message is encrypted independently. This is by far the simplest type of block cipher and is hardly ever used in practice when data secrecy is a serious concern. The most popular mode of block cipher encryption is the cyclical block chaining, or CBC, method. In this mode, the block to be encrypted is *XORed* (see the following Note) with the previous block before encryption begins. This means that two identical blocks may encrypt to different representations. Another popular mode of block cipher is called *output feedback cipher*, or OFB. Instead of operating on individual blocks, the secret key is used to generate a string of data the same length as the data to be decrypted. The text is then XORed with this generated "key."

Some of the common block ciphers in use are the Advanced Encryption Standard (AES) and the Data Encryption Standard (DES).

NOTE

XOR is the industry-standard term for *eXclusive OR*. One of the simplest forms of digital encryption is to XOR some plaintext in binary form with a "key" of the same length. This procedure compares two binary numbers of the same length digit by digit, producing another binary number of the same length. For each position in the number, if the two binary digits are identical (either both 1s or both 0s), the result is a 1 in that position of the result.

For example, if we compute:

10010010 XOR 11111111

the result is 10010010, the same as the original number. If we compute:

10010010 XOR 00000000

the result is 01101101—the exact bitwise inverse of the first number.

A great property of XOR is that for any binary numbers of the same length A and B, the following property holds:

A XOR B = C

means that

C XOR A = B

and

C XOR B = A

This is very useful in cryptography, because if we XOR some plain text with a key, we get our resulting cipher text (encrypted data). Then if we XOR the cipher text with that key again, we get the plain text—symmetric key cryptography at its purest!

Monoalphabetic Substitution Ciphers

Monoalphabetic substitution is a system of encryption whereby every occurrence of a particular letter in the plaintext message is replaced by the same exact cyphertext letter. One of the best-known and earliest monoalphabetic substitution ciphers is the Caesar cipher. In this scheme, every letter is replaced by the letter that appears three letters later in the alphabet. So, for example, *A* is replaced with *D*, *B* is replaced with *E*, and so on. There are several other well-known monoalphabetic substitution ciphers, such as the Atbash cipher (used in the Bible) and the substitution used in Edgar Allen Poe's poem *The Goldbug* (discussed in *The Mezonic Agenda*).

There are several types of attacks against this type of encryption. The simplest is the known plaintext attack, where we know both the plaintext and ciphertext for a particular message and can thus deduce the substitution that was used. Another powerful attack is *frequency analysis*, whereby we compare the frequency of the occurrence of letters in the ciphertext with the average frequency of occurrence of those letters in whichever language we suspect the plaintext is written in.

Polyalphabetic Substitution Ciphers

Unlike monoalphabetic ciphers, in which a single character-for-character substitution is done, polyalphabetic substitution ciphers use multiple substitution methods, or alphabets, for encryption. Consider, for example, a cipher in which a letter in position x of the plaintext is replaced by the letter x characters ahead of it in the alphabet. Using this scheme, the plaintext *aaaa* would encrypt to *bcde*, and the plaintext *ball* would encrypt to *ccop*. Polyalphabetic ciphers can be more difficult to attack. For example, frequency analysis is far less effective unless the attacker knows the number of alphabets used and to which positions in the plaintext these alphabets are applied. Several effective methods of attack such as known plaintext exist here also.

> **NOTE**
>
> One of the best-known and most influential cryptographic machines was used in World War II. In 1918, German engineer Artus Scherbius patented a unique encryption machine called the Enigma. The machine encrypts messages by substitution using rotors—cylinders containing wiring that maps input letters onto output letters. The encrypted letter is then illuminated on a light panel. As rotors move with each keystroke, the cipher letter changes, even if the same letter key is repeated. The Enigma became a key tool for German military services to encrypt secret transmissions during World War II. Although the Enigma machine produced ciphertexts that were insidiously difficult to crack, cryptanalysts in the United States and the Allied Forces were able to decipher a fair number of these intercepted messages. It is estimated that the Allies' ability to encrypt Enigma messages shortened the war by as much as two years.

Asymmetric Encryption

Witfield Diffie and Martin Hellman first publicly proposed asymmetric encryption in their 1977 paper, "New Directions in Cryptography." To encrypt a message in asymmetric encryption, a different key is used than the one used to decrypt that message. Asymmetric key cryptography has become very popular for transmitting digital messages such as e-mail, through the use of public and private keys in a system called *Public Key Infrastructure,* or PKI. PKI typically works using a public and private key pair. A user who wants to send an encrypted message can get the intended recipient's public key from a publicly accessible location. When the recipient gets the message, he or she decrypts it with a private key, to which no one else should have access.

In the sections that follow, we outline some important implementations of asymmetric encryption.

RSA

The RSA encryption algorithm is named after its inventors, Rivest, Shamir, and Adelman.[4] It is probably the best-known and most frequently used asymmetric algorithm. Its key length varies between 512 and 2048 bits. The block size is also variable but must be smaller than the key's. The resulting ciphertext is the length of the key. The public key consists of a product of two large primes and a fixed number. Cracking RSA encryption boils down to factoring a large number into its primes, which is provably difficult computationally. In 1998, under the label of the RSA-Challenge, 22,000 people with 50,000 processors participated over the Internet in a distributed brute-force attack to crack the RSA code. It took 39 days.

ElGamal

As opposed to RSA, which is based on the product of primes, the ElGamal algorithm is an asymmetric key encryption algorithm based on discrete logarithms. The ElGamal algorithm is implemented in several public packages, such as recent versions of Pretty Good Privacy (PGP). ElGamal can be used for public key encryption and decryption as well as for digital signatures. Conceptually, ElGamal is similar to other crypto systems based on discrete logarithms, such as Diffie–Hellman.[5] These algorithms are generally believed to be fairly robust, and breaking them boils down to solving the discrete logarithm problem.

Cryptography and *The Mezonic Agenda*

The Mezonic Agenda is rife with encryption. One of the first challenges that international security expert Chad Davis faces when the hacker Baff Lexicon hands him a cryptic CD is to decrypt one of the files included on the CD. The file, it turns out, is encrypted with a polyalphabetic substitution cipher. The book also talks about one of the more famous monalphabetic substitution ciphers to appear in literature through Edgar Allen Poe's poem *The Goldbug*. This poem contains a great example of how monoalphabetic substitution ciphers work and—if the message is long enough—how they can easily be cracked using frequency analysis. Later, Chad Davis must crack a message that has been encrypted using arguably the most famous cipher, the Caesar Cipher.

In general, cryptography is an integral part of any electronic system that must keep secrets. When the original Internet voting system, SERVE, was proposed in the United States, all data was transmitted from a voter's machine to a central vote repository in encrypted form. Many encryption algorithms are provably strong, but they are often made weak through improper implementation. For example, encryption is very good at protecting data in transit or at rest but can often be broken when that data is in use by an application. Whenever data is in use, the protection of the encryption scheme is reduced to the security of the software implementing that encryption. Currently, every software protection scheme has been broken, so care must be taken when implementing encryption and when assessing the true security it provides.

References

1. Sources: world.std.com/~cme/html/timeline.html and all.net/books/ip/Chap2-1.html.

2. Sources: See note 1 .

3. Ellis, Davis, "The Spook's Secret Sculpture Garden," *Time,* March 18, 1991.

4. R. Rivest, A. Shamir, and L. M. Adleman, *Cryptographic Communications System and Method.* U.S. Patent 4,405,829, 1983.

5. W. Diffie and M. E. Hellman, "New Directions in Cryptography." *IEEE Transactions on Information Theory*, Vol. IT-22, November 1976, pp. 644–654.

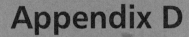

Appendix D

Buffer Overflows

Topics in this Appendix:

- Stack Overflows
- Heap Overflows
- Buffer Overflows in *The Mezonic Agenda*

Introduction

Code Red, MS Blaster, Nimda, SQL Slammer, Nachi ... these words have struck fear in the hearts of system administrators over the past several years. They are all *worms*—malicious pieces of code that do damage to a computer, spread to other computers, and have cost consumers over $5 billion in damages worldwide.[1] Many people use the terms *computer virus* and *computer worm* interchangeably, but there is one primary distinction: Viruses require the user to do something to become infected, such as click on an e-mail attachment, whereas worms spread without human intervention.. These particular worms share another common trait: They all spread using a software flaw known as the *buffer overflow*.

Buffer overflow vulnerabilities account for more than 70 percent of all known exploited security flaws in software. These flaws are among the most dangerous in software because many can (and have) been used to completely take over a victim's machine by executing arbitrary instructions. These types of flaws exist in a wide range of software running on various platforms, including Windows, Linux, and UNIX.

The nature of the flaw and the power that it gives an attacker mean that a system can be completely exposed. Imagine the ability to steal all document files on a machine by sending a few network packets, or formatting a Web server by entering data through a Web form. All these activities have been done in the past by an attacker crafting a buffer overflow exploit.

Buffer overflows exist because many programming languages do not inherently check the length of user data before that data is copied into a memory location of fixed size. When this happens, it's likely that the application will write past the bounds of the allocated memory buffer, allowing an attacker to change the values of other data stored in memory. For the most common types of buffer overflows—those that occur in a structure in memory called the *stack*—this usually means that an attacker can force an application to execute arbitrary instructions. Buffer overflows can occur in other areas of memory, too, such as the *heap*, which is a structure in which memory is dynamically created and freed during application execution. Because computer languages generally do not check the length of user data, the responsibility to ensure that input data does not lead to program errors or exploits falls on the programmer.

Languages such as C and C++ make it relatively easy to *accidentally* code a buffer overflow vulnerability. Some particularly dangerous C functions are *strcpy()*, *sprintf()*, and others that move or copy data from one location to another. These functions begin to place data in memory at the starting address of the target memory buffer but continue to store the data in subsequent addresses, essentially ignoring the bounds of the buffer. If the space set aside to store this data is on the stack, the result is that data can overwrite the *return address* of the current function or subroutine. When this happens, an attacker can take control of the application. In the sections that follow, we take a closer look at stack and heap overflows and their consequences.

Stack Overflows

Stack buffer overflows are currently the most exploited class of software flaw. The concept of a *stack buffer overflow* is that data placed on the *stack* overruns the space allocated for it, often overwriting the return address of the current function in memory. The *return address* is the address at which the application begins executing instructions once the current function is done executing. To understand how stack overflows occur, let's consider a simple C program that prints the text contents of a file.

NOTE

This application was compiled with the Visual Studio .NET compiler. It can easily be ported to other platforms and compilers, however, by removing the call to the user32.dll function *MessageBoxA* and removing the windows.h header file.

```c
#include <windows.h>
#include <stdio.h>
#include <conio.h>




int PrintFile(FILE* file)
{
        //Declare local variables
        int len;
        unsigned char data[512];

        //Clear the memory allocated for data
        memset(data,'\0',512);

        //Calculate file length
        fseek(file, 0, SEEK_END);
        len = ftell(file);
        fseek(file, 0, SEEK_SET);

        //Read the file contents into the data buffer
        fread(data, 1, len, file);
        fclose(file);

        //Print the file contents from "data" until we hit a null byte
        printf("File Contents: \n\n%s\n\n", data);

        //If we went past the bounds of data we end up overwriting the return
        //address!
        return 0;

}



int main(int argc, char* argv[])
```

```c
{
    char fileName[1024];

    //Make sure file name was entered
    if (argc < 2)
    {
        printf("Please specify file name as a commandline parameter.");
        return 0;
    }

    strncpy(fileName, argv[1], 1024);

    //Open the file and make sure we succeeded
    FILE* fp = fopen(fileName, "rb");

    if (!fp)
    {
        MessageBox(NULL, "Invalid file", "Error", MB_ICONSTOP | MB_OK);
        return 0;
    }

    //Call the PrintFile function to print the file's contents
    PrintFile(fp);

    printf("Press any key to continue...\n");
    while (!kbhit())
        Sleep(50);
    getch();

    return 0;
}
```

We can see that the *data* buffer is set up to hold 512 bytes of data. We will therefore start with the simple test case of a file with 500 occurrences of *a*, which we created and saved as test1.txt. Compiling the application as stackof.exe and running it on our test file gives the result shown in Figure D.1.

Figure D.1 Running the PrintFile Application on a File with 500 Characters

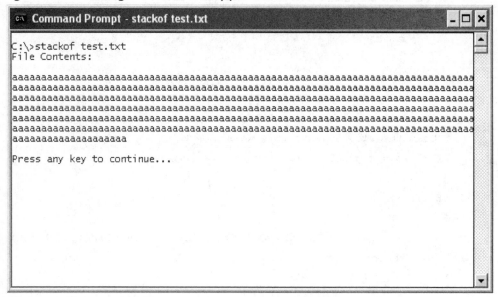

The *data* variable is declared as a local variable in the function *PrintFile*. Figure D.2 shows how the stack is likely to look once we are inside the *PrintFile* function. In the figure we see that 512 bytes of memory were allocated for the data variable. Several bytes below this, we see the 4 bytes that hold the *PrintFile* function's return address.

NOTE

There exist many stack protection methods that attempt to prevent the exploitation of buffer overflows. Interesting implementations include the /GS flag in Visual C++, StackGuard, and the enhancements made to Windows in Microsoft's Windows XP Service Pack 2.[2] Any of these may change how the stack of this sample application is actually implemented in memory. Figure D.2 shows the stack of a compiled version of the application without benefit of these technologies.

As the figure also shows, strings grow toward lower memory addresses. Studying this figure, it is easy to see that the return address could be overwritten if we were to load a file with more than 512 characters.

Figure D.2 Stack within the *PrintFile* Function

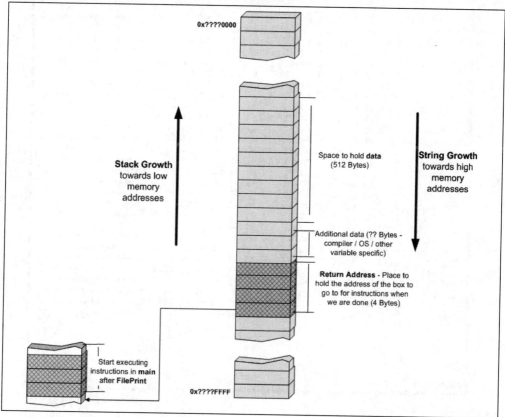

We now add 24 more instances of *a* to our file, giving a total of 524 characters that will be read into *data*. We will rename this file *test2.txt*. Figure D.3 shows the new text file opened in a hex editor.

Figure D.3 New Text File Opened in a Hex Editor

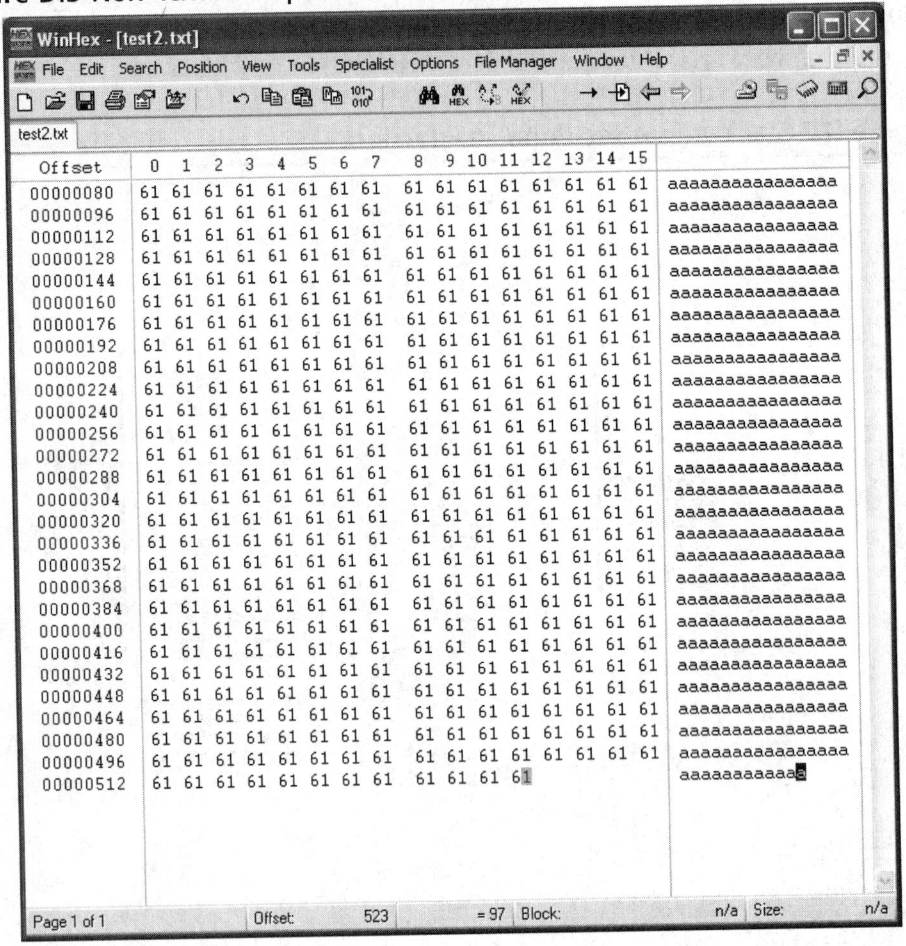

The *fread* function that is used to put the file's contents into the *data* buffer does not do any bounds checking and will therefore write past the end of the buffer. What we expect, then, is that the return address will be overwritten with *a* (61 in hex). Figure D.4 shows the result when we run the application using the input file test2.txt.

Figure D.4 Result of Application Using the Input File Test2.txt

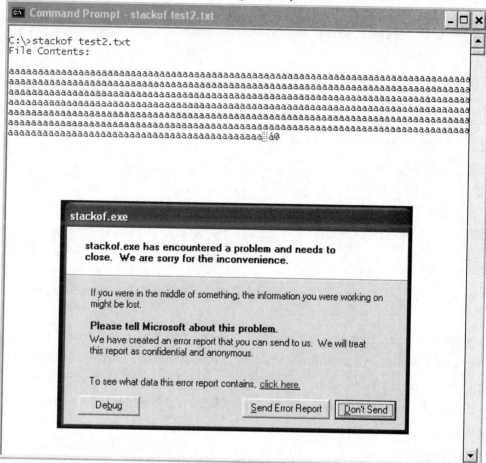

We see that the application has crashed. We can get more insight into the crash by running the application under a debugger. Figure D.5 shows the result.

Figure D.5 Running the Application Under a Debugger

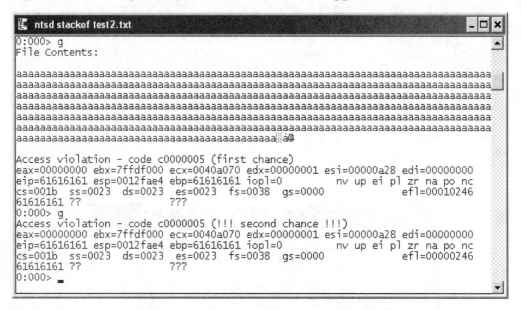

Here we see that the application has crashed because it's trying to execute instructions at memory address 0x61616161! Data from the file has written past the bounds of the *data* variable and overwritten the return address of the *PrintFile* function. When the function was finished executing (in other words, when it reached the command *return 0*), the return address was placed into the *Extended Instruction Pointer* register EIP. The EIP register holds the memory address of the next instruction to be executed. In this case, the application is trying to execute instructions stored at address 0x61616161, an invalid address, and thus the application crashes.

This is the basic anatomy of a stack-based overflow. With limited skills, an attacker who knew of the presence of a buffer overflow could insert a random long string in the right place and crash the target application. Buffer overflows, however, can have much more serious consequences. In the next section we discuss how stack overruns are exploited by attackers.

Exploiting Stack Overruns: An End-to-End Windows Example

Many stack overruns are exploitable by inserting a large amount of data into a field. This data is then stored in a buffer too small to hold it, and the result is that the return address of the current function is overwritten. When this situation occurs, we gain the power to manipulate the execution flow of the application.

One thing we could do is to force the application to execute a different section of the application's code than was intended. For example, we could force the application to display the message box (coded as a separate part of the application) that says "invalid file." Figure D.6 shows our application in the OllyDbg debugger.

Figure D.6 Application in the OllyDbg Debugger

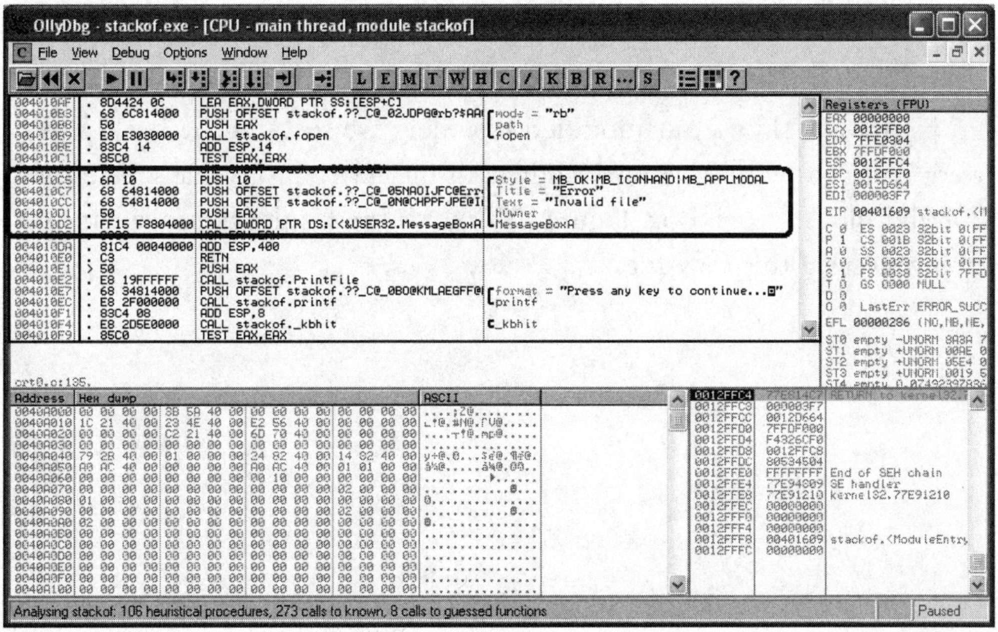

We can see that the instructions that invoke that message box start at the virtual memory address 0x004010c5. If we place this address in the location of our file that overwrites the return address of the *PrintFile* function, we can point the application to these instructions and thus force it to create this message box. This memory address must be placed in reverse order in the text file because of the little endian convention of Intel x86 processors.

> **NOTE**
>
> *Little endian* means that the least significant byte of any multibyte data field is stored at the lowest memory address. This means that when we write data as a machine code parameter, we must place it in reverse byte order. For example, the memory address 0x00403020 is written as 20304000 on a little endian system. The Intel x86 family of processors and their clones use little endian representation, whereas some other processor families such as SPARC use *big endian* (most significant byte first). Whenever you are writing machine code or Shell code, it is critical to know the so-called "endianness" of the processor on which that code will run!

Figure D.7 shows our modified file. Here we see that the last 4 bytes were replaced by the memory address of the instructions that create the "invalid file" message box. Figure D.8 shows the result when we run our application on this new file.

Figure D.7 Modified File

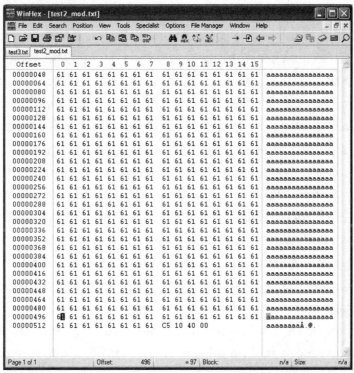

Figure D.8 Application Run on New File

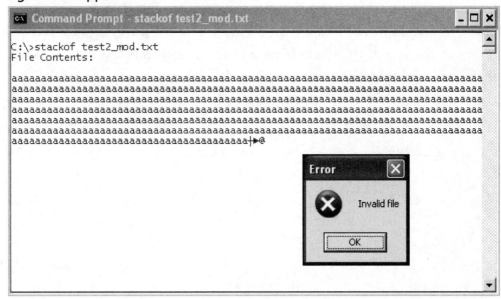

This is a key step. We have artificially changed the execution path of the application through data! In this case we have essentially forced the application to "jump" to the piece of code that creates the "invalid file" message box. An attacker's ultimate goal is to change the value of the return address so that it points to other attacker-supplied data on the stack. An attacker can then enter data values into the application that will be interpreted as machine instructions. These instructions are commonly referred to as either *shellcode* or *op-code*. In our running stackof.exe example, we will now illustrate how an attacker might take advantage of this buffer overrun. Our goal is to make stackof.exe launch a message box with "The Mezonic Agenda" as both the caption and the text of the box. This is not something the application was designed to do, and the code to do this is not present in the source code. We are faced with the challenge of manipulating the application's execution purely through data.

We already know that we can overwrite the return address of the function *PrintFile* and thus, ultimately, control the value of the EIP register. Our next step is to find a location in memory that contains some more of our data—data that we can then point EIP to, essentially telling the application to interpret this data as machine code. After an overrun has occurred, the most common place to look for our data in memory is at the top of the stack. The Extended Stack Pointer (ESP) register always points to the top of the stack. If we add some *a*s to our test2.txt file and look at the application in the OllyDbg debugger, we can see that data contained in the file—in this case, a bunch of *a*s—is indeed at the top of the stack, as shown in Figure D.9 (bottom-right corner).

Figure D.9 ESP Register; Data Is at the Top of the Stack

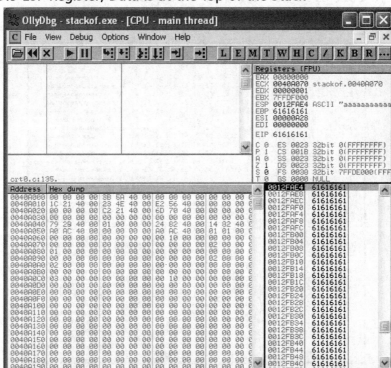

Here is an example piece Shell code used to exploit stackof.exe, where the offsets given are in the data file:

```
00000512   61 61 61 61 61 61 61 61   E4 FA 12 00 6A 00 68 00   aaaaaaaaäú..j.h.
00000528   FB 12 00 68 00 FB 12 00   6A 00 FF 15 F8 80 40 00   û..h.û..j.ÿ.ø @.
00000544   6A 00 FF 15 28 80 40 00   4D 65 7A 6F 6E 69 63 20   j.ÿ.( @.Mezonic
00000560   41 67 65 6E 64 61 00 61   61 61 61 61 61 61 61 61   Agenda.aaaaaaaaa
```

Figure D.10 shows our code as part of our new text file named exploit.txt.

Figure D.10 Code as Part of New Text File Exploit.txt

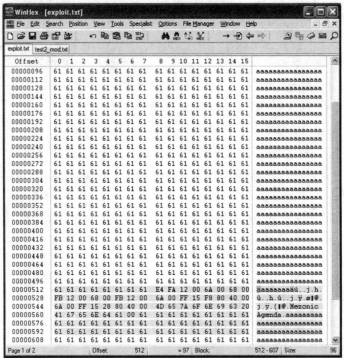

Offset 520 of the file contains the address to be loaded into the instruction pointer (0x0011fae4). This address points to the data right after it, or offset 524 in the file. Following is a step–by–step description of the Shell code used in our exploit file. The machine code for each instruction is listed on the left and can be mapped directly back to the code shown in our exploit file in Figure D.10.

To begin our exploit, we first prepare to call *MessageBoxA* by pushing its parameters onto the stack. The definition of the *MessageBoxA* function is shown in the following:

```
int MessageBox (HWND hWnd, LPCTSTR lpszText, LPCTSTR lpszCaption, UINT nType);
```

Parameters are pushed right to left, so the first thing to push is the last (fourth) parameter (*nType*). This parameter is the style of message box to create. In this case, we pass zero, which should give us the standard informational message box with an OK button.

```
6a00            push    0x0
```

Next, we push the third parameter of *MessageBoxA* onto the stack. This is the text that appears as the title of the message box. Address 0x0012fb00 as seen in the following line of code, which contains the string *Mezonic Agenda*:

```
6800fb1200      push    0x0012fb00
```

Continuing, we push the second parameter of *MessageBoxA* onto the stack. This is the text that appears as the contents of the message box. Again we push address 0x0012fb00 for the string *Mezonic Agenda*.

```
6800fb1200      push    0x0012fb00
```

Finally, we push the first parameter of *MessageBoxA* onto the stack. This is a window handle to the parent of the message box. This is not required, so we pass NULL, or zero.

```
6a00            push    0x0
```

Now all that remains is to call the *MessageBoxA* function. It is best to avoid inserting direct calls to system application program interfaces (APIs), a way of interacting with the application through code, in exploit code, because these system APIs are at different locations on different versions of the operating system. In Windows, an import table is present in every executable. Windows uses this table to figure out which functions an executable uses and places the real addresses to the APIs in the same table. This table is always loaded into the same location for a given version of an executable. Since the address is constant, we just need to find the place in the import table to which Windows writes the actual API addresses at load time. Using the NTSD debugger, we can easily search and locate these places.

To find an API in the import table, we first get the address of the API we're interested in using the *x* command. For example, to find the address of the *MessageBoxA* API, enter the following command:

```
x user32!MessageBoxA
```

Note that it is important that you give the DLL the API resides in when using this command. On our machine (Windows XP SP1), we get the following results:

```
77d6b00a   USER32!MessageBoxA
```

This states that the *MessageBoxA* function is at address 0x77d6b00a on this system. Note that these results may vary depending on the version of user32.dll on the machine. Now we need to use this information to find the import table entry in the application. To do this, use the *s* command, which searches memory for data. The *s* command expects a range of addresses to search, so first we need to know where our target executable has been loaded into memory. The *ModLoad* line in the NTSD output near the top (see Figure D.11) provides this information for the targeted executable module. For this exploit, this line looks like this:

```
ModLoad: 00400000 0040c000   stackof.exe
```

This states that hexdump.exe is loaded between addresses 0x00400000 and 0x0040c000. Now we want to search this area of memory for the known address of the API we are looking for. For the example data given, the following command will perform this search:

```
s 00400000 0040c000 0a b0 d6 77
```

Notice that the addresses given in the *ModLoad* line are given as the first two arguments to the *s* command. Following these two addresses is the data to search for, given a byte at a time. Again, the bytes in the address must be given backward due to the way the Intel processor stores data in memory (remember the little endian format discussed earlier). This command will locate any occurrences of the API's address in the executable. For this exploit, the search returned the following results:

```
004080f8   0a b0 d6 77 00 00 00 00-00 00 00 00 62 9f 16 41
...w........b..A
```

Figure D.11 Output from the NTSD Debugger as We Try to Find the Address of *MessageBoxA*

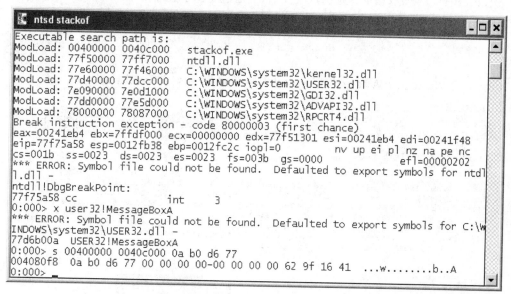

The address given on the left is the location we are looking for. This is where Windows stores the address of the *MessageBoxA* API when it loads the stackof.exe executable. To use this in exploit code, we simply do an indirect call on the address found with the *s* command:

```
ff15f8804000    call    dword ptr [004080f8]
```

This code will call *MessageBoxA* on any version of Windows, as long as we are using the same version of stackof.exe. When the *MessageBoxA* function is called, it pops all the parameters off the stack. After pressing OK on the message box, control is returned to the next instruction we've overwritten onto the stack (the next values in our text file).

Now we want to exit, so we call the *ExitProcess* function in kernel32.dll. This function takes a single parameter, which is an exit code. We will give zero as our exit code, so we push zero onto the stack.

```
6a00            push    0x0
```

Now all that remains is to call the *ExitProcess* function. The address of the function is found in the same way we found the address of *MessageBoxA*. Using this method, we find that 0x00408028 is the import table entry for *ExitProcess*. Armed with this information, we call the *ExitProcess* function and the application terminates (see Figure D.12):

```
ff1528804000      call      dword ptr [00408028]
```

Figure D.12 Result When the Exploit File Text File Is Viewed Using Stackof.exe

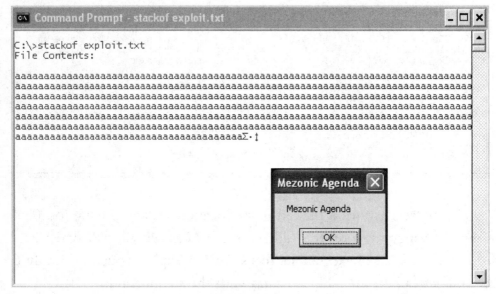

We have successfully bent the will of this executable through data! Although attackers are rarely interested in using buffer overflows to displaying message boxes, other tasks can be performed in much the same manner. Most exploit code begins by loading networking libraries and creating remote connections. We would hazard a guess that 80 percent of C programmers are not aware of how easily an attacker can take advantage of a code flaw such as the one shown here. Our hope in showing this example is to educate programmers and security professionals on the true dangers of these sorts of errors. In the next section we will look at a related problem—the *heap overflow*.

Heap Overflows

The *heap* is an area of memory where storage is dynamically allocated and freed during execution, as necessary. The heap is a very awkward memory structure due to its dynamic nature. It is filled with interspersed blocks of allocated and free memory that are linked together. Conceptually, we can think of the heap as a Web site with only *forward* and *back* links. Each page stores some information, and then the *forward* link takes you to the next place where information is stored. There are a few ways you could traverse the site: Go to the first page and keep clicking the *forward* link, or explicitly type in the Web address of the page you desired.

Various platforms and compilers keep track of heap data in different ways. Typically, each block of data is encased with headers that point to the next allocated block of memory in the heap using a *linked list*. When memory is allocated or freed, the pointers contained in these structures are updated appropriately.

When a *heap overrun* occurs, this link information is essentially corrupted, and any attempt to follow the link from the corrupted block usually causes the application to crash. There are several ways in which heap overruns can be exploited. One of the most trivial is to use the overflow to overwrite data in an adjacent memory location on the heap. Other more elaborate exploits involve manipulating the link information itself to eventually force the application to write an arbitrary value to an arbitrary address. This is the equivalent of a stack exploit and essentially gives an attacker control of the running process.

Let's take a look at a typical example. The following code listing is for heapof.exe, which attempts to store user data in a buffer of a fixed length:

```
#include <stdio.h>
#include <stdlib.h>
#include <string.h>
```

```c
int main(int argc, char* argv)
{
        //Allocating space for loc1 and loc2 on the heap
        char *loc1 = (char *)malloc(10);
        char *loc2 = (char *)malloc(10);


        //Setting loc1 to "111111111"
        memset(loc1, '1', 9);
        loc1[9] = '\0';


        //Setting loc2 to "222222222"
        memset(loc2, '2', 9);
        loc2[9] = '\0';


        printf("loc1 starting address = %p\n", loc1);
        printf("loc2 starting address = %p\n\n", loc2);


        printf("Distance from end of loc1 to beginning of loc2 on heap = %p",
        loc2 - loc1 - 0xA );
        printf("\n\nValue in loc1: %s", loc1);
        printf("\nValue in loc2: %s", loc2);


        //Here we use the especially dangerous 'gets' function which doesn't
        //do bounds checking to store user input in loc1
        printf("\n\nEnter new value to be placed in loc1 with gets(): ");
        gets(loc1);


        //If the input is longer than the length of loc1 plus the distance
        //between the two locations then we will start to overwrite loc2
        printf("\n\nValue in loc1: %s", loc1);
        printf("\nValue in loc2: %s", loc2);


        //Trying to free the memory locations. If the heap is corrupt then
        //this will likely cause the application to crash.
        printf("\n\nPress enter to (try) and free loc1...");
        getchar();
```

```
        free(loc1);


        printf("\n\nPress enter to (try) and free loc2...");
        getchar();
        free(loc2);


        return 0;
}
```

When we execute this code with a short input string, we get the result shown in Figure D.13.

Figure D.13 Result from Executing Code with a Short Input String (No Overflow)

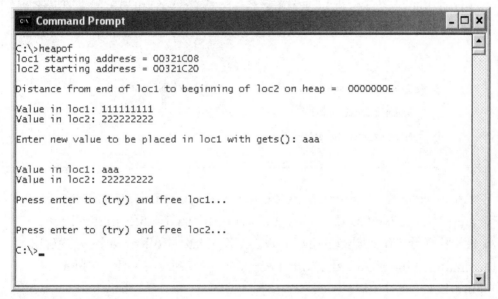

In Figure D.13 we can see that the application behaved as expected, with the value *aaa* as the entered string. Let's analyze this output in more detail. For this particular compiled version, we see that the distance between the end of the memory reserved for *loc1* and the starting address of *loc2* is 0xE, which is 14 bytes. Therefore, if we enter a value that is 25 characters long, the length of *loc1* (10) plus the distance between *loc1* and *loc2* (14) plus 1, we should write the last character of the entered value as the first character of *loc2*. Let's first take a look at what the heap would look like before we entered our string. In Figure D.14 we see that the memory reserved for *loc1* contains all ones, terminated by a NULL, and that the memory reserved for *loc2* contains all twos, terminated by a NULL.

Figure D.14 Memory Allocation

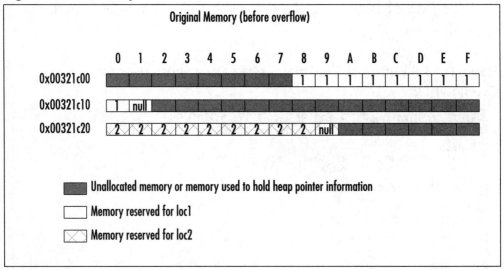

After we enter our string of 25 *a*s, we expect that *loc1* will be overwritten by *a* as well as the space between the two buffers. Finally, we expect that the first character in *loc2* will be an *a* followed by a NULL terminator. This means that our heap should look something like Figure D.15.

Figure D.15 A Picture of Memory After the Overflow

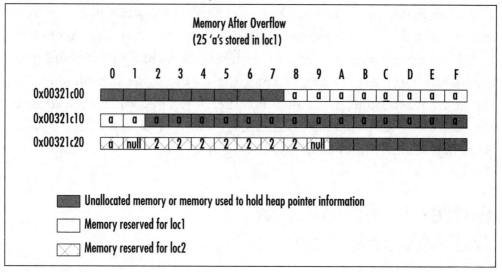

When the *printf* function is called, it will start at the beginning address given and continue to print data until it encounters a NULL. Therefore, we expect that when *loc1* is printed, the result will be 25 occurrences of *a*, and when *loc2* is printed, we will see only a single *a*. Figure D.16 shows that this is indeed the case.

Figure D.16 The Result of Running the Application with Enough Data to Overflow a Buffer

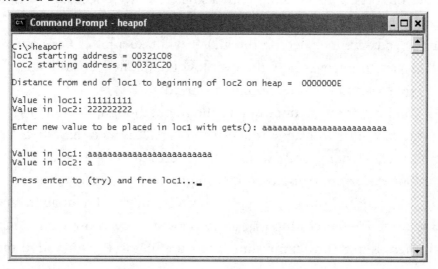

When we try to "free" the memory addresses, however, the application crashes, because important housekeeping information about the heap was corrupted when we overwrote the memory between the two buffers. Still, heap exploitation can be a powerful attack technique, with the simplest result being the ability to change the data in some variable that should be inaccessible. As alluded to earlier, several people have leveraged the heap housekeeping code to gain full control of an application. Although such techniques are interesting, they are beyond the scope of this overview.

Buffer Overflows in
The Mezonic Agenda

We would be remiss in writing a novel on voting and computer security without including a buffer overflow or two. Early in the book, Chad Davis gives a 30,000-foot view of buffer overflows to a group of conference attendees. Near the end of the book, however, a critical buffer overflow in the vote-counting server turns out to be the key to someone manipulating the fictitious election described in the book. In the counting software, Davis encounters a heap overflow, one that lets an attacker control the number of votes to be counted with a single file. We encourage you to go through the process that Davis does in the book and play with the counting software included on the CD. It will take a bit of detective work on your part to uncover how the overflow is exploited, but this appendix should give you all the background you need!

Beyond the software discussed in the book, though, the buffer overflow still continues to plague modern software. Advances have been made in tools such as source code scanner that alert a developer when "dangerous" functions are being used that might lead to a buffer overrun condition. Many of the source scanners, however, suffer from an abundance of false positives—indicating that there is a buffer overflow vulnerability when there is not, thus diminishing their usefulness. To compound the problem, many application developers have to deal with the issue of legacy components. These are software components that might have been written some time ago and were not subjected to the secure coding standards of newer components, which means that they are likely to harbor vulnerabilities such as buffer overflows.

Several efforts are in progress that are trying to fix the general stack overflow problem both at the compiler and operating system level. Several platforms, for example, have been "hardened" against typical buffer overflow exploits, such as upcoming versions of Windows and some flavors of Linux (www.immunix.org). These efforts are certainly a step forward, but the future of buffer overflow exploits remains unclear, and it is doubtful that they've been marked for extinction just yet.

References

1. *Computer Economics*, www.computereconomics.com.

2. Andersen, S., and Abella, V., "Changes to Functionality in Microsoft Windows XP Service Pack 2—Part 3: Memory Protection," *Microsoft Support Document*, www.microsoft.com, August, 2004.

3. Howard, M., and LeBlanc, D., *Writing Secure Code, 2nd Edition*, Microsoft Press, 2002.

4. Cowan, C., Pu, C., et al., "Detection and Prevention of Buffer-Overflow Attacks," *Proceedings of the 7th USENIX Security Symposium*, San Antonio, TX, January 1998.

Appendix E

Steganography

Topics in this Appendix:

- **Types of Steganography**
- **Steganography in** *The Mezonic Agenda*

Introduction

Steganography is the art of transmitting and receiving a message hidden within a publicly accessible medium. In the world of computers, this usually means embedding secret information in a picture or sound file that can be easily e-mailed, downloaded, or posted online. In this appendix we will go over the various types of steganography used today along with a couple of examples, and discuss how steganography was used in the *The Mezonic Agenda*.

One of the earliest forms of steganography was used in ancient Greece, where a message would be tattooed on a man's shaven, bald head. The hair would then be allowed to grow back and the man would travel to his destination where his hair would be shaved again and the message read. World Wars I and II saw much use of steganography, among other forms of communications, including the use of microdots. These dots were used to mark an end of a sentence much like the dots on the pages of this book. The difference was that the dots contained a large amount of data due to their resolution; the human eye just could not detect these hidden messages.

More recently, steganography—commonly known as *stego*—has been used by national security agencies, corporations, and even terrorist organizations. Outside of the political realm, there is also proof that stego has been used by earlier societies. Recently there has been much interest in possible hidden codes in the Torah and other scriptures sparking controversy among the religious community. When implemented properly, steganography is very difficult to detect and even when it is detected, the information may be even more difficult to extract and decipher.[1,2,3,4]

Types of Stego

Stego relies on a carrier medium to transmit hidden data to the intended recipient. Figure E.1 shows a generic diagram of how stego may be used. Notice that the data to be concealed may be additionally encrypted for added security. The difference between steganography and cryptography is that in cryptography, the data is encrypted or locked. For example if we were to ship a million dollars on an open-bed truck, we could do so by putting the money in a safe and loading the safe on the truck. Anyone could see that a safe was being shipped and assume something valuable is in the safe, but only the person or persons with a key could open it. The protection offered by the safe is analogous to the data security provided by encryption: we know something has been protected and we are trying to unprotect it. If we wanted to apply the principal of steganography to ship the money, then we could put that money in ice cream bars, for example, and drive an ice cream truck in plain sight to its intended recipient. Even though anyone could stop and steal the ice cream bars, chances are no one would suspect what lay hidden inside.

Figure E.1 How Data Is Hidden in Stego

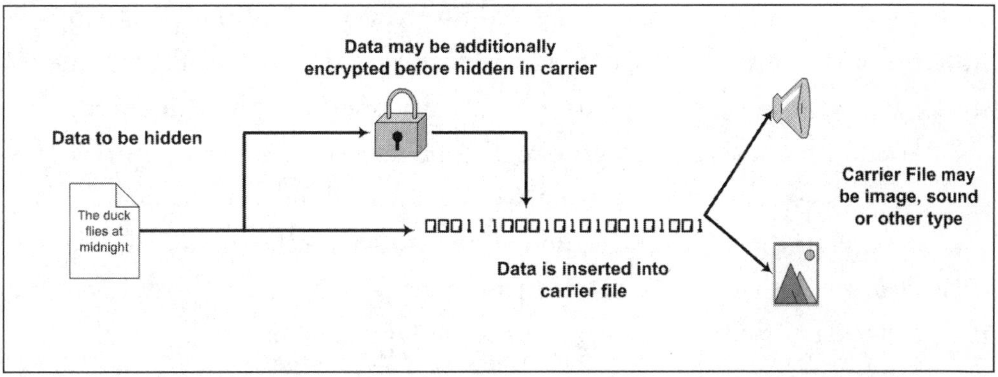

There are essentially three types of stego techniques used today (outlined as the "New Classification Scheme" in Eric Cole's *Hiding in Plain Sight: Steganography and the Art of Covert Communication*). Those three types are:

- Insertion
- Substitution
- Generation

Insertion Stego

As the name implies, insertion stego relies on *inserting* the secret data within a carrier medium. Consider files, for example. Most file formats contain an EOF marker, signifying the end-of-file. Data could be inserted after this marker and would not risk damaging the carrier file's quality. The problem with this type of stego is that if large amounts of data are to be hidden, the size of the carrier file will change quite dramatically, giving away the fact that something more than a simple image or audio file is being shipped. Consider, for example, the picture in Figure E.2 that was taken in Paris and is named tower.jpg. The file data.doc is inserted into this image and the new image created is named towernew.jpg, shown in Figure E.3. Though the images appear identical, the size of tower.jpg compared to towernew.jpg are quite different, as shown in Figure E.4, which contains Windows Explorer and the file specs along with data.doc—the file to be inserted into tower.jpg. Without altering how the image is displayed, data has been inserted into the file and the image would likely carry this data to the intended recipient undetected.

Beyond files, insertion stego can also be used to insert data into a wide variety of carriers such as network packets. There are several fields, for instance, in the TCP/IP header of network packets, such as the *do not defragment* field, that can be altered to convey a message without changing the packet data itself.

Figure E.2 480x640 JPEG Image of the Eiffel Tower in Paris

Figure E.3 Eiffel Tower Image with data.doc Inserted

Figure E.4 File Size Difference between Tower.jpg and Towernew.jpg

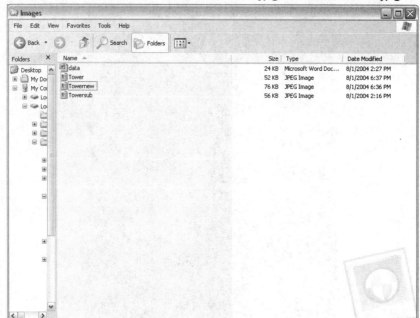

Substitution Stego

At a high level, substitution steganography works by replacing some data in a carrier file or medium with data that conveys a message. For digital information, most practical applications involve taking the least significant bits (LSB) of data in the carrier file and replacing them with the data to be hidden. This works well with image and sound files because a minute change in the LSB of a pixel's color or a note's sound is literally impossible to notice by the naked eye or ear.

How Does It Work?

Image files contain information to draw pixels: little dots that are assigned a color. In many image file formats, colors are determined based on a red, green, and blue value (RGB), each of which has 256 different shades ranging in value from 0 to 255. In this system, a RGB value of 0,0,0 is black and 255,255,255 is white. There are a total of 16,777,216 color combinations possible. Figure E.5 shows a general diagram of how substitution stego works. Notice that the data to be hidden is broken up and distributed among the LSB of the carrier file. Additionally, algorithms may be used to randomly distribute the hidden data so that it is even more difficult for someone to intercept and decipher the data without knowing this algorithm. In general, only half of the least significant bits usually need to be replaced because there is a good chance that the LSB may already be set to the value we need as a matter of coincidence. Sound files work in much the same way by storing the least discernable frequencies in the LSB location(s).

Figure E.5 Substitution Stego Outline

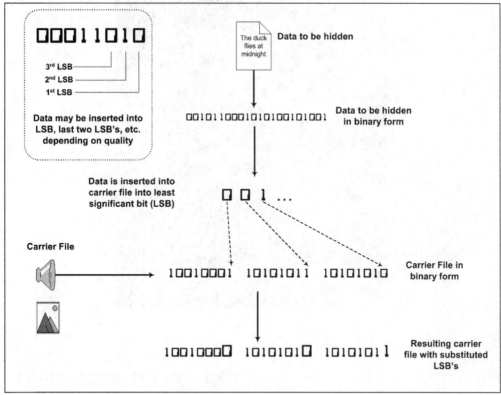

A Quick Example

Taking the same unaltered picture in Figure E.2 and inserting the file data.doc via a substitution method gives Figure E.6, a new file named towersub.jpg. Notice the much smaller difference in file size as seen earlier in Figure E.4. If the data to be inserted were significantly smaller than the carrier file there is no difference in size.

Figure E.6 tower.jpg with data.doc Substituted—Resulting File Is Towersub.jpg

Generation Stego

Generation stego uses the data to be hidden as the basis for generating a sound file or image file as opposed to working with an existing carrier and then embedding data within it. Popular files for this type of stego are images and sound files with abstract qualities. For example, fractals have mathematical properties that can be based on the data to be hidden. Likewise sound files such as WAV files can be generated using the data to be hidden as the actual sound data.

Another form of generation stego that has been used for many years is text generation. In this type of stego, the text to be hidden is combined with other text to form a completely irrelevant message. For example, if you wanted to send the secret message, "Strike at midnight," you could send the message:

"Sam, there's rain in Kansas! Everyone at the Mac is drenched. Nick is going home tonight."

Taking the first letter of each word in this message gives:

"**S**am, **t**here's **r**ain **in** **K**ansas! **E**veryone **at** **t**he **M**ac **is** **d**renched. **N**ick **is** **g**oing **h**ome **t**onight."

or,

"StriKEatMidNight"

One other method is to take a message and use it to create a completely different text via grammar rules that choose what word to use based on the words of the hidden text. A web site known as Spam Mimic does just that. The web site can be found at www.spammimic.com. This web site allows the user to enter a small message and have a spam-like encoded message created based on the user's text.[5]

Steganography in *The Mezonic Agenda*

In the fictional part of this book, the Mezonic Corporation uses network steganography to embed hidden messages bound for video cards on user machines. This data is then interpreted by the video cards into suggestive messages that are subtly displayed to computer users. Specifically, the company changes the *order* that network packets are sent and they use this ordering to conceal information. This is a method of network steganography, one that has been known for several years. The Transmission Control Protocol (TCP) is responsible for ensuring that packets sent using this protocol arrive at their destination. The receiving device keeps track of which packets have been received and which are missing using a packet *sequence number*. For a particular connection, a starting sequence number is established at connection time using an interactive exchange of packets known as the *handshake*. When a new packet is sent, the sequence number is increased by the size of the packet and if a packet arrives out of sequence, the receiving device will wait a specified period of time for the missing packet before informing the sender. This process slows down the data transmission but it ensures that data isn't corrupted or lost in the process.

When missing packets arrive, the packet data is placed in the correct order and passed off to the intended destination program running on the receiving machine. Out-of-sequence packets are a common occurrence and rarely cause a noticeable difference in communication, which makes packet sequence steganography an attractive means of communicating hidden data over the network. Problems occur, however, when other network devices such as firewalls process the network traffic before it reaches its destination. The risk is not that the communication will be detected, but that the network device will resequence the packets in the correct order before forwarding them to their destination.

Other forms of network steganography involve stuffing information in obscure fields in the TCP/IP packet header. Although these methods are often more reliable, detection can be much easier because inspecting the packet headers will reveal that the header has been purposely tampered with, as opposed to out-of-sequence packets, which has several possible causes such as collisions, packet loss, or router delays.

The possibility of steganography in electronic voting is less of a concern than information leakage through covert channels. Whereas steganography is about purposely trying to hide a piece of information in a communications medium, covert channel information leakage can either be purposeful or accidental. Take, for example, the vote files used in the fictitious election of *The Mezonic Agenda*. These files are supposedly named using a random and unique number such as 185720387.vte. Imagine, however, if the function to generate these random numbers was seeded based on the voter's social security number. In an ideal world, the resulting numbers would still indeed be truly random but in practice, machines actually produce pseudo-random numbers, which, if we knew the mechanism used to generate them, may allow us to reconstruct who that vote belongs to! There have been several highly publicized hacks using the principle of predictable pseudo-random number generation. One of the most entertaining involves the prediction of supposedly randomly shuffled cards during virtual Texas Hold'em poker games hosted by PlanetPoker Internet cardroom.[6] Using the algorithm the company had implemented to shuffle cards, the researchers were able to make predictions about which cards would be dealt during a game. Incidents like this demonstrate that information is leaked in unusual ways and that companies involved in such critical public interest roles as facilitating elections need to be vigilant.

References

1. www.torahcodes.co.il/

2. www.ldolphin.org/torahcodes.html

3. www.bereanpublishers.com/Apologetics/a_hidden_torah_secret.htm

4. Cole, Erik. *Hiding in Plain Sight: Steganography and the Art of Covert Communication.* Wiley, 2003

5. www.stegoarchive.com/

6. www.cigital.com/papers/download/developer_gambling.pdf

The Mezonic Agenda Hack

Contest Rules

The Mezonic Agenda Hack is a game of skill, which tests your ability to hack the results of a mock election. The Mezonic Agenda Hack is provided by Syngress Publishing, Inc. (" Syngress").

Your submission will be reviewed by a single judge chosen by Syngress to determine a single winner. It is expected that Hugh Thompson and Spyros Nomikos, authors of The Mezonic Agenda, will be the judges. There will be one prize of: a Black Hat Vegas 2005 Pass and a suite of Syngress security books, with an estimated market value of $2000.

Acceptance of Contest Rules

Registering for and/or participating in The Mezonic Agenda Hack as offered on this web site signify your agreement to be bound by the most current version of these Contest Rules. Contest Rules are subject to change; Syngress may modify these Contest Rules at any time by posting replacement Contest Rules on this web site.

No Entry Fee

There is no entry fee or purchase necessary to register for and/or participate in The Mezonic Agenda Hack.

Eligibility

To be eligible for and/or participating in The Mezonic Agenda Hack, you must meet the following eligibility requirements:
A) Be a United States citizen or US permanent resident; and
B) Be 18 year of age or older

Applicable Law; Void Where Prohibited

The law governing contests under state and federal law will apply. You agree to comply with all applicable laws, statutes and regulations in relation to this contest. The Mezonic Agenda Hack, is not offered outside the United States.
The Mezonic Agenda Hack may not be legally permissible in certain areas. The Mezonic Agenda Hack is void where prohibited.

Ineligible Persons

The following persons are ineligible to participate in The Mezonic Agenda Hack or receive any prize: Syngress Publishing, O'Reilly Media, Inc., and the authors, and their employees, officers, and directors and their subsidiaries, and affiliates (and the immediate family members of all the above); and any other person with access to non-public information regarding the operation of The Mezonic Agenda Hack. For purposes of this section, immediate family members include parents, siblings, spouses, children, or any other person permanently residing in the same household with such employee, officer, or director.

Deadline

All submissions for participants to be included in The Mezonic Agenda Hack must be made and received no later than January 20, 2005.

Registration

Registration for The Mezonic Agenda Hack may be done only through Syngress. Syngress and Hugh Thompson and Spyros Nomikos have no responsibility for any submissions that are lost or misplaced due to errors in telecommunications, processing, storage or for any other reasons.
To be eligible for consideration, applications must include all information requested.

Reporting to IRS

If you should be awarded the prize, you may be required to provide your Social Security number and complete an IRS form 1099 as a condition of the award. Failure to provide to do so when requested may result in your disqualification, at Syngress' option.

Contest Criteria for Selection of Winner

The Mezonic Agenda: Hacking a Presidency Contest challenges you, the reader, to interact with the book and CD, decrypt its contents, and ultimately control the fate of a mock US Presidential Election. Contestants will attempt to vote for themselves as the winning candidate during our "simulated" election to be held in early 2005. Contestants must use their hacking skills, along with strategy, to manipulate the results of the Mezonic "mock" election.
Any eligible contestant can download the software from the Mezonic Agenda: Hacking a Presidency website (www.mezonicagenda.com) without having to purchase the book. The book, though, will help the reader better understand how the software works, teach them software hacking skills and ultimately aid in its exploitation.
Prizes include a free pass to the 2005 Black Hat Briefings in Las Vegas and a suite of security books from Syngress Publishing.
Syngress may require any participant receiving any prize to provide Syngress with proof that he or she is eligible to participate according to the eligibility requirements hereunder.

Acknowledgement of Proprietary Rights

By registering for and/or participating in The Mezonic Agenda Hack you acknowledge that all information contained on Syngress' web site with regard to The Mezonic Agenda Hack is be protected by one or more valid copyrights, patents, trademarks, trade secrets, or other proprietary rights, and that all such rights, are owned by Syngress or its licensors or suppliers. You may not modify, publish, participate in the transfer or sale of, create derivative works from, or in any way exploit this information.

Promotional Activities

By registering for and/or participating in The Mezonic Agenda Hack you agree and allow your name, picture, voice, likeness, and/or biographical information to be used for promotional purposes including but not limited to printing, publishing, audio and video recording and broadcast and use in any media and at any time without compensation. You agree to cooperate reasonably in such promotion if you are a winner.

Submissions

All submissions to The Mezonic Agenda Hack shall become, and shall remain, the sole property of Syngress. Syngress shall exclusively own all rights to, and shall be entitled to unrestricted use of, all such submissions without compensation to you. No submissions will be returned.

Accuracy of Information

You represent that all information that you supply in The Mezonic Agenda Hack is complete and accurate. Knowingly submitting incomplete or inaccurate information may result in immediate termination of your participation in The Mezonic Agenda Hack and forfeiture of any prizes to which you may otherwise be entitled, at Syngress' option.

Odds

The results of The Mezonic Agenda Hack will depend on the number of participants and the skill level of the players participating in The Mezonic Agenda Hack and therefore cannot be calculated mathematically.

Selection of Winners

The winners of The Mezonic Agenda Hack will be determined by the judge. By registering and/or participating in The Mezonic Agenda Hack you agree to be bound by the judge's decision, which will be final.

Announcement of Winners

A final winner will be determined and selected on or about February 15, 2005. The winner will be notified and announced by email or phone on February 21, 2005. Information regarding the winner will be on this web site for a reasonable time.

Taxes

Winners are responsible for any and all local, state and federal taxes that may be due as a result of winning in The Mezonic Agenda Hack.

Disqualification

Syngress reserves the right to terminate your participation and eligibility in The Mezonic Agenda Hack for any of the good reason including but not limited to submission of any inaccurate information, fraud or any breach of the terms of this Agreement.

Limitation of Liability

By registering for and/or participating in The Mezonic Agenda Hack you agree that Syngress shall not be liable for or responsible for any damage, loss, or injury resulting from participating in The Mezonic Agenda Hack. SYNGRESS AND HUGH THOMPSON AND SPROS NOMIKOS MAKE MAKES NO REPRESENTATIONS OR WARRANTIES OF ANY KIND EXPRESS OR IMPLIED.

Governing Law and Disputes

These Contest Rules will be governed and construed in accordance with the laws of Massachusetts, not including principles of conflicts of law. The state and federal courts located in Boston Massachusetts will have sole and exclusive jurisdiction and venue over any legal action arising from this Agreement or the relationship of the parties.

Entire Agreement

These Contest Rules, in current for or as Syngress may modify them, constitute the entire agreement between you and Syngress and cannot be modified by you.

Severability

If any portion of these Contest Rules is deemed void or unenforceable, then that provision shall be deemed severable from these Contest Rules and shall not affect the validity and enforceability of the remaining provisions.

GENERAL: This License Agreement constitutes the entire agreement between the parties relating to the Product. The terms of any Purchase Order shall have no effect on the terms of this License Agreement. Failure of Syngress to insist at any time on strict compliance with this License Agreement shall not constitute a waiver of any rights under this License Agreement. This License Agreement shall be construed and governed in accordance with the laws of the Commonwealth of Massachusetts. If any provision of this License Agreement is held to be contrary to law, that provision will be enforced to the maximum extent permissible and the remaining provisions will remain in full force and effect.

*If you do not agree, please return this product to the place of purchase for a refund.

Syngress: *The Definition of a Serious Security Library*

Syn·gress (sin–gres): *noun, sing.* Freedom from risk or danger; safety. See *security*.

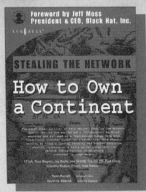

Stealing the Network: How to Own a Continent

131ah, Russ Rogers, Jay Beale, Joe Grand, Fyodor, FX, Paul Craig, Timothy Mullen (Thor), Tom Parker, Ryan Russell, Kevin D. Mitnick

The first book in the *"Stealing the Network"* series was called a "blockbuster" by Wired magazine, a "refreshing change from more traditional computer books" by Slashdot.org, and "an entertaining and informative look at the weapons and tactics employed by those who attack and defend digital systems" by Amazon.com. This follow-on book once again combines a set of fictional stories with real technology to show readers the danger that lurks in the shadows of the information security industry... Could hackers take over a continent?

ISBN: 1-931836-05-1

Price: $49.95 US $69.95 CAN

Zero Day Exploit: Countdown to Darkness

Rob Shein, Marcus H. Sachs, David Litchfield

This is a realistic and downright scary tale of cyber-terrorism. It takes the reader from the casinos of Las Vegas to the slums of Manila to FBI Headquarters, as an elite team of security hotshots race to stop Islamic terrorists from crippling the economies of the Western world. Written by the world's leading counterterrorism experts, which makes it all the more chilling for its authenticity.

ISBN: 1-931836-09-4

Price: $49.95 USA $69.95 CAN

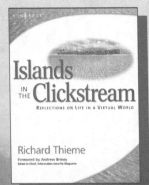

Richard Thieme's Islands in the Clickstream: Reflections on Life in a Virtual World

Richard Thieme is one of the most visible commentators on technology and society, appearing regularly on CNN radio, TechTV, and various other national media outlets. He is also in great demand as a public speaker, delivering his "Human Dimension of Technology" talk to over 50,000 live audience members each year. *Islands in the Clickstream* is a single volume "best of Richard Thieme."

ISBN: 1-931836-22-1

Price: $29.95 US $43.95 CAN

Hardware Hacking: Have Fun While Voiding Your Warranty

Joe Grand

Do you want to run Linux on your Xbox? Ever dream of building a theater-quality entertainment system in your basement using a bunch of junk? See no reason why you can't open your garage door with your Palm Pilot? If you answered yes to any of these, buy this book.
Joe Grand is President and CEO of Grand Idea Studio, Inc., a product design and development firm that brings unique inventions to market. His creations consumer devices, medical products, video games and toys, are sold worldwide

ISBN: 1-932266-83-6

Price: $39.95 US $59.95 CAN

Hacking a Terror Network: The Silent Threat of Covert Channels

Russ Rogers

Written by a certified Arabic linguist from the Defense Language Institute with extensive background in decoding encrypted communications, this cyber-thriller uses a fictional narrative to provide a fascinating and realistic "insider's look" into technically sophisticated covert terrorist communications over the Internet. The accompanying CD-ROM allows readers to "hack along" with the story line, by viewing the same Web sites described in the book containing encrypted, covert communications.

ISBN: 1-928994-98-9

Price: $39.95 US $57.95 CAN

Inside the SPAM Cartel
Spammer X

Authored by a former spammer, this is a methodical, technically explicit expose of the inner workings of the SPAM economy. Readers will be shocked by the sophistication and sheer size of this underworld. "Inside the Spam Cartel" is a great read for people with even a casual interest in cyber-crime. In addition, it includes a level of technical detail that will clearly attract its core audience of technology junkies and security professionals.

ISBN: 1932266-86-0

Price: $49.95 US   72.95 CAN

Penetration Testing with Google Hacks
Johnny Long,
Foreword by Ed Skoudis

Google, the most popular search engine worldwide, provides web surfers with an easy-to-use guide to the Internet, with web and image searches, language translation, and a range of features that make web navigation simple enough for even the novice user. What many users don't realize is that the deceptively simple components that make Google so easy to use are the same features that generously unlock security flaws for the malicious hacker. Vulnerabilities in website security can be discovered through Google hacking, techniques applied to the search engine by computer criminals, identity thieves, and even terrorists to uncover secure information. This book beats Google hackers to the punch, equipping web administrators with penetration testing applications to ensure their site is invulnerable to a hacker's search.

ISBN: 1-931836-36-1

Price: $49.95 USA $65.95 CAN